W9-CMJ-921

122424

ESSENTIAL KNOWLEDGE AND SKILLS FOR BACCALAUREATE SOCIAL WORK STUDENTS IN GERONTOLOGY

CARNEGIE LIBRARY
LIVINGSTONE COLLEGE
SALISBURY, N. C. 28144

Editors: Robert L. Schneider, Virginia Commonwealth University
Nancy P. Kropf, Virginia Commonwealth University

A Joint Publication of:

Council on Social Work Education, Washington, DC
Virginia Commonwealth University, School of Social Work, Richmond, VA

CARNEGIE LIBRARY
LIVINGSTONE COLLEGE
SALISBURY, N.C. 28144

122494

Robert L. Schneider   Nancy P. Kropf

ESSENTIAL KNOWLEDGE AND SKILLS FOR BACCALAUREATE
SOCIAL WORK STUDENTS IN GERONTOLOGY

Copyright © 1989 by   Council on Social Work Education and
                      Virginia Commonwealth University, School of Social Work

All rights reserved.

Library of Congress Catalog Card Number: 89-061493

ISBN: 0-9623138-1-5

Printed in the United States of America

The Virginia/Louisiana Undergraduate Social Work
Curriculum Project in Gerontology, 1987-88
(#03AT0243-01 USDHHS Administration on Aging Grant)

TABLE OF CONTENTS

PREFACE

In 1984, as a result of an Administration on Aging (AoA) funded curriculum and faculty development project, the Council on Social Work Education (CSWE) published six important texts designed to expand and strengthen the capability of social work faculty to prepare graduate students for practice with older persons and their families. CSWE is now pleased to publish jointly with Virginia Commonwealth University School of Social Work this volume, a part of the Undergraduate Social Work Education and Gerontology Series. Its aim is to assist faculty to prepare undergraduate social work students for work with aged populations. The two volumes of this series are a product of an AoA grant to the School of Social Work at Virginia Commonwealth University in collaboration with Grambling University's School of Social Work. Together with the earlier volumes, they provide a major resource in attempting to fulfill the ultimate goal of the AoA grants, i.e., to improve the quality and quantity of the social work labor force providing services to the elderly.

Although the focus of the Undergraduate Social Work Education and Gerontology Series is on baccalaureate social work education, some of the material will also prove useful to faculty teaching graduate students. Many of the topics covered in these two volumes, e.g., foundation curriculum and such skills as discharge planning and case management, are also taught in MSW programs.

As is the case with the 1984 volumes, these volumes will not only provide valuable material for use in classroom teaching and field instruction coordination, but will also help faculty refine and further develop gerontological curriculum content. This is particularly important at the undergraduate level because it provides essential knowledge and skills for those students who, upon receipt of the BSW degree, assume practice positions serving the elderly. For those who enter MSW programs, this material will provide strong motivation to elect a gerontology specialization, and, for those who do, a rich base for advanced study.

Donald W. Beless
Executive Director
Council on Social Work Education

May 1, 1989

ii

INTRODUCTION

The 1987 report, <u>Personnel for the Health Needs of the Elderly through the Year 2020</u>, indicates that, as a result of the rapidly increasing numbers of persons 65 years of age and older, the need for trained health services personnel such as social workers is likely to expand substantially in the coming decades. Planners argue that well prepared social workers with education and training in gerontology can provide more appropriate, effective, and sensitive care in more efficient and economical ways than practitioners without such training. In 1984, Dr. T. Franklin Williams, the Director of the National Institute on Aging, stated that he did not know the number of social workers needed, but he was confident that "more social work services are needed now and in the future with the increasing number of frail older persons." He noted that social workers would be needed to assist older persons and their families to consider options for long-term care, to advocate for them, to help staff day care programs, home services and geriatric evaluation clinics.

The Bureau of Labor Statistics notes that the most favorable job prospects for social workers in the 1980s and beyond includes services to the aged. But the most visible feature of today's social worker assisting the aged is the lack of gerontological content in their pre-service formal education. Educators and schools of social work have responded to this situation with different degrees of enthusiasm. In 1981, educators founded the National Committee for Gerontology in Social Work Education and by 1984, it had over 300 members across the nation. Graduate schools of social work developed concentrations in gerontology at a remarkable rate, increasing from 36% in 1981 to 50% in 1984. Less was known about undergraduate programs in social work. In 1986, it was reported that 50% of the programs had increasing interest on the part of students in the field of aging.

Nevertheless, serious gaps remain in the academic training of social workers. Only 4% of the National Association of Social Workers (NASW) members consider work with older persons to be their primary field of practice. Only 5% of the doctoral students in social work education specialized in the geriatric field. Fifty-three percent, or half of the individuals identified as gerontological social work faculty in graduate schools, had any specialized training in gerontology. Only about 10% of all BSW faculty reported any special preparation in the field of aging.

From 1983-85, the Administration on Aging (AoA) supported the Council on Social Work Education's effort to incorporate the integration of gerontological content into social work curricula and to develop a model curriculum for specialization at the graduate level. An assessment, <u>The Current Status of Gerontology in Graduate Social Work Education</u>, and a four volume work, <u>The CSWE Series in Gerontology</u>, were developed and disseminated nationwide to faculty and schools.

In Fall, 1987, AoA awarded funding to the Schools of Social Work at Virginia Commonwealth University and Grambling State University to enhance the quality of gerontological social work curricula and to strengthen the capacity of baccalaureate social work programs to prepare workers for effective practice in the field of aging. A study, <u>Current Status of Gerontology in Undergraduate Social Work Education: Virginia and Louisiana, 1987-88</u>, and a 2 volume work, <u>Undergraduate Social Work Education and Gerontology Series</u>, were produced and disseminated to BSW programs across the country.

This volume, <u>Essential Knowledge and Skills for Baccalaureate Social Work Students in Gerontology</u>, is part of the undergraduate series mentioned above. It provides faculty with content and materials necessary for current practice with the aged, such as case management, discharge planning, older women and older minorities. A second volume is entitled <u>Integrating Gerontology into the BSW Curriculum: Generalist Practice, Human Behavior and the Social Environment, Social Policy, Research, and Field Instruction</u>. Its specific focus is assisting faculty in teaching about aging in the basic social work courses of an accredited BSW program. Together, these volumes constitute a comprehensive resource to BSW programs which may wish to strengthen their curriculum in gerontological social work.

How to Use This Volume

The design and content of this volume are intended to promote the incorporation of aging content into undergraduate social work courses. Faculty will discover that by using these materials, they can easily present traditional concepts and skills and simultaneously introduce new knowledge and practice techniques from the field of aging.

Among the distinctive features of the chapters are:

Comprehensive Teaching Aids

Included in each chapter are an introduction, learning objectives, an outline of the chapter's contents, an 18-20 page text with key topics, content and research findings, discussion questions, audio-visual resources, annotated and general bibliographies, and classroom learning activities.

Case Studies or Vignettes

Each chapter contains 2 or 3 case studies of gerontological social work practice. Students can put themselves in the place of the social workers and begin to formulate their own approach to practice and problem solving. In Appendices A and B, guidelines are provided to the instructor on how to use a case study as a teaching method and specific questions are provided to assist the students and teacher in analyzing various dimensions of the situation from a social work perspective.

Adaptability

The chapters are designed in such a way that the instructor may use sections or units of the materials without incorporating all of the content. For example, the section on interviewing may be "lifted out" of the chapter and used for in-class demonstrations without covering all of the content on aged human behavior. An easy-to-read outline in the early pages of the chapter permits instructors to review and choose topics that will be most pertinent to topics that they may wish to present.

The development and production of these volumes owes a debt to a number of groups and individuals. The editors wish to recognize and thank the following:

- Dean Grace E. Harris, Virginia Commonwealth University School of Social Work, and Dean William Pollard, Grambling State University School of Social Work, for their support and willingness to provide the necessary resources to undertake and complete the AoA grant project.

- Dr. Pill J. Cho, Professor, Grambling State University School of Social Work, for his tireless efforts in coordinating the project, its activities and liaisons in the state of Louisiana.

- Dr. Donald Beless, Executive Director of the Council on Social Work Education, was very helpful to us as we proposed a joint publication venture. The Council is now playing a major role in disseminating these important documents.

- The authors of the chapters who are listed in Appendix F. We appreciate very much their patience with our editorial suggestions and recommendations for revisions.

- The members of the Advisory Board who are listed in Appendix D. These individuals, from across Virginia and Louisiana, assisted us enormously in the original design and scope of the project and its materials. We hope that they recognize their contributions between these pages.

- The Faculty Liaisons from the 19 undergraduate programs in social work education in Virginia and Louisiana who are listed in Appendix E. The liaisons, one from each program, formed a network that communicated effectively with their colleagues and with the project staff and editors. It is impossible to implement this type of project without the help of those who "link" it all together.

- Mr. Robert Jones, Administration on Aging Region III Office in Philadelphia, who served as our contact throughout the project. Bob helped us through several twists in the road and we are grateful to him.

- Ms. Debbie Costigan, a Project Associate who served as a Research Assistant as well as an author in her own right. Our thanks for many hours of eye-straining research and follow-up on lost references.

- Ms. Lila Garlick, Project Secretary and Assistant to the Principal Investigator. Ms. Garlick coordinated so many activities and pieces of paper that only the telephone company and the duplication service personnel know the true extent of her help. Our special thanks goes to her.

- Ms. Sally Companion, Secretary and Typist extraordinaire! These manuscripts literally would not be available without the able and expert assistance of Ms. Companion. Her devotion and commitment to this task are beyond normal description and we only rejoice that we were lucky enough to have enjoyed her services.

We hope that all faculty will test our materials, attempting to integrate some aspect of aging and gerontological social work practice into their courses. Our profession and our schools face a major challenge to provide an adequately trained cadre of social work professionals in the coming decades to care for the aged. We hope that these materials will assist you and promote the effectiveness of our caring and constructive profession.

Robert L. Schneider, DSW
Editor and Principal Investigator

Nancy P. Kropf, MSW
Associate Editor

Virginia Commonwealth University
School of Social Work
Richmond, VA

July, 1989

CHAPTER 1

SOCIAL WORK IN HOME HEALTH & COMMUNITY CARE SERVICES

by Nancy P. Kropf

Introduction

Home health and community care services are important components of a comprehensive long-term care system. These services support many older people who find themselves with limited resources and health concerns. For example, a 65-year-old widow who breaks her hip may no longer be able to manage her household alone. A 75-year-old man who has his driver's license revoked may be unable to shop for groceries or medications. Unfortunately, a common consequence for an older person needing such assistance is placement into a nursing home. Community or home care is advocated as an alternative to nursing home placement, with 20-40% of all placements in nursing homes judged to be inappropriate or preventable (Star, 1982). Many older people who receive some type of support are able to remain in their own homes and communities. Support can come from a variety of sources: those in a person's informal network, such as family, friends and neighbors, or formal network, such as home health programs and community care services.

Social workers provide important services in home and community care systems. They are instrumental in assessing needs and linking a person with appropriate support systems. For example, the 65-year-old woman may be eligible for a visiting homemaker and a health aide to assist with household and medical tasks. The 75-year-old man may have neighbors who agree to take him on their weekly shopping trip. He also could be transported to a meal site for a daily lunch program. Combining support from family, friends and formal programs can delay or prevent nursing home placement. Effective social workers utilize the informal and formal support networks to help many older people remain in their own homes and communities. Social workers contribute to one of the most important goals in long-term care which is maintaining the independence of the older person.

Learning Outcomes

After completing this chapter, students will be able to:

- Identify an array of home health and community services.

- Distinguish between formal and informal support networks.

- Prepare a service plan for an older person using community and home health services.

- Compare the brokerage and consolidated models of home health and community services systems.

Outline of Key Topics and Content Areas

Home Health & Community Care Services in Long-Term Care

Definition of Long-Term Care
Continuum of Long-Term Care Services
Reasons for Home Health and Community Care Services
Demographics
Psychosocial Issues
Health Care Costs

Informal Support Networks

>Family Caregiving
>Friends and Neighbors
>Religious Affiliations
>Self Care Groups and Mutual Help Systems

Formal Support Networks

>Home-Based Services
>Community Services
>>Care Services
>>Congregate Programs

Model Programs

>Brokerage or Channelling Models
>>Triage
>>Five Star Homebound Elderly Program
>>Upjohn Health Care Services
>>Natural Gatekeeper Program
>Consolidated Models
>>Integrated Continuing Care Program
>>On Lok
>>East Kentucky Health Center

Summary of Key Topics and Content Areas

Home Health & Community Care Services in Long-Term Care

Definition of Long-Term Care

Long-term care is often misconstrued to mean nursing home care. Nursing homes are an important part of long-term care, but the total system is not limited only to institutional services. The following is offered as a more generic definition of long-term care.

>Long-term care can be defined as those services designed to provide diagnostic, preventative, therapeutic, rehabilitative, supportive and maintenance services on a recurring or continuous basis for individuals of all age groups. These services are provided in a variety of institutionalized and non-institutionalized care settings, including the home, with the goal of promoting the optimal level of physical, social and psychological functioning. Individuals in need of long-term care services are defined as persons who have chronic physical and/or mental impairments. (Virginia Long-Term Care Council, 1985, p. 2)

Individuals with some limitations in functioning may also benefit from long-term care services. This definition includes much broader services than those provided within a nursing home.

Continuum of Long-Term Care Services

A comprehensive long-term care system usually includes diverse and flexible services which are provided along a continuum of care. Figure 1 is a schematic representation of an array of services recommended for a comprehensive long-term care system (Brody & Masciocchi, 1980). As depicted, the continuum can be broken into three services settings. One type, institutional settings, provide a 24-hour residential service. These places are most appropriate for individuals who need continuous, intermittent or acute treatment. The second type, community care programs, provide services to older people at various sites around the community, including health, nutritional, legal or social assistance. The third type is home health services. These services are provided within someone's home by an agency representative or social worker. The continuum of care represents services to individuals with multiple or severe impairments, to people who require nursing home care, and to the elderly who have minimal needs, such as a place to socialize with others.

Social workers in the long-term care system are employed in a variety of settings, such as hospitals, nursing homes, governmental agencies or home health care agencies. They are responsible for performing many different functions, depending upon the goals of their agencies and the needs of their clients. In determining a long-term care service plan for an older client, the social worker must assess how the client's unique needs can be met while preserving the greatest amount of autonomy for the person. A major role of all social workers in this system is continued assessment of the changing needs of their clients and linkage to the resources which best address those needs.

Reasons for Home Health and Community Care Services

Demographics. The number of older people has being growing dramatically. Current predictions indicate that this growth will continue into the next century. One reason for the increased interest in long-term health care is the increasing number of older people in society. Between 1900 and 1980, the general population of the United States increased by 200%, with the over 65 age group increasing by 700% (from 3 million to 25.5 million people). Future projections indicate that the over 65 population will double between 1980 and 2030 with the biggest increase in the over 85 age group (Rabin & Stockton, 1987). These figures forecast a society with a larger ratio of older people, especially those who are the "oldest-old." Not only can our society expect to have more older members, but our oldest members will be represented in even greater numbers than previously.

Advancing age by itself does not necessarily mean there will be a greater need for long-term care services. However, certain health conditions are more prevalent in the older population. As people age, the number of chronic conditions such as arthritis, cardiac problems or dementia also increases. One estimate is that five out of six people who are 65 years or older possess at least one chronic health condition (Harkins, 1981). Chronic conditions can result in functional impairments, such as the inability to dress, cook meals, or leave the home. When these limitations occur, assistance from family, friends or service programs can help prevent or delay placement into a nursing home for the older person.

Psychosocial Issues. The increase in impairments of older people affects more than just biological or physical functions. Social workers with elderly clients need to assess the psychosocial implications of their clients' limitations. For example, the 75-year-old man who loses his driver's license also loses a sense of independence. Social workers help older clients receive services which best address their physical and psychosocial needs. This 75-year-old man may be referred to a social worker for a meal program since he can no longer get to a grocery store. However, effective social work practice with this man will address not only his need for meals but also his need to maintain some feelings of independence.

Figure 1.
Long-Term Support System

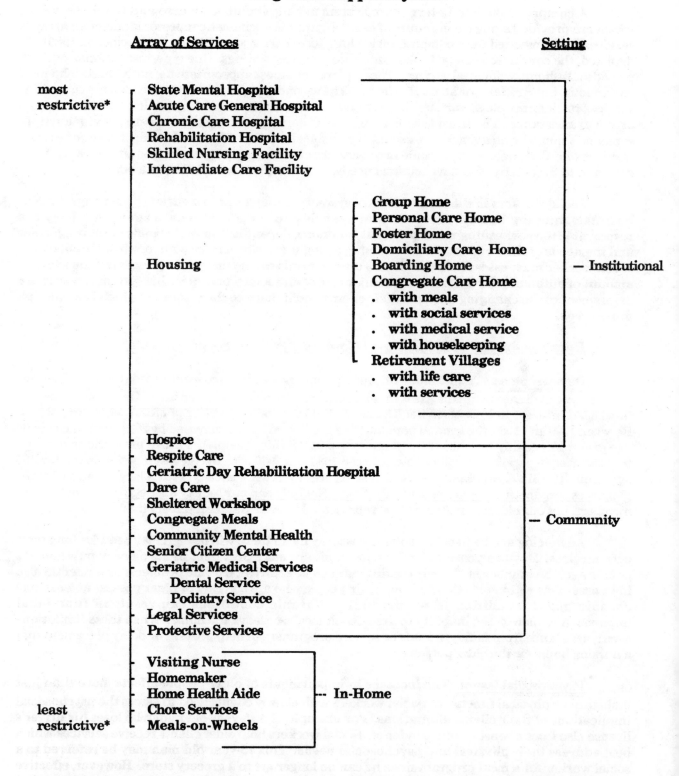

Array of Services   **Setting**

most
restrictive*
  - State Mental Hospital
  - Acute Care General Hospital
  - Chronic Care Hospital
  - Rehabilitation Hospital
  - Skilled Nursing Facility
  - Intermediate Care Facility

  - Housing
      - Group Home
      - Personal Care Home
      - Foster Home
      - Domiciliary Care Home
      - Boarding Home   — Institutional
      - Congregate Care Home
        . with meals
        . with social services
        . with medical service
        . with housekeeping
      - Retirement Villages
        . with life care
        . with services

  - Hospice
  - Respite Care
  - Geriatric Day Rehabilitation Hospital
  - Dare Care
  - Sheltered Workshop
  - Congregate Meals
  - Community Mental Health   — Community
  - Senior Citizen Center
  - Geriatric Medical Services
      Dental Service
      Podiatry Service
  - Legal Services
  - Protective Services

  - Visiting Nurse
  - Homemaker
  - Home Health Aide   --- In-Home
least
restrictive*
  - Chore Services
  - Meals-on-Wheels

* The classification of from most to least restrictive is a general view of services and may vary
  within each service.

Source: Brody & Masciocchi, 1980/

4

An important part of psychosocial adjustment to receiving services is the value that older people attach to their home environment. Most older people desire to remain in their own homes and communities, places which have real and symbolic value. While many older people begin to experience limitations in functioning, many resist leaving their own homes and communities. The desire to feel connected to others is a part of human nature, regardless of a person's age. With support from an older person's family, friends, neighbors and established services, even very frail people are able to remain at home. Psychosocial issues of aging are as important as physical issues in assessing service needs.

Family caregivers of older people need to be considered when evaluating the psychosocial issues of aging. Most older people who need assistance in daily living receive support from family members. Family caregiving is estimated to comprise 80% of total care of the elderly (Silverstone & Burack-Weiss, 1982). Older people are not "dumped" into nursing homes because their families do not want to help in care. Families continue to provide care to older members, many of whom are very frail. The importance of family caregiving cannot be underestimated since this support may be the very reason that many impaired older people stay out of residential institutions. A study by Silverstone and Burack-Weiss (1982) found that nursing home residents had substantially less family support than community dwelling elderly. This difference was greater than differences by severity of health conditions between the two groups. Psychosocial issues of long-term care support need to include family issues since this support frequently prevents or delays nursing placement for an older person.

Health Care Costs. Health care costs for the aging population are major long-term care issues. Policy makers involved with estimating economic costs for caring for an aging population note that costs of care have been increasing rapidly and steadily, especially nursing homes. Between 1971 and 1982, our population increased by 12% but nursing costs increased from $5.6 billion to $27 billion per year. These figures represent an increase of 382% and threaten the solvency of governmental programs (Stone & Newcomer, 1985). The current payment system under Medicaid and Medicare is very expensive and is structured to provide institutional, not home or community services. This situation contributes to the high rate of inappropriate placement of older people into nursing homes since they cannot afford to pay for health services that are not covered by either Medicaid or Medicare (Stone & Newcomer, 1985). The escalating costs of nursing home placement have forced service providers and politicians to investigate home health and community care services as less costly alternatives to nursing homes.

Cost issues, however, cannot be separated from quality of care issues. For example, an older widow who lives alone may have a health condition which prevents her from cooking, driving or doing heavy housework. Her family and neighbors can provide some help, which is supplemented by an in-home meal delivery program and home health aide. This constellation of support systems allows the woman to remain in familiar surroundings, have contact with various people of her support networks and maintain a high degree of decision-making within her life. Even if a nursing home placement would be a less costly alternative, the quality of her life would not be proportionate to the financial savings. Unfortunately, the quality issue is too frequently overlooked in assessing the costs of long-term care.

Informal Support Networks

Most support of an older person is supplied by the family. The family unit is just one of the components of an informal support network. A definition of an informal network is a series of linkages along which information, emotional reassurances, and services flow to and from a person and his or her exchange relationships. These services may be economic, social, or emotional (Hooyman, 1983). The members of an informal network usually have emotional ties to an older person. A paid housekeeper, for example, maintains a different relationship with an older person than a daughter or neighbor who assists with cleaning. Members of informal networks provide important services to elderly people and their contribution needs to be acknowledged and supported. The following section will review some of the systems included in an informal support network, highlighting important issues for social workers.

Family Caregiving

The family is the primary and preferred source of support for older people in the United States. Cantor (1985) describes the structure of support operating in our society as "hierarchal-compensatory", with family as the most preferred source of assistance, followed by friends, and lastly governmental or formal agencies. Within this structure, an older person would probably receive the majority of support from family, with friends compensating for functions not performed by family. Any remaining gaps would be filled by formal agencies, such as health care or meal services. Within the family structure, various members provide different functions and support for an older member (Wenger, 1984). The majority is provided by either a spouse or an adult child. Additionally, most family caregivers are women (Day, 1985).

Most families will undertake major sacrifices to provide care for an older member. Even when the person is very impaired, families make great attempts to continue to provide care (Cantor, 1985; Shanas, 1979). Caregiving has many rewards but also includes demands. Social workers and other professionals need to be extremely sensitive to the stresses and strains of caregiving. Identifying the demanding aspects of caregiving is an initial step in social work interventions planned to buffer or relieve stress. Caregiving strain can be categorized into these types: financial, physical, or emotional (Zimmer & Mellor, 1982). Financial strain is from the actual expense of caregiving, such as money used for medications for an older person or gas to take someone shopping. Another financial strain is from the "opportunity cost" of care, or the things which someone gives up to assume a caregiving role. For example, a daughter who quits a job to care for her mother gives up the money from employment. In this example, the daughter is relinquishing her "opportunity" to receive a salary. A study of family caregivers in Virginia found that caregivers spent an average of $72 a month in financial support of an older member living in the community. Additionally, this group averaged over 122 hours per month providing care, assisting with very basic skills such as toileting, dressing and feeding (Virginia Long-Term Care Council, 1985). Caregivers are providing economic support and forfeiting other activities to provide care to a relative.

Physical exertion is a second caregiving type of strain. Physical demands of caregiving can be great. Someone who requires assistance in toileting or bathing needs to be lifted, moved, and positioned. Continued assistance can result in injuries for the caregiver. Since the majority of family caregivers are spouses or adult children, they may be experiencing some physical limitations themselves (Day, 1985). A situation of a 65 year old providing care to an 88 year old parent is one of the "younger-old" person caring for the "older-old." The multiple demands on a caregiver's time contributes to physical strain. The stress of trying to juggle responsibilities becomes exhausting and physically draining. Many caregivers work full time jobs, have children and assist an older parent. Little time is left for these people, who are often called the "sandwich" generation, to attend to their own health needs, such as exercising or eating balanced meals.

A third type of strain experienced by family caregivers is emotional. Having a personal relationship makes the experience of caregiving emotionally charged. Since some people are quite frail, fears of hurting the older person are common. Decision-making becomes a source of strain when the responsibility of health or residential decisions are assumed by the caregiver. What happens, for example, when a son thinks his mother should not continue to live alone, but his mother refuses to move? These decisions become even more complicated when other family members choose sides, splitting families into different factions. Guilt and conflict can ensue for a family.

The constant progression of certain ailments is highly emotional for a family. For example, a grandparent with Alzheimer's disease may not be able to remember the names of the grandchildren or even recognize their faces. The potent relationship between family caregivers and an older member increases the emotional components of care.

Social workers helping older clients and their families need to be sensitive to the strains of caregiving. Understanding family issues is an important part of social work practice with the aging population. Certain programs and services can "help the helpers" provide support (Zimmer & Mellor, 1982). Based upon the tasks families perform, two main types of programs are especially effective (Clark & Rakowski, 1983). One type is educational, providing caregivers with information about caring for an older person. Information on the normal aging process, medical conditions, possible community resources, and interaction with professional and medical staff have been found to be useful. A second program deals with emotional aspects of care. Support groups give caregivers a place to socialize with others, ventilate feelings and get away from providing care for a few hours.

While these interventions are beneficial for families, financial strain may continue to be a problem since public policy in America does little to assist caregiving families. Social workers and other professionals should advocate for policy to provide some kind of financial support. Specific proposals include subsidies to families who provide care, increased coverage of home health services by Medicare, Medicaid and private insurance, and more flexibility in employment schedules of caregivers.

Friends and Neighbors

Friends and neighbors are other resources within an older person's informal support network. Even when older people have interactions with adult children, friends and neighbors may be better suited to perform certain tasks (Cantor, 1979). Frequently friends live closer to an older person than family members and respond quickly in cases of emergency. When a family lives a long distance away, they rely on information from neighbors about their relative's functioning. A neighbor who notices that newspapers are piling up on a porch or a friend who notices that cigarette butts are extinguished on living room chairs can provide information about the individual's functioning. Friends and neighbors are main sources of support for older people with no family (Cantor, 1979). For example, a couple may ask the widow who lives next door to holiday dinners. Friends from church may assist the woman by transporting her to services. Even when family members are very involved, friendships allow people to have different types of relationships. Friends provide a sense of intimacy, especially important when an older people loses a significant other, such as a spouse (Hooyman, 1987).

Since friends and neighbors are important resources in an older person's network, they should not be overlooked in social work practice with older people. These people are familiar faces for an older person and provide a connection to the larger society. Just looking out a window and knowing the names of people passing on the street can be a source of security, assistance and comfort for an older person. Social workers can foster supportive relationships between an older person and neighbors. Social workers must also be sensitive to an older person's desire to remain connected to friends and communities.

Religious Affiliations

In addition to family, friends and neighbors, older people belong to various voluntary groups. Religious affiliations such as churches and synagogues, are the most common type of voluntary organization for older people (Huttman, 1985). Religious ties continue to be important sources of support for older people, especially for the current cohort who were raised during a religious era. Besides the spiritual and fellowship benefits from belonging to a congregation, many churches and synagogues have special programs for older members. These programs include outreach ministries to homebound or hospitalized members, special transportation to worship services, special services for the hearing or visually impaired, and meals or grocery supply programs. For older people in rural areas where there are few agency support programs, churches are major resources in providing community elderly with services (Hancock, 1987). A program by Catholic Social Services in New Mexico, for example, organized an Outreach Program for community elderly. This program is run through various churches but was linked to a community agency to provide training and consultation to volunteer service providers (Anker & Trumbower, 1985). Volunteers are also used as referral sources for the elderly who need additional services, such as therapy or financial assistance. These churches provide a vital outreach service to link community elderly with needed programs and services.

Self Care Groups and Mutual Help Systems

Self care and mutual help groups, while not limited to the elderly, may have special relevance for this age group. "Self-care refers to actions that individuals take to promote their own well-being or that of their families and friends. Mutual help groups are comprised of individuals who share a common condition and meet to give each other support" (Bernadette, Wright, Minkler, & Fullarton, 1981, p. 50). A major advantage of both groups is the emphasis on self determination of the members, who actively participate and structure the group experiences. Some gerontologists stress the need for more of these kind of groups, since too frequently projects are started and maintained by professionals, not older members (Haber, 1983). An example of a mutual help system is a monitoring group for recently diagnosed diabetics where members help each other stay on diets and take medications. Another example is the STAES program in St. Louis. This program trains elderly volunteers to provide services such as telephone reassurance, socializing, and shopping assistance to other elderly community members. Additionally, these volunteers maintain regular contact with assigned neighbors and are sources for referrals if other needs arise (Morrow-Howell & Ozawa, 1987). Self care and mutual help systems allow elderly participants to be both recipients and providers of service to others.

Although self care and mutual help groups have the goal of members helping one another, social workers are important components of a successful system. Social workers are instrumental in identifying a need for a group and assisting members with the group's organization. Social workers are trained in group process and supervising volunteers. These skills are assets in starting and maintaining self care and mutual help systems. Social workers also are sources of referral for potential members. Being active in groups benefit elderly clients by promoting their own problem solving and health promotion process.

Summary

An informal network includes family, friends, neighbors and members of voluntary groups. Each of these are actual or potential resources for an older person. Social workers can be involved with all these informal groups. Because social workers are trained in understanding family dynamics, group processes, community organization and volunteer management, they possess knowledge and skills to intervene in a variety of ways within an informal network. For example, family caregivers can be linked to respite services to buffer the strains of caregiving. Friends and neighbors can be used as information sources about an older person's functioning. Churches and synagogues can be organized to provide a telephone reassurance program. Since the majority of care for an older person is provided by informal systems, effective social work practice includes support to members of this network.

8

Formal Support Networks

Formal support networks are those services and agencies which are established to meet the needs of older people. Agencies in the formal service network include governmental agencies, state agencies or public systems. Formal network services also include private non-profit agencies, such as Catholic or Jewish Social Services, and proprietary agencies such as private clinics or private in-home nursing services. The formal service network may provide services such as nursing care, social work or housekeeping. This relationship between a formal service provider and an older person is different from that of members of the informal network who maintain a more personal bond. Social workers are employed in most formal agencies. Because the formal service network is large, complex and confusing, social workers in community agencies must be familiar with the different agencies available to the older client, the services provided, and any eligibility requirements to use the services.

An important issue is how this formal network interfaces with an established informal support network of the clients. Formal services do offer numerous benefits to clients, such as being staffed by trained professionals, having special equipment, and receiving money from the government. The current philosophy of service delivery is to have agencies and professionals bolster existing support mechanisms, such as families and friends, and fill in the service gaps or service need (Chappell, 1985; Huttman, 1985). For example, a daughter believed that her aging mother should be called daily to confirm her condition. However, restrictions at the daughter's job prevented her from placing calls. The daughter contacted an agency to discuss this problem. The agency social worker linked the daughter to a telephone reassurance program sponsored through a local church. Now the phone program contacts the mother on week-days and the daughter continues to retain responsibility for weekend calls. This type of collaboration by informal and formal supports meets the needs of the aging person and assists the caregivers.

Home-Based Services

Home health care services are those which are provided to people within their own home. These services are needed because of a functional limitation which prevents the older person from leaving home. For example, a person who is bedridden cannot get out to receive services in the community. Even though a person is quite frail, home-based service may provide more appropriate assistance than hospitals or nursing homes. Home-based care has several advantages over institutional settings, including:

1. the possibility of being less costly. One home care project in New York eliminated the need for a $35 million dollar hospital in the community. Another study in Philadelphia estimated that home health care costs average $35 per day compared to an average semiprivate hospital room costing $152 (Irwin, 1982).

2. the elimination of an institutional atmosphere associated with medical settings. People receiving services in their homes do not experience the isolation, disruption and institutional atmosphere of nursing homes and hospitals (Oktay, 1978).

3. the health benefits of convalescing in familiar surroundings. At home, people can recover amid family members and friends.

For many reasons, interest in home health care services has been increasing and studies continue to assess cost and care issues.

The goal of home-based services is to decrease, delay or prevent nursing home or hospital admission. Services provided within the home assist an elderly person in a variety of ways. Homebound people typically require multiple services provided by a number of health care providers. For example, nurses and physical therapists assist with medication and muscle rehabilitation. Home health aids assist with less complicated medical procedures, such as changing bandages, positioning or transferring. Homemakers attend to personal care areas, such as meal preparation, dressing and housekeeping. Home-based people may require any or all of these services, depending on their abilities and supports. A well-integrated health care plan includes physical assistance, household management and attention to psychosocial issues of the homebound elderly.

When older people cannot leave their homes, they are not able to get groceries or prepare meals, and may not even feel like eating properly. Meals on Wheels is a meal delivery program to home-bound individuals. This program serves one or two meals per day to people unable to get around in the community. The primary function is to prepare and deliver meals, but has the added function of providing home-bound elderly with a few minutes of social visiting. Most of the meals are delivered by volunteers who deliver to the same individuals daily. An established route has the added advantage of allowing the volunteers to monitor the homebound person. Many of these volunteers are themselves older people (Gelfand, 1984). Like self help groups, older volunteers for this program become the service providers to other older people, benefiting both the volunteer and the homebound elderly.

Social workers in home health care are often responsible for coordinating the various professionals and organizations involved in caring for a homebound client. Often social workers act as liaisons for clients with health care agencies and insurance providers, including Medicaid and Medicare. Social workers help the family and client adjust to service providers entering the home and providing care. Reassessment of clients' needs are an on-going part of social work in home-based care. Clients who are improving may need some services reduced while other clients may need additional services over time. An effective service plan needs to adapt to the changing needs of the clients and their informal supports.

Social workers in home health care also need to be aware of potential limitations of these services. Many private insurance companies do not provide coverage for services within a client's home. Medicare and Medicaid funds also have restrictions on what type of home services can be reimbursed. Medicare policies do not consider social work as a primary service. Social work services are covered only if ordered by a physician and do not cover psychosocial concerns of illness, such as adjustment issues or family issues involved in treatment (Blue Cross of Greater Philadelphia, 1987). Another problem is the unavailability of health care services. Rural areas or poorer communities may not have the necessary resources to provide a well-integrated home health care service.

Community Services

Unlike home health services, community programs provide services to many older people simultaneously. This system has two major benefits: it is able to provide services to a large number of people and gives older people an opportunity to socialize with peers. Two types of community services will be discussed. One type is the care services offering temporary supervision or assistance for an older person and temporary relief for the caregivers. Care programs serve those elderly with mental or physical impairments which prevent them from staying alone. The second type of community service is congregate programs which mainly attract the older person with preserved functional and mental abilities. These programs are provided at various community sites where older individuals gather together to receive a service, such as a meal. Unlike home-based services, community programs are designed for the elderly who are ambulatory or mobile.

Care Services. Community care sites provide temporary care for the elderly person allowing their caregivers to attend to other tasks, such as working, shopping, socializing or relaxing. These services have an added advantage over home care services because the people have an opportunity to socialize with others. The following paragraphs review the different types of community programs available for the elderly and their caregivers.

For caregivers of an impaired person, leaving the home for any reason may mean finding and paying someone else to provide temporary care to an impaired family member. Even small trips to the grocery store can become complicated, involved and costly. Respite care services provide relief for caregivers enabling them to use time for something other than caregiving. A definition of respite care is "... short-term temporary care for disabled or chronically ill people living at home" (Joyce, Singer, & Isralowitz, 1983, p. 153). There are many models of respite services, some provided within a person's home and others at some community site. Community respite care can be in adult foster care or nursing homes. For example, a family going on vacation can arrange for an elderly parent to stay in respite while they are away. In-home respite is usually for a short time, perhaps a few hours so a couple can have a night out together. Used on a regular basis, respite services can help prevent or decrease the feeling of entrapment by caregivers. Having periodic breaks from the responsibility of providing care, family members can attend to tasks, personal matters or simply have a needed break.

Adult day care centers provide a supervised environment for the elderly who are unable to remain alone. Although similar to respite care, day care centers require regular attendance while respite services are scheduled around certain times or events. Many caregivers use adult day care because they are working and must be out of the home. Most day care centers are small, averaging about 15-20 clients with a staff ratio of 1:5 or 1:7. Maintaining this size and ratio prevents the development of an institutional atmosphere (Gelfand, 1984). Day care centers typically provide some type of programing for their participants, such as crafts, individual or group projects. Individual plans are drawn up for participants of the centers based upon medical, social and functional assessments. Staff is available to assist day care participants with special needs, such as ambulation difficulties, taking medications, or toileting needs.

Hospices provide services to the terminally ill. While not specifically designed for older people, this population is frequently diagnosed with conditions appropriate for hospice care. Since these programs deal with the terminally ill, or those for whom there are no cures, the focus of care is providing comfort measures for the patient and the family. Issues of bereavement and grief are discussed openly with patients and families and the hospice team assists in making appropriate plans. Hospice teams use an interdisciplinary approach, providing physical, social, emotional and spiritual care. Teams usually include a physician, nurse, social worker, clergy member and volunteers (Williams & Anderson, 1986). As with respite services, care can be provided within the person's home or within various community structures such as a hospital or community health agency. Regardless of the setting, hospice care promotes the quality of life for patient and family, not just its extension.

Congregate Programs. Congregate programs provide services to the elderly and opportunities for socializing at various community sites. Two types of congregate programs will be discussed: the Congregate Meal Program and the Multi Purpose Senior Center.

The Congregate Meal Program is a federal program authorized in 1973 by the Older American Act. This program provides a hot meal for the elderly at various places within the community. Typical meal sites include churches, school cafeterias, or senior centers. This program provides for the nutritional needs of older persons who may be at high risk for malnutrition. Barriers to proper nutritional eating include inadequate finances to purchase food, inability to prepare or purchase groceries, or the lack of desire to eat. Eating involves psychosocial

11

factors; people who are depressed or lonely may have less desire to eat. Congregate meal sites address both the nutritional and social aspects of eating. While all people over 60 years of age are entitled to this program, sites are planned with special attention to low-income older people.

Many people take advantage of the congregate meal program. In 1980, over a half a million meals were served at 13,000 sites nationally, and almost two-thirds served to low-income clients (Huttman, 1985). Frequently, meal sites provide some programing on issues or activities of interest to the elderly. Examples of typical offerings are a lecture by a dietician on low-cost meal preparation, organized card games or health promotion exercises.

The Multi Purpose Senior Center is another type of congregate program. These centers were established by the Older American Act and began receiving federal funding in the mid 1970s. Senior centers follow a holistic approach to the health of older people, offering an array of services within a centralized location (Gelfand & Gelfand, 1982). Senior centers are found within local communities across the nation, offering older community members a place to gather, socialize and receive services and information. While different locations stress different programs based upon community needs and desires, program offerings fall into two major categories (Gelfand, 1984). One type is recreation/education programs. Seniors can choose from activities such as drama, lectures, arts and crafts, physical fitness and many others. The second type of program focuses on services delivered through the center. Representatives from community agencies such as Social Security, legal centers, or housing authorities often have hours within senior centers. Community services can be delivered within the centers, such as meal programs, health screenings or day care. Multi Purpose Senior Centers provide opportunities for community seniors to become involved with others and receive needed services at accessible locations.

Many of the community programs outlined above have social workers on staff. Depending upon program goals, the social workers may become involved in a variety of services. For most community programs, a major issue is transportation to and from the community site. Social workers may be involved in coordinating transportation for clients or linking with other community agencies for shared services. Community advocacy and organization tasks are others ways social workers coordinate transportation for clients who use public transportation to community programs. Some issues for negotiation with public transportation staff are reduced rates for people over 60 years, arranged stops close to community programs, and accessible transportation vehicles for people with physical limitations. Transportation coordination between families, such as a Share-a-Ride program, is an additional idea for social work intervention.

Besides transportation coordination, social workers in community services play a major role in coordinating services for program clients and families. For example, a single daughter who lives with her 85 year old father uses day care services while she works. Her work schedule varies, and she frequently works in the evenings or on weekends when the day care center is closed. Social workers knowledgeable about other forms of respite care in the community can assist the daughter in structuring a plan so her father is cared for while she works these shifts. Figure 2 is a problem/ solution inventory which can be used as a checklist by social workers and families (Hooyman, 1983). Possible problems of the elderly person are identified along with ways of solving the problems. Families should be encouraged to use these resources to prevent strain and stresses of caregiving.

Summary

Social workers in community systems are frequently involved with families or caregivers of the older clients, as well as the clients themselves. Sometimes work with the families involves discussions and assurances about the quality of services provided. With respite care, for example, the social worker may have to plan the transition of a family into a service (Ellis, 1986). Families

Figure 2.
Problems/Solution Inventory

Problem	Possible community resources
Difficulty arranging transportation to employment, volunteer site, senior center, medical appointment, etc.	Carpools; with neighbors, families of other older people, fellow volunteers or workers City provisions for older people; reduced bus fares, taxi cab scrip, "Trans-Aide" Volunteer services: Red Cross, Salvation Army, church organizations for emergency or occasional transportation
Living alone and fearing accidental injury or illness without access to assistance	Telephone check-up services: through local hospitals, or friends, neighbors, or relatives Postal alert: register with local senior center; sticker on mail box alerts letter carrier to check for accumulation of mail Newspaper delivery: parents of the delivery boy or girl can be given an emergency phone number if newspapers accumulate Neighbors: can check pattern of lights on/off
Needs assistance with personal care such as bathing and dressing	Private pay for hourly services: home aides from private agencies listed in phone book Visiting Nurse Association; services will include aide services when nurses are utilized Medicaid/Medicare: provisions for home aides are limited to strict eligibility requirements but such care is provided in certain situations Student help: posting notices on bulletin boards at nursing schools can yield an inexpensive helper Home sharing: sharing the home with another person who is willing to provide this kind of assistance in exchange for room and board
Needs occasional nursing care and/or physical therapy	Visiting nurse: services provided through Medicare or Medicaid or sliding scale fees, must be ordered by a physician Home health services; private providers, Medicare and Medicaid reimbursement for authorized services Veterans Administration Hospital Home Care: for veterans over 60 years old for specific situations

Figure 2. Problem/Solution Inventory (continued)

Problem	Possible community resources
Difficulty cooking meals, shopping for food, and arranging nutritious diet	Home-delivered meals: "Meals on Wheels" delivers frozen meals once a week, sliding fees Nutrition sites: meals served at Senior Centers, churches, schools, and other sites Cooperatives: arrangements with neighbors to exchange a service for meals, food shopping, etc.
Not enough contact with other people; insufficient activity or stimulation; loneliness and boredom	Senior centers: provide social opportunities, classes, volunteer opportunities, outings Church-sponsored clubs: social activities, volunteer opportunities, outings Support groups: for widows, stroke victims, and general support Adult day care: provides social interaction, classes, discussion groups, outings, exercise
Difficulty doing housework	Homemaker services: for those meeting income eligibility criteria Service exchanges: with neighbors and friends, i.e., babysitting exchanged for housework help Home helpers: hired through agencies or through employment listings at senior centers, schools, etc. Home sharing: renting out a room or portion of the home, reduced rent for help with housework
Forgetful about financial affairs; eyesight too poor for balancing checkbook and reading necessary information	Power of attorney: given to friend or relative for handling financial matters Joint checking account: with friend or relative for ease in paying bills Volunteer assistance: available from the Red Cross, Salvation Army, church groups, senior centers, and other organizations
Needs assistance with will, landlord-tenant concerns, property tax exemptions, guardianship, etc.	Senior citizens' legal services Lawyer referral service: offered by the county bar association City/county aging programs: hot lines for information and assistance in phone book

Source: Hooyman, 1983

planning on using a respite placement for any length of time may have reservations or guilt about going away and leaving a parent in a nursing home. Introducing the family to the system gradually by discussing the specific respite program, visiting the respite location and perhaps arranging a trial stay allows both family and older member to become familiar with the surroundings before a longer respite time is planned.

Home-based and community services are cost effective and humane methods of serving the health, social and emotional needs of the elderly. While community programs serve people who have some mobility, even very frail people are assisted by home-based services. Social workers have important functions in coordinating and delivering these services.

Model Programs

Several model programs will be outlined below to illustrate how some localities have instituted home health and community service systems. These programs are administered under different auspices, e.,g., hospitals, community mental health centers, and agencies on aging. Model programs can be classified into two types, brokerage or channelling models, and consolidated models (Zawadski & Ansak, 1983).

Brokerage or Channelling Models

Brokerage (also called channelling) models of service are methods of making home-based and community care more accessible and less costly for the elderly. Within these models, existing community services are modified or expanded to make service options more comprehensive. Channelling models are designed to link people needing long-term care to appropriate services within the community. The goal of these programs is to match a client's needs with existing services in order to prevent or delay nursing home admission.

Triage. Triage is a community health care system in Connecticut. This project was started in 1974 as a reaction by the Connecticut State government to escalating Medicare/Medicaid costs (Quinn, Segal, Raisz, & Johnson, 1982). The system waives certain restrictions of Medicare/ Medicaid by allowing people to receive services that they normally would not under those plans. Triage is a reimbursement system that pays for existing community resources, such as home-based care or medical services thereby integrating the client into available community systems. The Triage system chooses from a wide range of existing services, those which will best contain or decrease functional limitations of the elderly. The waiver system assures that these services will be paid so recipients are not required to purchase them with their own resources. If this system were not available, many consumers could not afford to pay for these services. An evaluative study of the Triage users and traditional Medicaid/Medicare users (Hodgson & Quinn, 1980) found that Triage participants had improved morale, a greater sense of control over their own lives, and enhanced family support over time. Costs of the program were reasonable and did not cost more than the rate under the Medicare system.

Five Star Homebound Elderly Program. A second brokerage program is the Five Star Homebound Elderly Program in Chicago (Star, 1982). This program was started in 1976 by hospitals in a northern suburb to serve homebound clients. The goal of the program is to bring medical services to the clients in their homes. These clients are unable to travel to community health services putting them at risk for nursing home care. The project uses a team of medical professionals: physicians, a dentist, a podiatrist, nurses, home health aides and social workers. Clients have access to a variety of services such as a routine dental check or assistance with psychosocial adjustment to an amputation. Since services are provided within the clients' homes, professionals can assess environmental factors in health care. For example, a patient would not recover from pneumonia if there is no heat in the home. Excluding physician costs, the program is less expensive to operate than nursing home care.

Upjohn Health Care Services. Upjohn Health Care Services is a model located in rural Florida. This program began in 1973 and serves approximately 200 people (Pride Institute Journal, 1982). The majority of people using these services are elderly and have some type of health problems. Many of these older people had difficulty gaining access to adequate health care under the previous system. One reason for the difficulty was a large number of in-migrating people who did not understand the health services system. A second reason was an inadequate transportation system. The third barrier was the attitude of the community toward health care professionals. Physicians were distrusted and hospitals were viewed as places where you went to die. The Upjohn model modified the existing system to minimize these barriers. Under this program, visiting nurses and health aides made house calls to the elderly in the community. Referrals to this program came from other older persons who were using this system which minimized access barriers. Additionally, using health service professionals and staff is less threatening. The home environment is also a less threatening place for treatment procedures and solves transportation problems. In designing a model program for this rural community, Upjohn evaluated the needs of the elderly and structured ways to overcome barriers to adequate health care.

Natural Gatekeeper Program. Another type of program uses natural gatekeepers in the community. Many people have interactions with an elderly person such as the mail carrier, newspaper carrier, and meter readers. A program between the Virginia Department for the Aging and Virginia Power links a gatekeeper to the frail elderly. Started in July, 1987, the program trains meter readers to notice signs of potential problems in homes of the elderly. In cases where there are indicators of a possible problem, such as broken windows or piled newspaper, the reader alerts the appropriate agency, which investigates the situation or notifies designated family members.

Consolidated Models

A second model of service delivery is consolidated health care programs. This model combines numerous services into a single location or agency. Integrating services together decreases the fragmentation found in traditional health care services. Typically an older person goes to a physician's office for a check-up, a dentist's office for dental work and a hospital for physical therapy. This fragmentation of services is confusing and exhausting for older people and their caregivers. The consolidated model makes health care accessible and less frustrating since numerous services are provided at one location.

Integrated Continuing Care Program. The Integrated Continuing Care Program (ICCP) is an integrated health care system operating in Massachusetts. This program merged an existing case management program with the visiting nurses program to create a more comprehensive system (Wolf, Halas, Green and McNiff, 1986). Clients entering the program receive a complete assessment and a care plan based upon needs. Now clients are required to have only one initial assessment, and services are planned through one agency, not several. An evaluation of this model found results to be quite positive for the program, measured by client satisfaction, cost and quality of care. This model is noteworthy as it merged an existing, yet fragmented service delivery system into a consolidated one.

On Lok. Another consolidated model of care is the On Lok Senior Services Center of San Francisco. The catchment area for this project includes many older people of limited income and diverse ethnic backgrounds. On Lok started in 1979 when the community commissioned a study on the feasibility of building a nursing home. The study discovered that a nursing home would be extremely expensive and the community decided to try an alternative program. On Lok is a comprehensive system including medical services such as audiology, podiatry and dentistry, social services, day care, meal services and an HMO program (Yee, 1981). Even when a client is hospitalized or admitted to a nursing home, services continue to be provided to the person. The On Lok model has a positive impact on health care in the community. The majority of elderly who chose to participate in On Lok services have continued to use them (Zawadski & Ansak, 1983).

   East Kentucky Health Center. An example of a consolidated rural model is the East Kentucky Health Center. This center was started by two physicians in 1972. The program uses a team approach, employing professionals, paraprofessionals, and volunteers to assist rural elderly with health care needs (Pride Institute Journal, 1982). The center is run by a protocol manual which is a list of procedures written by professionals corresponding to the most common diagnoses at the center. In addition, outreach visits are made to the more isolated elderly, helping family and patient to understand and participate in practices to enhance health. This model frees up physician time, enabling doctors to see more severely sick patients. Using other personnel also allows health procedures to be fully explained to the patient. The addition of extra staff time means health information is made clearer to patients, enhancing their ability to comply with treatment.

   These models are a sample of the programs around the country providing community based long-term care. They reflect the efforts of professionals responding to the need for consolidated and comprehensive services. Hopefully, additional models and demonstration projects will influence policy makers and services providers to consider community and home-based services as viable, cost-effective and humane methods of caring for our elderly population.

Chapter References

Anker, L., & Trumbower, J. A. (1985). Congregations reach out to the homebound. Aging, No. 351.

Bernadette, M., Wright, L. D., Minkler, M., & Fullarton, J. (1981). Self-care and mutual help. Report of the technical committee on health maintenance and health promotion. White House Conference on Aging.

Blue Cross of Greater Philadelphia. (1987). Medicare Home Health Provider Bulletin (Home Health Aging Bulletin No. 87-14). Philadelphia: Author.

Brody, S. J., & Masciocchi, B. A. (1980). Data for long-term care planning by health systems agencies. American Journal of Public Health, 70 (11).

Cantor, M. H. (1979). Neighbors and friends: An overlooked resource in the informal support system. Research on Aging, 1(4).

Cantor, M. (1985). Families: A basic source of long-term for the elderly. Aging, No. 349.

Chappell, N. L. (1985). Social support and the receipt of home care services. Gerontologist, 25(1).

Clark, N. M., & Rakowski, W. (1983). Family caregivers of older adults: Improving helping skills. Gerontologist, 23(6).

Day, A. T. (1985). Who cares? Demographic trends challenge family care for the elderly. Population Trends and Public Policy, Population Reference Bureau, Inc.

Ellis, V. (1986). Introducing patients and families to respite. In R. J. V. Montgomery & J. Prothero (Eds.), Developing respite services for the elderly. Seattle: University of Washington Press.

Gelfand, D. E. (1984). The aging network (2nd ed.). New York: Springer.

Gelfand, D. E., & Gelfand, J. R. (1982). Senior centers and social support networks. In P. Biegel & A. Naparstek (Eds.), Community support systems and mental health. New York: Springer.

Haber, D. (1983). Promoting mutual help groups among older persons. Gerontologist, 23(3).

Hancock, B. L. (1987). Social work with older people. Englewood Cliffs, NJ: Prentice Hall.

Harkins, E. B. (1981). Social and health factors in long-term care: Findings from the statewide survey of older Virginians. Richmond: Virginia Commonwealth University, Virginia Center on Aging.

Hodgson, J. H., & Quinn, J. L. (1980). The impact of the Triage health care delivery system upon client morale, independent living and the cost of care. Gerontologist, 20(3).

Home health care for the rural elderly: Experiences in Florida and Kentucky. (1982). Pride Institute Journal, 1(2).

Hooyman, N. (1983). Social support networks in services to the elderly. In J. K. Whittaker & J. Garbarino (Eds.), Social support networks: Informal helping in the human services. Chicago: Aldine.

Hooyman, N. (1987). The importance of social supports: Family, friends, and neighbors. Unpublished document.

Huttman, E. D. (1985). Social services for the elderly. New York: Free Press.

Irwin, T. (1982). Home health care: When a patient leaves the hospital. Public Affairs Pamphlet, No. 560.

Joyce, K., Singer, M., & Isralowitz, R. (1983). Impact of respite care on parents' perceptions of quality of life. Mental Retardation, 21(4).

Morrow-Howell, N., & Ozawa, M. N. (1987). Helping network: Seniors to seniors. Gerontologist, 27(1).

Oktay, M. S. (1978). Home health care for the elderly. Health & Social Work, 3(3).

Quinn, J., Segal, J., Raisz, H., Johnson, C. (Eds.). (1982). Coordinating community services for the elderly: The Triage experience. New York: Springer.

Rabin, D. L., & Stockton, P. (1987). Long-term care for the elderly. New York: Oxford University Press.

Shanas, E. (1979). The family as a social support system in old age. Gerontologist, 19(2).

Silverstone, B., & Burack-Weiss, A. (1982). The social work function in nursing homes and home care. Journal of Gerontological Social Work, 5(1/2).

Star, J. (1982, June). Living on their own. Chicago Magazine.

Stone, R., & Newcomer, R. (1985). Health and social services policy and the disabled who have become old. In M. P. Janicki & H. M. Wisniewski (Eds.), Aging and developmental disabilities: Issues and approaches. Baltimore: Paul H. Brookes.

Virginia Long-Term Care Council. (1985). Study of the public and private cost of institutional and community based long-term care. Richmond, VA.

Wenger, G. C. (1984). The supportive network: Coping with old age. London: George Allen & Irwin.

Williams, J., & Anderson, H. (1986). Hospice. Caring, 5.

Wolf, R. T. Halas, K. T., Green, L. B., & McNiff, M. L. (1986). A model for the integration of community-based health and social services. Home Health Care Services Quarterly, 6(4).

Yee, D. L. (1981). On Lok senior health services: Community-based long-term care. Aging, Nos. 319-320.

Zawadski, R. T., & Ansak, M. L. (1983). Consolidating community-based long-term care: Early returns from the On Lok demonstration. Gerontologist, 23(4).

Zimmer, A. H., & Mellor, M. J. (1982). The role of the family in long-term home health care. Pride Institute Journal of Long-Term Home Health Care, 1(2).

Discussion Questions

1. What is a definition of long-term care? Why are home health and community care programs important components of a long-term care system?

2. What are three areas of stress and strain for family caregivers? How can social workers intervene to minimize or buffer the stress of caregiving?

3. How is a formal support network different from an informal network?

4. How do home health and community care services differ? What are typical social work functions in both kinds of services?

Learning Activities

Activity #1. Someone I'm Not

In this exercise, students assume identities of older people. Students answer a number of different questions based upon their perceptions of an older person's life. Small group discussions allow students to compare how different older people have different life experiences.

Before class, the instructor outlines four different identities of an older person and records them on index cards. Four sample identities are listed below:

1. A 75-year-old black woman in poor health living alone in a high crime urban area

2. A 62-year-old white married man in good health living with his wife

3. An 85-year-old white woman living in a nursing home who is blind from diabetes

4. A 77-year-old Hispanic woman caring for her 79 year old husband who is bed-ridden

19

Each student receives a card with one of the four identities. On sheets of paper, students respond to the following questions as if they were the older person.

1. What is your favorite activity?

2. How do you prepare your meals?

3. How often do you see family members?

4. How do you view your future?

5. Overall, are you happy with your life?

Instruct the students to form groups of four members, each containing all four identities. The number of members per group will remain constant but the number of groups will vary depending on the class size.

Have students discuss their responses to the questions and compare how people of different identities responded.

If time permits, have the entire class discuss similarities and differences within their answers.

Activity # 2. Where Has My Time Gone?

In the following exercise, students are sensitized to the amount of time caregivers of the elderly spend performing that role. Students are first asked to outline a typical week. Then they are asked to adjust this schedule to provide caregiving tasks for an elderly relative.

At the beginning of the exercise, the instructor distributes two copies of the Activity Worksheet (see attached sample).

Students are asked to choose a typical week in their life, and fill in the worksheet with activities performed within the time slots for each day of the week. For example, classes could be filled in for Monday/Wednesday/Friday, 9 AM- Noon.

Next the instructor tells the class the following story:

You are the only relative who lives in the same town as your Aunt Emily. She is 74 years old and widowed. She is in the hospital with a broken hip which occurred when she slipped on ice outside her apartment. She is about to be discharged and cannot live by herself for at least 3 months. Since no other relatives are available to help, she is coming to live with you while she convalesces. She currently gets around with a walker but requires help in the following areas:

Preparing meals
Dressing and undressing
Bathing
Toileting
Dispensing medication which needs to be refrigerated. She takes her medication
    orally at breakfast, lunch and dinner.
Laundering clothes

Where Has My Time Gone? Activity Worksheet

Time	Sunday	Monday	Tuesday	Wednesday	Thursday	Friday	Saturday
Midnight - 6 AM							
6 AM - 9 AM							
9 AM - Noon							
Noon - 3 PM							
3 PM - 6 PM							
6 PM - 9 PM							
9 PM - Midnight							

Next, students use the second Activity Worksheet. They plan what their week would look like if they had to fit these caregiving responsibilities into the normal routine. They fill out the second sheet, altering their schedule to assist Aunt Emily.

After the students have completed their worksheets, they discuss how their lives would change if they became caregivers of an older person. Ask the students questions such as: What activities were cut to make room for caregiving tasks? How much personal time do you have left? How would you feel if you really had to work under the caregiving schedule?

Activity #3. All In A Day's Work

In this exercise, the classroom must be equipped with either a large chalkboard or a flipchart.

The instructor divides the board or chart into 3 sections. Mark each section with one of the headings: Home Health Aide, Adult Day Care Worker, Meals on Wheels Volunteer.

One at a time, the instructor reads each of the three jobs listed below.

1. You are a home health aide. You go into older people's homes on a daily basis. Your responsibility is assisting with their personal care needs and housekeeping chores.

2. You are an adult day care worker. You supervise seven older people during the weekdays.

3. You are a senior citizen who volunteers for Meals on Wheels. You deliver lunches to twenty older people during weekdays.

After the instructor reads each job description, students are told to read each of the following questions one at a time.

1. Imagine a typical client. How would you describe the person's home, appearance and functioning level?

2. Describe how you assist your clients. What exactly does your job require you to do with your clients?

3. Do you like your job? What is your favorite part of the job? What is your least favorite part?

After a sufficient amount of time, ask the students to respond orally to the questions. Record summaries of the answers on the board or flip chart under the corresponding heading.

After the three questions are completed for the first job, move on to the second one and then the third.

After all questions have been completed for all jobs, ask students to assess how the different service roles compare. Ask students for opinions about the relationship that social workers will have to these employees.

Case Studies

(Please review Appendices A and B for guidelines on teaching gerontological social work by using case studies)

Case #1. A Healthy Mrs. Heath

"I'm tired of being in this hospital and want to go home." These are the first words Mrs. Heath tells Ann Blake, the hospital social worker.

Mrs. Heath is a 63 year old widow who lives alone in an apartment. She is currently hospitalized for a fractured leg. She was admitted two days ago after falling in her church parking lot. Her private insurance policy fully covers any medical procedures performed while hospitalized. Mrs. Heath has no other medical problems and is expected to have a successful healing process. Her discharge date is scheduled in one week. However, Mrs. Heath will need assistance after her discharge. Ann Blake, the hospital social worker, has been contacted to assist in discharge planning for this patient.

Mrs. Heath is expected to have her leg in a cast for a month after her release from the hospital. Her physician predicts that she will be able to walk with a walker soon after her return home. Due to her lack of strength and the size of her cast, he thinks mobility will be limited while she uses her walker. She needs to return to the hospital biweekly to monitor the healing process and to have the cast setting checked.

Ms. Heath tells the social worker that she gets along well with others in her apartment complex, most of whom are retired and widowed. After the death of her husband four years ago, she moved into this complex so she wouldn't be so lonely. She and her husband were "always on the go" and she felt very lost right after his death. She and the other widows in the apartment complex socialize frequently, such as going shopping together, eating out and seeing movies. Her room is already beginning to fill with cards and plants from her friends. She is anxious to return to her apartment and resume her life activities. Although she has two adult children, both are married, work and have families. Her son lives in another state and her daughter several miles away. Although Mrs. Heath has a good relationship with both children, she does not want to convalesce in their homes. She stated that she would "go crazy living there. I'm used to my own place now, you know. Right after Arnie, my husband, died, I stayed with my daughter for a month. What a mess! I love my grand kids and my poor granddaughter had to move out of her room so I could have a place to stay. A twelve-year-old girl needs her own room. I was out of place. No, I won't go back there to stay. I'm used to my apartment with my friends and my beautiful pet kitty, Sugar."

Mrs. Heath has expressed much frustration with this accident. She is particularly worried that she may not be able to prepare meals, attend to personal hygiene needs and drive her car. Mrs. Heath is very active in a number of groups, including her church, a senior citizens club, and her group of women friends. She receives a good pension from her husband's employment and is financially secure. As the hospital social worker, Ann Blake's responsibility is to make sure that Mrs. Heath has the assistance she needs after her return home.

Written by: Nancy P. Kropf

Case #2: The Pressing Needs of Mrs. Preston

"My mother has been acting different lately. Her behavior really has me concerned." Alice Marshall begins to describe the unusual way her mother has been acting.

Mrs. Preston, Alice's mother, is a 78-year-old widow. She has lived alone since her husband's death twenty years ago. She is in good health, except for high blood pressure which is controlled by diet and medication. She gets along well with her neighbors, all of whom she knows by name. Her favorite activities are baking, watching TV, and going for walks. Until recently, she has been managing her household very well.

Two months ago, neighbors contacted Alice with concerns about Mrs. Preston. On three or four occasions, neighbors observed her walking through the neighborhood in her pajamas and slippers. She has also accused the newspaper and postal carriers of trying to break into her house, although she has known these people for years.

Alice describes changes within her mother's normal housekeeping routine. Her mother was an immaculate housekeeper. Recently, things have been out of order. Dirty clothes are piled in corners of the room. Dishes are stacked on living room furniture caked with food. Numerous hazards were discovered in the kitchen, such as newspaper placed on top of the burners. All of the pots were badly burned, and black ants were crawling over the counter and dirty dishes. "But the hardest part," Alice stated," is her denial. She insists that the pans have been scorched for years. I know that's not true. One Saturday I spent the entire day cleaning her house. I washed the dishes, laundered her clothes, sprayed the ants. One week later, the place was a mess again."

Alice contacted her brother who lives in town. For two weeks they have been taking turns going to their mother daily. Since both have jobs and families, these trips are demanding of their time. Alice has also started to prepare meals for her mother as she suspects that her mother is not continuing her diet. Alice is worried that her mother needs more assistance than she and her brother can provide. She concludes with the statement, "Even though she doesn't want to, Mother may have to move to a nursing home."

Written by: Nancy P. Kropf

Audio Visual Resources

Coordinated Community Service for the Elderly   30 min., 16 mm color

The film is an attempt to show how a coordinated community program works for the elderly. The film stimulates students' thoughts on planning and implementing new service programs for their communities.

CONTACT: Department of Mental Health and Mental Retardation, Office of Geriatric Services, P.O. Box 1797, Richmond, Virginia 23214 (804-786-8044).

In Care of: Families and Their Elders   30 min., film

This film is a set of documentaries taped in homes of caregivers across the country. It reveals the daily struggles and contributions of families members in caring for elderly relative. Hugh Downs narrates.

CONTACT: Anna H. Zimmer, MSW, Brookdale Center on Aging of Hunter College, 425 E. 25th Street, New York, New York 10010 (212-481-5066).

<u>My Mother. My Father</u>   33 min., 16 mm or videotape

This documentary is the winner of five national awards. The film takes a look at four families as they deal with the stresses of caregiving for an aging parent. While not attempting to provide students with any answers, the film takes an honest look at the way families make individual choices about caregiving.

CONTACT: Linda Bloise, Terra Nova Films, Inc., 9848 S. Winchester Avenue, Chicago, Illinois 60643 (312-881-8491).

<u>Someone I Once Knew</u>   30 min., 16 mm, 1983

This film focuses on the plight of the victims of Alzheimer's Disease and their families. Through the reactions of the families, the students can see the frustration these families face. The film examines this disease from a medical, physical and emotional point of view. It helps sensitize students to the need to support the caregivers of the Alzheimer patient.

CONTACT: Department of Mental Health and Mental Retardation, Office of Geriatric Services, P.O. Box 1797; Richmond, Virginia 23214.

<u>We've Come of Age</u>   12 min., videotape, 1972

Shows the need of community elderly to join together for mutual help in this youth-oriented society. The film makes students aware of the problems of growing older in American society.

CONTACT: Ruth B. Finley, Information Resources Center of Virginia Center on Aging & Geriatric Education Center, P.O. Box 229-MCV Station, Richmond, Virginia 23298 (804-786-1525).

Annotated Bibliography

Andreoli, K. G., Musser, L. A., & Reiser, S. J. (1986). <u>Health care for the elderly: Regional responses to national issues</u>. New York: Haworth Press.

    This book is a report on a conference of the same name held in Texas in 1985. Thirty-one distinguished speakers presented and discussed material on topics about the future of health care for elderly. One chapter specifically deals with the place of home health and community services in long-term care.

Axelrod, T. B. (1978). Innovative roles for social workers in home-care programs. <u>Health and Social Work</u>, 3(3).

    This article describes the various roles social workers play in home health agencies. In order to provide comprehensive programs to the in-home client, social workers can be instrumental at both direct practice and administrative levels of home health care.

Gelfand, D. E. (1984). <u>The aging network</u> (2nd ed.). New York: Springer.

    This book is a good overview of the different types of services forming a network for the elderly. The introduction includes the legislative basis for programs and services. Each chapter is a description of a different service or program within the aging service network. The structure of the book is easily adaptable to many classroom uses, such as assigned student readings or illustrative material.

Hooyman, N. (1983). Social support networks in services to the elderly. In J. Whittaker & J. Garbarino (Eds.), Social support networks: Informal helping in the human services. Chicago: Aldine.

This chapter discusses the role of the informal support system in providing community services to the elderly. Practice problems with the elderly are described and a problem-solving inventory for workers and families is proposed. The chapter also describes the different projects in existence which have the goal of creating or strengthening social supports of the elderly.

Hooyman, N., & Lustbader, W. (1986). Taking care. New York: Free Press.

The book is written for professionals and caregiving families. It provides information on the dilemmas of caregiving and provides practical tips for families about how to allow their family member to maintain as much independence as possible. It sensitizes professionals to the tasks of providing care to an impaired family member.

Oktay, M. J. (1978). Home health care for the elderly. Health and Social Work, 3(3).

This article describes the growth of in-home health care services. It also describes the different roles of social workers within the home health care system. Three case examples are included to illustrate the roles and functions of social workers.

Rabin, D., & Stockton, P. (1987). Long-term care for the elderly: A fact book. New York: Oxford University Press.

This book discusses different issues that the long-term care system currently faces. One chapter deals specifically with the population using home-based services, including their functional ability and their sources of support. The chapter also includes current information about financing in-home services.

Silverstone, B., & Burack-Weiss, A. (1982). The social work function in nursing home and home care. Journal of Gerontological Social Work, 5(1/2).

This article describes the functions of social workers with elderly clients in nursing homes or their own homes. The authors discuss the auxiliary function model for practice, which includes an assessment of the client's own resources and the role of the social worker in filling identified gaps.

Wenger, G. C. (1984). The supportive network: Coping with old age. London: George Allen & Irwin.

The author discusses the different types of support available to the elderly. Included are the services which can be provided by the different networks, such as family, friends, and health services. The author includes a whole chapter of examples of elderly people using these supports to remain in the community.

General Bibliography

Ansak, M. L. (1983). On Lok series health services: A community care organization for dependent adults. Pride Institute Journal of Long-term Home Health Care, 2(1).

Brummel, S. W. (1984). Senior companions: An unrecognized resource for long-term care. Pride Institute Journal of Long-term Health Care, 3(1).

Cantor, M. H. (1979). Neighbors and friends: An over-looked resource in the informal support system. Research on Aging, 1(4).

Chappell, N. L. (1985). Social support and the receipt of home care services. Gerontologist, 25(1).

Clark, N. M., & Rakowski, W. (1983). Family care givers of older adults: Improving helping skills. Gerontologist, 23(6).

Clayton D. E., Schwall, V. L., & Pratt, C. C. (1984-85). Enhancing linkages between formal services and the informal support systems of the elderly. Gerontology and Geriatrics Education, 5(2).

Day, A. T. (1985). Who cares? Demographic trends challenge family care for the elderly. Population Trends and Public Policy. Population Reference Bureau, Inc.

DuBois, P. M. (1980). The hospice way of death. New York: Human Science Press.

Garner, J. D., & Mercer, S. O. (1982). Meeting the needs of the elderly: Home health care or institutionalization? Health and Social Work, 17(3).

Gelfand, D. E., & Gelfand, J. R. (1982). Senior centers and social support networks. In P. Biegel & A. Naparstek (Eds.), Community support systems and mental health. New York: Springer.

Getzel, G. S., & Mellor, J. M. (Eds.). (1984). Gerontological social work practice with the community elderly. New York: Haworth Press.

Kane, R. L., & Kane, R. A., (1980). Alternatives to institutional care of the elderly: Beyond the dichotomy. Gerontologist, 20(3).

Kohen, J. A. (1983). Old but not alone: Informal social supports among the elderly by marital status and sex. Gerontologist, 23(1).

Lurie, E. R., Kalish, R., Wexler, R. L., & Ansak, M. L. (1976). On Lok senior day health center. Gerontologist, 16.

Morrow, H. N., & Ozawa, M. N. (1987). Helping network: Senior to seniors. Gerontologist, 27(1).

Quinn, J., Segal, J., Raisz, H., & Johnson, C. (Eds.). (1982). Coordinating community services for the elderly: The triage experience. New York: Springer.

Ross, H. K. (1983). Neighborhood family: Community mental health for the elderly. Gerontologist, 23(3).

Shanas, E. (1979). The family as a social support in old age. Gerontologist, 19(2).

Silverman, P. R. (1976). Mutual help groups. Berkeley, CA: Sage.

Silverstone, B., & Burack-Weiss, A. (1983). Social work practice with the frail elderly and their families: The auxiliary function model. Springfield, IL: Charles C. Thomas.

Smyer, M. A. (1984). Working with families of impaired elderly. Journal of Community Psychology, 12(10).

Weeks, J. R. (1984). Aging concepts and social issues. Belmont, CA: Wadsworth.

Williams, J., & Anderson, H. (1986). Hospice. Caring, 5.

Wilson, P. A. (1981). Expanding the role of social workers in coordination of health services. Health and Social Work, 6(1).

Wolf, R. S., Halas, K. T., Green, L. B., & McNiff, M. L. (1986). A model for the integration of community-based health and social services. Home Health Care Services Quarterly, 6(4).

Zawadski, R. T., & Ansak, M. L. (1983). Consolidating community-based long-term care: Early returns from the On Lok demonstration. Gerontologist, 23(4).

Zimmer, A. H. (1982). Community care for the aged: The natural supports program. Journal of Gerontological Social Work, 5(1/2).

Zimmer, A. H., & Mellor, M.J. (1982). The role of the family in long-term home health care. Pride Institute Journal of Long-Term Home Health Care, 1(2).

CHAPTER 2

SOCIAL WORK IN NURSING HOMES

by Stephen D. Stahlman

Introduction

While social workers have been employed in health care settings since 1905, their involvement in nursing home facilities is a recent phenomenon dating to the 1960s. Nursing homes are one of many facilities which provide long-term care to elderly individuals. Long-term care refers to health, personal care and social services delivered over a sustained period of time to persons who have lost or never achieved some capacity for self care (Kane & Kane, 1987). Long-term care, whether continuous or intermittent, strives to provide care for the elderly in an environment which supports a high degree of autonomy for the older person.

While other age groups are recipients of long-term care services, the elderly constitute the largest consumers of long-term care, primarily through nursing home placement (Kane & Kane, 1987). In the past, long-term care referred specifically to institutional placement. Today the term implies a continuum of services such as home health care, respite care, hospice care and other services that are provided to meet the needs of the elderly.

Over the past twenty years, there has been an increase in the number of persons over 65 as well as an increase in the number of nursing homes. These increases have provided new opportunities for social workers in health care. They have also raised questions concerning the quality and cost of health care, the role of the social worker in nursing home facilities, and the bioethical dilemmas that have been created by advances in medical technology.

This chapter provides a description of nursing homes such as characteristics of residents, levels of care and staffing patterns. Three models of social work practice in working with the elderly are presented. Issues that relate to health policy and professional practice are also discussed. Lastly, future issues that affect the quality, cost of and access to care are considered.

Learning Outcomes

After completing this chapter, students will be able to:

- Describe pertinent characteristics of nursing homes including levels of care, staffing patterns and client population.

- Identify the role and function of social workers in nursing home care.

- Discuss the complexities of ethical decision making found in nursing home care.

- Identify future trends and issues in health care that will affect the elderly in nursing home facilities.

Outline of Key Topics and Content Areas

Nursing Home Demographics

      Development of Nursing Homes in Health Care
      Types of Facilities
      Resident Profile
      Staffing Patterns

Models of Social Work Practice

      Auxiliary Function Model
      Advocacy Model
      Intergenerational Family Model

Issues for Social Work

      Policy Issues
            Medicare and Medicaid Costs
            Effects of DRGs
            Certification Requirements

      Practice Issues
            Standards for Social Work Practice
            Interventions with Families
            Ethical Decision Making
            Interdisciplinary Approach

      Future Trends
            Quality of Care
            Access to Care
            Cost of Care

Summary of Key Topics and Content Areas

Nursing Home Demographics

Development of Nursing Homes in Health Care

While the growth of the modern day nursing home is a post 1930s phenomenon, the practice of providing care to elderly in private homes dates back to the early 1900s. Pegal (1981) indicates that at the beginning of the 1900s, as many as one thousand such homes existed. Most of these homes were owned and operated by philanthropic, charitable organizations, and churches. Many of the homes for the elderly at the turn of the century were a result of various immigrant self-help groups who wished to provide for their own. These homes were primarily custodial in nature and most often referred to as convalescent or rest homes. Most were very small and the administration consisted of family "mom" and "pop" operations. Nearly half the homes had no financial requirements for payment. In some homes, residents who were able-bodied were expected to contribute their share of work around the facility (Pegal, 1981).

Few changes occurred in long-term institutional care for the elderly from the early 1900s to the 1930s. The Social Security Act of 1935 was instrumental in the creation and development of the modern day nursing home. Title I of the Social Security Act established grants-in-aid to states, and Old Age Assistance (OAA) established federal responsibility for the care of the helpless by providing financial assistance (Vladeck, 1980). Even though cash assistance was given to the elderly, the provisions made clear that benefits would not be provided to individuals who were residing in any public institution such as a poor farm or almshouse. This act signaled the end of the poor farms and almshouses and marked the beginning of other living alternatives for the elderly. Proprietary homes began to emerge which provided services to the elderly, who now had resources to pay for such services.

Since the 1930s, the nursing home industry has experienced phenomenal growth due to the increase of health care needs of the elderly population. The reasons for this growth are varied and complex. Over the past fifty years, the advances in medical technology have increased longevity. Since more people are living longer, there has been an increase in the number of chronic conditions that are present among the elderly. In addition to increased longevity, a growing number of families have two wage earners outside the home, reducing the possibility for providing home care for aging parents. As society has become increasingly mobile, children may be unable to provide care for an aging parent.

Federal grants and loans were also made available which encouraged nursing home growth. The Hill-Burton Act of 1946 is an example of one such program. This government sponsored program initially provided direct grants for the construction of 350,000 beds in over 6,000 health care facilities. In 1954, the Hill-Burton Act was amended to provide grants for the construction of nonprofit nursing homes, giving further incentives for growth.

The amendments of the Social Security Act in 1965, commonly known as Medicare and Medicaid, significantly changed the way in which health care for the elderly would be paid. The purpose of the Medicare program was to provide a health insurance plan for those over the age of 65. The Medicare program is federally funded while Medicaid, on the other hand, is a federal/state partnership program designed to provide health care to certain disadvantaged and low income groups. A large percentage of Medicaid funding is spent on nursing home care. In 1983, 52.1% of all Medicaid expenditures were for this type of care (Holahan & Cohen, 1986).

Types of Facilities

The term "nursing home" typically refers to residential facilities in which at least 50% of the residents receive nursing services (Beaver & Miller, 1985). Homes that receive reimbursement from Medicare or Medicaid must be certified by the federal government as intermediate care facilities (ICFs) or skilled nursing facilities (SNFs). Care in SNFs and ICFs is covered by Medicaid but Medicare coverage is permissible only in SNF facilities. Kane and Kane (1987) indicate that, "although SNFs have stricter regulatory requirements, the differences in the care needs of residents are notoriously obscure" (p. 54). The data from the 1985 National Nursing Home Survey reveal that 27.7% of certified facilities were ICFs, additionally 18.3% were SNFs and 29.8% had both levels of certification. Of all nursing homes in the country, 75.9% were certified.

Nursing home sponsorship can be one of three categories. A nursing home may have proprietary ownership, designed specifically for profit. Nearly 75% of all nursing homes are proprietary. Nursing homes may also have voluntary ownership in which the facility is most likely run by a non-profit religious institution. Approximately 20% of the nursing homes have voluntary ownership. The third category of sponsorship is governmental. These facilities are run by state, and local municipalities. Nursing homes in the Veterans Administration would be an example of this category. See Table 1 for a summary of selected characteristics of nursing home facilities.

Table 1.
Selected Nursing Home Characteristics, 1985

Facility Characteristics	Nursing Homes		Nursing Home Beds	
	Number	Percent Distribution	Percent Distribution	Beds per Nursing Home
Total	19,100	100.0	100.0	85.0
Ownership				
Proprietary	14,300	74.9	69.0	78.4
Voluntary Nonprofit	3,800	19.9	22.8	97.6
Government	1,000	5.2	8.1	131.9
Certification				
Certified Facilities	14,400	75.8	88.8	99.4
SNF Only	3,500	18.3	19.0	88.0
SNF/ICF	5,700	29.8	44.6	127.0
ICF Only	5,300	27.7	25.2	77.2
Not Certified	4,700	24.6	11.3	38.9
Bed Size				
Less than 50 Beds	6,300	33.0	9.3	23.9
50-99 Beds	6,200	32.5	27.4	71.7
100-199 Beds	5,400	28.3	43.2	130.0
200 Beds or More	1,200	6.3	20.1	272.3
Census Region				
Northeast	4,400	23.0	22.8	84.4
North Central	5,600	29.3	32.7	94.9
South	6,100	31.9	30.1	80.0
West	3,000	15.7	14.4	78.6
Affiliation				
Chain	7,900	41.4	49.3	101.5
Independent	10,000	52.4	41.9	68.1
Government	1,000	5.2	8.1	131.9
Unknown	100	0.5	0.7	116.0

Source: 1985 National Nursing Home Survey. Adapted from National Center for Health Statistics data (Strahan, 1987).

Resident Profile

In 1986, the number of persons over the age of 65 numbered 29.2 million, representing 12.1% of the United States population (American Association of Retired Persons, 1987). This number represents a 14% increase since 1980 compared to only a 5% increase in the under-65 population. As a group, the elderly represent one out of every eight Americans. Of particular interest is the older population group (age 75-84) which is the fastest growing segment in the United States. As indicated earlier, the elderly population will continue to increase at a much faster rate than any other age group, with the largest increase expected between the years 2010 and 2030, when the "baby boom" generation reaches 65. Figure 1 illustrates the projected growth of the elderly population.

Figure 1.
Number of Persons 65+: 1900 to 2939
(in millions)

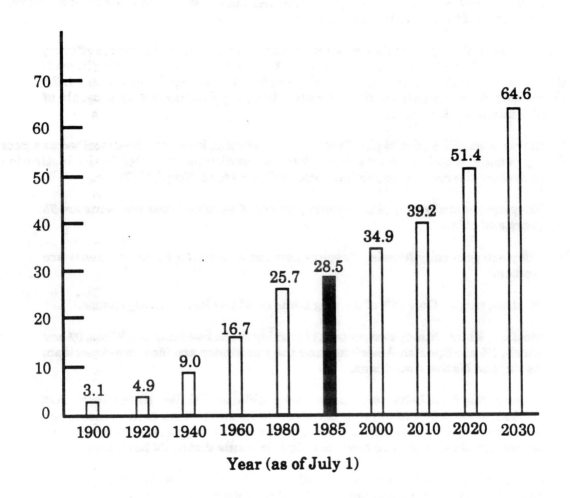

Note: Increments in years on horizontal scale are uneven.

Based on data from U.S. Bureau of Census

Source: American Association of Retired Persons, 1987

While it is important to understand the current and projected growth of the elderly, it is equally important to note that only a very small percentage of this population are living in institutionalized care at any given point in time. Currently, only about 5% (1.3 million) of the elderly live in institutional care settings, most of which are nursing home facilities. The percentage of elderly that live in institutional care dramatically increases with age. For example, only 2% of those elderly aged 65-74 live in institutional care, increasing to 7% for those elderly between the ages of 75-84. The percentages of persons age 85 or over living in nursing home care is 23.8% (U.S. National Center for Health Care Statistics, 1982).

What are the characteristics of a "typical" resident in nursing home care? Vladeck (1980) provides a description of the typical resident to be:

> . . . an 80 year old, white widow or spinster of relatively limited means, suffering from three or four chronic ailments. For most of the residents, the nursing home is their permanent place of residence until they die. The average length of stay is 2.5 years with only a small portion of patients being discharged as a result of rehabilitation services. (p. 13)

From this description, the "typical" resident in a nursing home can be described as a poor, white elderly female, who is suffering from chronic conditions who dies in the institution. Additional facts about the resident population include (Schneider & Kropf, 1987):

- They are generally very old. Seventy percent of nursing home residents are 75 years and older.

- They are generally female. Seventy percent of nursing home residents are women.

- Most are single. Only 12% of nursing home residents have a living spouse.

- Most are White. Ninety-two percent of nursing home residents are White, 6% are Black, 1% are Spanish-American, and the remainder are Mexican-American, Asian, and Native Americans.

- Many suffer from behavioral or mental problems. Studies have shown that between 33 and 80% of nursing home residents suffer from mental disorders. While most of these residents have some form of dementia, no one knows the percentage of residents who have reversible dementia that could be treated.

- Most have chronic or crippling disabilities and need help with the activities of daily living, including assistance with bathing, dressing or eating.

Today the resident population of nursing homes shows some changing characteristics, based in part on the implementation of the policy of Diagnostic-Related Groups (DRGs). The DRG system reimburses the hospital a flat fee based exclusively on the diagnostic category assigned to the patient. Hospitals are paid a predetermined price, based on the average cost of treating a patient with a particular diagnosis. The number of days of coverage and the rate of payment will differ for a patient with cardiac problems from someone with kidney failure.

Since the inauguration of the DRGs in 1984, studies have revealed that the average length of stay in hospitals has decreased (Bragg, 1986; Coe, Wilkinson, & Patterson, 1986). The concern of whether hospital patients are being released prematurely has implications for the nursing home population. If patients still need acute medical services, the nursing home becomes a possible alternative. In fact, nursing home populations are becoming more acutely ill and debilitated. This population will require greater specialization and more intensive care from nursing home staff.

Staffing Patterns

The personnel employed by a nursing home work in various departments, and contribute to the overall goals and needs of the resident population. The size and number of personnel vary considerably depending on the level of care and size of the total institution.

Schneider and Kropf (1987) provide an overview of the various departments and responsibilities that are found in most nursing home facilities. These include:

Dietary Department. The dietary program is responsible for planning and preparing the food served in a nursing home in accordance with state licensure regulations (and federal certification requirements if it is a certified facility). Special diets must be ordered by a physician.

Dietitian--is expert in planning menus, diets and dietary procedures. The dietitian is responsible for setting up special diets, as well as maintaining proper nutritional levels for residents.

Food Services Supervisor--is responsible for the daily preparation of foods, special diets, etc. He/she uses the menus developed by the dietitian.

Activities Department. Most nursing homes have an activities program. An activities program is a requirement for certification of ICFs and SNFs. Activities should be planned to be appropriate to the needs and interests of the residents and to enhance the quality of life.

Recreational Therapist (also called Activities Coordinator or Activities Director)--is responsible for developing, scheduling and conducting programs to meet the social and diversional needs of residents such as outside speakers, music, games, outings, parties, etc.

Nursing Services. Nursing Services generally includes RNs, LPNs, and nursing assistants/orderlies. These are the people who provide direct care to the residents.

Director of Nursing (DON)--is a registered nurse (RN) who oversees the entire nursing staff, including nursing supervisors, licensed practical nurses, nurses aides and orderlies. The DON is responsible for quality and safety in patient care.

Nursing Supervisor (also called charge nurses)--is responsible for nursing care to residents on a floor, or in an area or section, or the nursing home during a particular shift. May be an RN or LPN.

Registered Nurse (RN)--is a nurse with a minimum of two years of nursing school training.

Licensed Practical Nurse (LPN)--is a person who has completed one year vocational training in nursing. May be in charge of nursing in the absence of an RN. LPNs often administer medications and perform treatments.

Nursing Assistant/Aide/Orderly--are the people who supply 80-90% of the "hands-on" patient care given in nursing homes. Currently, there are no job qualifications established by states or the federal government for these positions.

<u>Administration</u>. The administration unit of a home may include the nursing home administrator, secretarial staff, accounting, and admissions. The nursing home administrator is usually required by state law to be in the home a minimum number of hours per week.

Nursing Home Administrator--is responsible for overall (fiscal, legal, medical and social) management and operation of the facility. Must be licensed by the Board of Nursing Home Administrators to operate a nursing home. This individual is ultimately responsible for all nursing home activities.

Medical Director--is the physician who formulates and directs overall policy for medical care in the nursing home. Usually only part-time (in the facility for 3-5 hours/month).

<u>Social Services</u>. Social Services departments are responsible for identifying the emotional, social and medically related needs of the patient. An assessment of each resident's needs should be found in his or her record and needed services should be incorporated into the care plan. If the services are not provided by the home, there are usually policies and procedures for referral.

Social Worker--is a person trained to identify medically related and emotional needs of residents and to provide services necessary to meet such needs. Most facilities have "social services designees" who provide services under the supervision of a social worker. Individuals working in social services usually do so on a part-time basis. "Designees" are frequently activities coordinators.

Reality Therapist--is a person trained to help reorient the disoriented patient to time, place and person.

<u>Housekeeping and Laundry</u>. Members of the housekeeping staff are usually responsible for basic housekeeping chores such as vacuuming floors, dusting, emptying waste cans, and cleaning furnishings. Most nursing homes have laundry facilities and provide clean bed linens and towels. The homes are also equipped to launder residents' clothing.

<u>Other Medical Staff</u>.

Attending Physicians--directly responsible for the care of residents. Residents must either choose their own physician or have one assigned by the nursing home to supervise their care.

Podiatrist--specializes in the diagnosis and treatment of diseases, defects and injuries of the foot.

Dermatologist--specializes in the diagnosis and treatment of diseases, defects and injuries of the skin.

Ophthalmologist--specializes in the diagnosis and treatment of diseases, defects and injuries of the eye.

Physical Therapist (PT)--trained in restoring the function of muscles in arms, legs, backs, hands, feet, etc., through movement, exercises or treatment. Usually a consultant to the facility. Sometimes physical therapy assistants carry out the plans of the therapists.

Occupational Therapist (OT)--trained to conduct therapy to restore the fine muscles of the hands and arms.

Models of Social Work Practice

In response to the demand for social services for residents in nursing homes, several social work practice models have been developed that provide frameworks for assessment and intervention with the elderly population in nursing home care. A description and discussion is provided below of three specific models: auxiliary function model, advocacy model and intergenerational family model.

Auxiliary Function Model

Silverstone and Burack-Weiss (1983) have developed a model specifically for working with the frail elderly. The frail elderly are identified as, "the old old (over 75) and other persons over sixty who suffer from impairments or enervating conditions that can temporarily or permanently interfere with autonomous functioning" (p. 5). The auxiliary function model is based on a systemic view of human behavior. Problems and solutions associated with aging are viewed as multi-dimensional rather than linear cause and effect. In addition, this model employs a problem solving framework to gather appropriate information and formulate a plan of action based on the data gathered.

With the frail elderly population, loss and depletion is a major theme. Silverstone and Burack-Weiss (1983) identify the various losses as primary and secondary losses. Primary depletion refers to those losses which are biological in nature. These losses may be external or internal. Examples of primary depletions include the sensory changes such as diminished eyesight, hearing or speech, and mental impairments.

Secondary depletions refer to those losses that are experienced by the elderly that accompany biological aging or are imposed by the age structure of our social system and other environmental deficits. For example as people age, the likelihood of the death of a spouse is increased. While secondary depletions are not confined to the frail elderly, they are experienced in greater frequency with this group. Additional examples of secondary depletions include changes in work status through retirement, loss of significant others, and financial changes.

Since the number of losses or depletions may be extensive, the desired goal of the auxiliary function model is to maximize the frail elderly person's adaptation through support. A supportive environment includes the use of significant others such as family, neighbors and friends. Within the context of this model, every effort is made to restore what is lost and conserve strengths and assets available to the frail elderly. Special attention is given to the adaptive response of the frail elderly. The responses to the primary and secondary depletions determine in part the level and type of intervention that is needed. Three specific responses to adaptation have been identified by Silverstone and Burack-Weiss (1983):

- The first adaptive response to depletion is that of restitution. "Restitution is the process of recovering a function that has been lost even if at a slightly diminished level" (p. 18). Restitution can occur through healing, spontaneous remission or external intervention.

- The second adaptive response to loss is that of compensation. Compensation involves the substitution of a lost object or increasing the function of an unimpaired part of the organism. For example, a person who has a leg amputated would increase the usage of their hands by using crutches. For depletions that occur at the secondary level, the compensation may include the development of new friendships to compensate for the death of significant others.

- The third adaptive response to primary and secondary depletion is accommodation. Accommodation should only be considered when restitution and compensation are not possible for the frail elderly. For example, when mental and physical disabilities have become chronic and the level of functioning has diminished significantly, restitution or compensation may be impossible. Accommodation may increase dependence, but services and support should be introduced to sustain the elderly person's functioning as much as possible.

Since the auxiliary function model focuses on the replacement of depletion, the degree to which restitution and compensation is possible is significantly influenced by the amount of resources that are available to provide support.

The function of the social worker in the auxiliary function model is to individualize the particular needs of each client. These tasks can be accomplished by preparation of a written statement identified as the study, assessment and plan (Figure 2). The study, assessment and plan serve as an organizing tool, a method of accountability, and a vehicle of interpersonal communication. The written statement identifies the various depletion of losses, how the client has responded to such losses and the development of short and long range objectives and corresponding tasks.

After the study, assessment and plan have been completed, the role of the social worker is to identify those support systems which will be used to carry out the auxiliary role. In many situations, this role will be performed by the family.

Advocacy Model

Many opportunities are provided in the nursing home setting for social workers to be advocates for the elderly resident. An advocate is a person who acts on behalf of another person when someone is not able to act on his/her own behalf. Hancock (1987) indicates that the social worker may carry out the role of patient advocate and "identify rules, regulations, practices and policies that are inconsistent with the rights of nursing home residents, or with the provision of care for the residents and to work toward their change" (p. 179).

Many nursing home practices affect patient care. These include: hiring practices which allow the employment of unqualified personnel, inadequate staffing, and any policy which would violate legal rights of residents. The social worker must work cooperatively with the nursing home administrator. However, in the role of patient advocate, the social worker must bring to the attention of the administrator those policies and conditions that impinge and violate the rights of residents. (See Figure 3 for the Bill of Rights for Nursing Home Residents in Virginia)

Besides the nursing home, the advocacy role extends to the community. The linkage between the nursing home facility and the community is a most important one. Communities can provide assistance and input through advisory boards. The community may be an important source of needed volunteers that help to link the facility with the surrounding area. In addition, educational programs can serve as an excellent marketing tool to provide information about programs and services that are available to the elderly in the community. One area often overlooked is the contributions the elderly can make to the community through such programs as Adopt A Grandparent.

Figure 2.
Outline of Study, Assessment, and Plan

1. STUDY

   A. Overview

      (1) Presenting problem and precipitating event
      (2) Referral Source
      (3) Client profile (face sheet)
         (a) Age, sex, marital status, race, religion
         (b) Family constellation
         (c) Socioeconomic and cultural influences
         (d) Environmental influences
      (4) Client and family behavior in interview situation
      (5) Professional contacts and consultation arranged

   B. Depletion and Losses

      (1) Primary: physical and mental
      (2) Secondary: social and economic

   C. Current Adaptation (Restitution, Compensation, and/or Accommodation)

      (1) Individual functioning
         (a) Activities of daily living
         (b) Problem-solving capacities
         (c) Affective and interpersonal behaviors
      (2) Environmental Functioning
         (a) Physical surroundings
         (b) Family: resources and problem-solving capacity
         (c) Service organizations
         (d) Other informal resources

   D. Previous adaptation

      (1) Developmental and situational crises
      (2) Life-style
      (3) Family exchange patterns

2. ASSESSMENT

   A. Summary of Study
   B. Interpretation: Reformulation of Problem

3. PLAN

   A. Long Range Objectives
   B. Short Range Goals
   C. Social Work Tasks

Figure 3.
Bill of Rights for Nursing Home Residents in Virginia

If you are a nursing home resident, it is your right by State law:

- To be informed of your rights and the rules and regulations governing you, and to be given a copy of the facility's policies and procedures upon admission.

- To be informed of available services and related charges.

- To be informed of your medical condition and to be involved in planning your treatment.

- To have your personal and medical records treated confidentially, and to have approval or refusal of their release.

- To be transferred or discharged only if:

    (1)   the transfer or discharge is appropriate for meeting your documented medical needs; or

    (2)   the transfer or discharge is necessary to safeguard you or other residents from physical or emotional injury; or

    (3)   the transfer or discharge is for the reason of nonpayment, except as prohibited by *Title XVIII or XIX of the Social Security Act and the Virginia State Plan for Medical Assistance.*

- To be consulted, along with your family or responsible party and attending physician, prior to transfer or discharge, and to be given at least five (5) days advance written notice of such transfer or discharge, except in an emergency involving your health and well-being.

- To be free from mental and physical abuse and to be free from unauthorized chemical or physical restraints.

- To not be required to perform services for the facility.

- To be treated with recognition of your dignity, individuality and privacy.

- To participate in social, religious and community activities.

- To use your personal clothing and possessions as space permits.

- To manage your personal financial affairs.

- To have private communication with persons of your choice and to send and receive unopened mail.

- To have privacy for visits with your spouse.

- To voice grievances and recommend changes in policy.

- To apply for and, if eligible, to receive Medicaid without restriction. This includes not being required to fulfill a specified period of residency in the facility before applying for Medicaid. No contract or agreement may require a deposit or other prepayment for Medicaid recipients, nor may the contract or agreement authorize the facility to refuse to accept retroactive Medicaid benefits.

- To receive information about the facility's admission policies, including any preference given. Nursing homes must disclose to applicants information on their waiting list, including but not limited to:

    (1) the number of persons on the waiting list;

    (2) the applicant's status in relation to the admission preferences of the facility; and

    (3) the dates when persons were placed on the waiting list.

For the exact wording of the rights, see Chapter 5 of the *Code of Virginia, Article 2, Title 32.1-127 and 32.1-138.*

Hancock (1987) identifies the Ombudsman program, National Citizens' Coalition for Nursing Home Reform, residents' councils, and legal rights of nursing home residents, as specific programs that promote advocacy for nursing home residents. The National Citizens' Coalition for Nursing Home Reform is a national organization formed in 1975 and seeks to improve long-term care systems and quality of life for residents. The Ombudsman program is federally mandated under the Older Americans Act. The nursing home ombudsman is an advocate for residents who have concerns about nursing home policy and operation. The nursing home residents' council is another federally mandated program. This council is a forum for the expression of patient concerns or input into policy-making in the facility.

Intergenerational Family Model

The model of intergenerational family treatment is an approach that can be used whenever an older adult is part of the family constellation (Greene, 1986). The model focuses on treating the older adult within the context of the family unit. One basic element in this model is the functional age of the older client. Functional age refers to the adaptational capacity in the biological, psychological and sociocultural areas (Greene, 1986). "An assessment of the individual from this perspective allows the caseworker and family alike to understand the structure of life and daily living habits of the older adult" (p. 19).

When bio-psycho-social changes occur in the older adult, changes also take place with other family members. Social workers cannot adequately address the older person's problems without realizing how the issues affect the entire family system. Interventions are designed to assist family members in their adaptation to functional age changes of an older family member. Family participation in treatment is encouraged. Social workers who employ the functional age model organize and interpret client information to arrive at a family-focused biopsychosocial assessment. The assessment includes how the changes in functioning of the older adult have altered the balance within the family system. Interventions are introduced that help restore individual and family functioning.

Issues for Social Work

Social workers in nursing home care are faced with many practice and policy concerns that have a direct effect on the clients they serve. They have an obligation to clients to be informed about practice and policy issues that affect programs and services. Policy issues such as Medicare and Medicaid costs, standards for nursing home care, and impact of diagnostic related groups (DRGs) are discussed below. Practice issues that have been identified for discussion include: interventions with families, ethical decision making and an interdisciplinary approach of working with the elderly.

Policy Issues

Medicare and Medicaid Costs. The Amendments to the Social Security Act of 1965 (Title XVIII and XIX), commonly known as Medicare and Medicaid, significantly changed the way in which health care of the elderly would be paid for. The Medicare Program provides a health insurance plan for those over age 65. Medicaid provides medical assistance for low income persons who are aged, blind, disabled or members of families with dependent children (Beaver & Miller, 1985). (See Table 2 for an overview of Medicare and Medicaid Services)

Figures 4 and 5 show how Medicare and Medicaid dollars are spent. Only 1% of the Medicare dollar is spent on nursing home care. Medicare does not provide for the type of custodial care typically provided in nursing homes. In 1984, 69% of Medicare expenditures were for acute care coverage in hospital settings. In contrast, Medicaid expenditures for nursing home care have continued to expand, from 52.1% in 1983 to 68% in 1984 (Holahan & Cohen, 1986; Kane & Kane, 1987). Federal Medicare outlays for the elderly have increased about 17% per year since 1970 and are expected to build to a deficit of $300 billion by 1995 (Inglehart, 1983).

National health care expenditures have risen dramatically in recent years. In 1986, expenditures totaled $458 billion, up from $75 billion in 1970, representing a compound annual increase of 12% (Standard and Poor's Industry Surveys, 1987). The reasons for the dramatic increase in health care expenditures are complex and varied. Rising demands and costs for health care have been created by the Medicare and Medicaid Programs of the 1960s. The increase in the number of elderly which require an increasingly larger percent of the health care dollar, and the level of medical technology which has created additional diagnostic tests and procedures all fuel the fires of increased costs (Standard & Poor's Industry Surveys, 1987).

The obvious question is: How are rising health care costs going to be paid for? Several efforts have been initiated to control the spiraling costs of health care. Morreim (1985) identifies the following attempts at cost containment which include: freezing physicians' fees, prospective payments like DRGs, mandatory establishment of rate setting commissions, and prior authorization of non emergency care for Medicaid patients. Other programs include the establishment of Health Maintenance Organizations (HMOs), and Preferred Provider Organizations (PPOs).

Effects of DRGs. One particular plan aimed at cost containment directly affecting the elderly is the Diagnostic Related Groups System (DRGs). Enacted in 1983 by Congress, the DRGs is a government program designed to provide incentives for cost containment of Medicare expenditures. Hospitals are paid a predetermined price for their services, a priced based on the average cost of treating a patient with a particular diagnosis (Dolenc & Dougherty, 1985). Since hospitals are reimbursed a flat rate, efforts must be made to make sure real costs do not exceed the amount that is reimbursable.

Table 2.
Summary of Medicare and Medicaid Programs

Program	Services Covered	Eligible Population	Copayments/User Charges
Medicare (Title XVIII of the Social Security Act) Part A - Hospital Insurance	In each benefit period (beginning with admission and ending 60 days after hospital or SNF discharge), 90 days of inpatient hospital care plus 60-day lifetime reserve; 100 days post-hospital SNF care; intermittent skilled home health care; limited hospice services. Hospitals are paid prospectively per admission according to patient's classification into one of 471 diagnosis related groups (DRGs). SNFs and home health agencies are paid per day and visit respectively.	All persons eligible for Social Security, younger persons with permanent disabilities or end-stage renal disease; also voluntary enrollees, 65 and over; most persons over 65 are covered.	The 1986 Hospital deductible is $492 plus a daily co-payment of $123 for days 61-90; lifetime reserve days have a copayment of $246. SNF care has a daily copayment of $61,50 for days 21-100.
Part B - Supplemental Medical Insurance	80% "reasonable and customary changes" for physician services, diagnostic tests, medical devices, outpatient hospital services, and laboratory services.	Those covered under Part A who elect coverage and pay monthly premium of $15.50 (1986). Medicaid pays premium for its recipients.	$15.50 monthly premium, $75 annual deductible and 20% copayment of reasonable or customary charges. In 1985, only 29.8% of physicians were "participating" physicians who accepted Medicare rates as payments in full. Extra charges beyond Medicare rates can be high.
Medicaid(Title XIX of the Social Security Act)	*Mandatory services for categorically needy:* Inpatient hospital, outpatient, SNF, limited home health, lab and x-ray, family planning, early and periodic screening, diagnosis and treatment for children through age 20; *Optional services* (vary from state to state): Dental care, therapies, drugs, intermediate care facilities, extended home care, private duty nurse, eye-glasses, prostheses, personal care services, medical transportation, home health services and homemaking. State can establish limits on the amount, duration, and scope of services. Under section 2176, as of 1982, DHHS can also waive certain Medicaid requirements to broaden coverage of community services to those who could otherwise require nursing home care.	Those who are known as "categorically needy" are automatically eligible: those who qualify for Supplemental Security Income (SSI), State Supplementary Payments (SSP), or Aid to Families with Dependent Children (AFDC). States have the option of covering certain needy families with unemployed parents, pregnant women with no eligible children, children under 18 and in school by including them in AFDC or covering them though they may not be eligible for AFDC. They also have the option of including the medically needy: those who do not qualify for public assistance by income but whose medical expenses effectively reduce their available income to categorical levels.	None, once recipient spends down to eligibility.

Source: Adapted from Kane and Kane (1987)

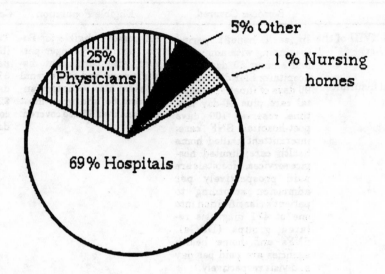

Figure 4.
Where the Medicare Dollar for the Elderly Went: 1984

5% Other

1% Nursing homes

25% Physicians

69% Hospitals

Source: Health Care Financing Administration, Office of Financial and Actuarial Analysis

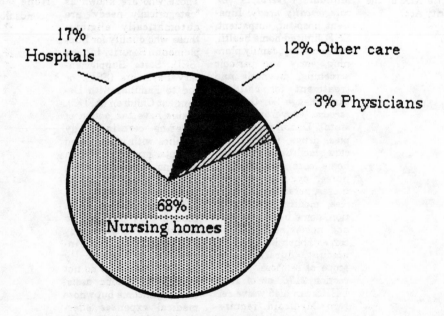

Figure 5.
Where the Medicaid Dollar for the Elderly Went: 1984

17% Hospitals

12% Other care

3% Physicians

68% Nursing homes

Source: Health Care Financing Administration, Office of Financial and Actuarial Analysis

One particular concern of health care professionals is the effect that DRGs will have on the quality of patient care. Since the implementation of DRGs, the nationwide average length of stay for Medicare patients in short stay hospitals decreased from 9.4 days in fiscal year 1983 to 7.5 days in fiscal year 1984 (Lyles, 1986). While this decrease in the average length of stay may signify greater efficiency of hospital use, many health care professionals fear that patients are being discharged "sicker and quicker."

Although too early to assess the full effect of DRGs upon patient care, some trends are beginning to emerge. One is that hospitals discourage admissions of seriously ill patients who require a longer length of stay than allowed under the DRG system. Such patients have been identified as "outliers" because they fall outside the range of reimbursement allowed by the DRG system. Already some hospitals are discouraging certain types of admission to keep down the number and amount of "outliers" (Meadors & Wilson, 1985). Dolenc and Dougherty (1985) indicate that hospitals will avoid seriously ill patients who will likely require a longer length of stay and will therefore most likely cost more than prospective payments allow. This trend has serious negative implications for the elderly since the severity of illness and number of chronic conditions both increase with age. While the intended effects of DRGs are to contain the spiraling cost of health care, patients who are discharged prematurely will create additional caregiving burdens on nursing homes and families.

Certification Requirements. Facilities that receive Medicaid or Medicare reimbursement must be certified. The certification requires compliance with minimal standards for care as set forth by the federal government. Schneider and Kropf (1987) provide a summary of the requirements of a skilled nursing facility. These include:

1. Compliance with federal, state, and local laws - It involves checking all licenses and registrations of facility staff (e.g., administrator, dieticians, etc.) and compliance with life safety rules and regulations.

2. Governing body and management - A facility must have a written policy for resident care that covers every aspect of medical and psychological treatment. This policy must be reviewed annually. There are also standards that pertain to disclosure of ownership, staffing patterns and staff development.

3. Medical direction - A facility must have a Medical Director who is responsible for implementing a resident care policy. The Director ensures that medical care is in compliance with federal and state regulations and meets the residents' needs.

4. Physician services - A resident may be admitted to a facility only through recommendation of a physician and must remain under the care of a physician throughout the resident's stay. The resident must be thoroughly examined within 48 hours after admission. The examining physician must prescribe a plan for medical and personal care and review that plan periodically. This plan is subject to peer review and should be adjusted as the resident's condition changes.

5. Nursing services - Skilled Nursing Facilities must have a Director of Nursing; a registered nurse on day duty, seven days a week; a charge nurse on each shift to supervise nursing activities; and a licensed practical nurse on duty 24 hours a day. Each resident should have a written plan of care. The director of nursing and the medical director review and revise the plan and make sure it is carried out. This plan of care includes a resident's diet, medication, physical therapy, physical limitations and psychosocial needs. Only an RN, LPN, a doctor or a

staff member with appropriate training can administer drugs. The drugs must be kept in a safe place, labeled, and dispensed according to a doctor's order. A complete record of each dosage and its effects must be kept. The physician who prescribes medication must do so in writing and review the orders frequently. Medication cannot be used as a convenience for staff members. Residents may use their own drugs with the approval of a physician.

6. <u>Dietetic services</u> - The facility must also have a dietician or a staff member responsible for nutrition who consults a dietician regularly. The dietician should consult with residents' physicians in determining any special needs. Restrictions should be noted in writing in the medical record. Those residents who need help eating must receive it. Residents also have a right to make suggestions about their diets and the dietician must take into account each resident's "food preferences and eating habits." Any change in a resident's eating habits should be noted for the physician.

7. <u>Special rehabilitative services</u> - Residents must be able to receive necessary rehabilitative treatment. If the facility cannot provide this service, it must enable the resident to get the service, or specify that it does not offer rehabilitation. The facility is responsible for helping residents to achieve the widest range of motion possible and at the same time, adjust to their physical limitations.

8. <u>Pharmaceutical services</u> - The facility should have someone who is responsible for the distribution of drugs. If this person is not a pharmacist, the facility should periodically consult with a pharmacist. There should be a periodic review of all drugs prescribed to a resident to ensure the drugs are working properly, without undesirable side effects.

9. <u>Laboratory and radiological services</u> - Facilities should either provide or arrange for the provision of x-rays, blood tests, and emergency treatment. Doctors' orders are needed for these services. Orders should be documented in the resident's patient care chart with a dated doctor's signature.

10. <u>Dental services</u> - Facilities should refer residents to dentists. They should help residents get to and from such services and keep the results of all tests as part of the resident's medical record. Facilities are responsible for daily oral hygiene and the maintenance of dentures.

11. <u>Social services</u> - Facilities must have a social service worker on hand or must have someone who acts as a liaison with a social service agency in the community. This person helps develop resident care plans and attends to residents' psychosocial and emotional needs. The worker maintains contact with each resident's family and informs them of the resident's rights.

12. <u>Resident activities</u> - The regulations are not specific with regard to residents' activities. The purpose of an activities program is to create an environment that is as near to normal as possible, thereby encouraging persons in a facility to exercise their abilities. An activities program should provide physical, intellectual, social, spiritual, and emotional challenges much in the same way that every day life in the community provides challenges. All that the standards require is that the facility provide adequate space and facilities, and an activities director. Residents may refuse to participate if they wish. Physicians must approve an activity plan and can limit residents' activities if they consider it medically necessary.

13. Medical records - The Medical Director and the Director of Nursing must maintain medical records for each resident. These are confidential and must contain notes on every aspect of the resident's medical condition and treatment. They must be up-to-date and signed. Only a doctor may make medical judgments. After each visit, the attending physician should note the resident's condition and review the plan of treatment, in writing, in the resident's medical record.

14. Transfer agreement - Nursing homes must have transfer agreements with a hospital so that when their residents require more skilled care, the homes can assist residents in receiving such care.

15. Physical environment - The physical environment of the facility must meet the standards of the Fire Code and the Life Safety Code.

16. Infection control - Each facility must have a disaster plan that is practiced regularly. Staff members should receive disaster preparedness training.

17. Utilization review - Facilities are required to have utilization review committees to ensure that quality care is provided efficiently, appropriately, and cost effectively. They focus primarily on expenditures and review residents' records and conditions to make sure that the facilities provide the appropriate level of care. They monitor treatment and residents' care plans. Members of the committee come from the staff of the facility and from the local community. They are physicians and health professionals, and they offer an evaluation of the medical needs of the resident. The utilization review committee should work closely with the administrative staff of the home to facilitate necessary changes in resident care. The facility must have an operational discharge planning program.

In addition, each state requires SNF and ICF facilities to be licensed. The state regulations vary from state to state, but are usually similar to the Federal regulations for certification above.

The purpose of state and federal regulations is to ensure that the facility has the capacity to provide adequate care. The regulations require that the building itself meets safety requirements, that procedures be established for infection control, that facilities employ staff or consultants with certain formal credentials, and that medical records meet certain requirements (Kane & Kane, 1987). The regulations provide only minimal expectations for staffing and operation.

Social workers should know that the federal regulations require the person designated as social service director to have an MSW or BSW from a program accredited by the Council on Social Work Education (CSWE). However, if that person does not meet the requirement, then a consultant with those credentials meets with the social service director. The term "social service designee" has been used to refer to those persons who are assigned social service responsibilities without professional social work training. In a comparison between social work consultants and social service designees, Gehrke and Wattenberg (1981) found that social service designees frequently identified the needs of the elderly, but were unable to provide many of the services needed. These authors cited lack of time and training for designees as reasons for the inability to provide care beyond the planning stage.

Practice Issues

Standards for Social Work Practice. The National Association of Social Workers (NASW) has developed standards of social work practice in long-term care facilities. According to these standards, social work objectives for long-term care include the following (NASW, 1981):

1. Provide direct social services to residents, their families, and significant others.

2. Assist residents, families and significant others to utilize appropriately and receive maximum benefit from the facility and the community-based social and health resources on a continuum throughout the stay of each individual from preadmission to discharge or death.

3. Strengthening communications between residents, their families, and significant others, and the program or facility staff.

4. Assisting the facility to achieve and maintain a therapeutic environment essential to the optimal quality of life and independent functioning of each resident and to provide for maximum participation of residents in planning activities and policies.

5. Promoting facility-community interaction through encouraging community involvement in the facility and resident and staff involvement in the community, developing linkages with a wide range of community resources, and participating in the assessment of the need for and planning for other long-term and health care resources.

Intervention with Families. Contrary to the myth that older people are isolated and alienated, the family is the primary source of social support for older people. The immediate family tends to be the major source of help during illness and the extended family ties the elderly to the community (Shanas, 1979). The availability of family is often a major determinant of whether an older person lives in a nursing home or in the community (Smyer, 1980). For every older person living in a nursing home, two or more equally impaired elderly live with and are cared for by family (Hooyman & Kiyak, 1988).

The decision to move a loved one into a nursing home facility is not easy. The social worker often works with the family members to assist in the transition. Mixed feelings such as a sense of relief, guilt, anger and loss are common. The social worker must be prepared to deal with the family's response to nursing home placement. The family can also be a tremendous source of information during the admission stage. Brody and Sparks (1966) have indicated that at the time when institutional care is requested, the family is in a state of crisis and the placement reveals family patterns and reoccurring themes in full strength. Greene (1982) suggests that the following questions can give the social worker insight concerning future interventions and also provide an opportunity for family members to discuss the crisis of institutionalization. These include: What were the major disabilities? What kind of assistance in daily living did the new resident require prior to admission? What were some of the problems and stresses each family member faced and how did they try to cope with them?

Once placement has been made, the social worker can be instrumental in providing families with instruction about the nursing home, establishing a mutual support group with other family members, and providing information on the particular disease or condition of the family member. The need for the family to keep in regular contact with the resident should be emphasized. Hooyman and Lustbader (1986) indicate that nursing home residents who have regular visitors receive better care than those without. When staff are aware that family members will follow-up on a resident's request, they are likely to fulfill it more quickly than in the absence of this expectation. The importance of the social worker working with family members from the pre-admission screening through discharge cannot be overemphasized. The family's involvement in the life of their loved one ideally continues after the placement has been made.

Ethical Decision Making. While social workers perform various roles in the nursing home, all will be confronted with situations and circumstances requiring decision making skills in bioethics. Broadly defined, bioethics refer to the ethical decisions that are made in health care. Blumenfield and Lowe (1987) indicate that an ethical dilemma can occur when there is a pull of divergent loyalties and interests. An ethical dilemma exists when acting on one moral conviction means behaving contrary to another one or when adhering to one value means abandoning another.

The expanding technologies of the medical field have increased the complexity of ethical decision making. The introduction of new technologies such as organ transplants, in vitro fertilization, genetic screening and life-sustaining support systems have led to increased complexities that could not have been possible even twenty-five years ago. These technological changes have made possible the ability to maintain life almost indefinitely through artificial life support systems, as in the case of Karen Quinlin. Once, the cessation of a heart beat determined death, but now, as a result of the advances in medical technology, the criteria for determining when death occurs have been the subject of much debate. As the level of medical technology advances, so does the level of complexity involving ethical decision making. The social worker who is employed in a nursing home must come to grips with such questions as: What action should be taken in life and death situations? Who should make such decisions and under what circumstances? What criteria should be used in arriving at a chosen course of action? How much and when should information be shared with residents with terminal conditions? Who should make decisions when the resident is unable to decide for him or herself? These are only a few of the many ethical questions that social workers confront in nursing home facilities.

Guidelines can be offered to assist the social worker with such difficult decisions. While not providing specific responses to specific issues, the National Association of Social Workers (NASW) Code of Ethics provides useful guidelines relevant to the worker's obligations to client, staff and the profession. The common theme that is present within social work and health care is the underlying concern about right and wrong with respect to the duties and obligations of the social worker. Questions concerning values and ethics have been apparent since the inauguration of the profession in the late nineteenth century; however, the subject has not received widespread, systematic attention in social work education (Reamer, 1985).

One decision making model that has been developed by Blumenfield and Lowe (1987) provides an understanding of the conditions which create the need to make an ethical decision. Accordingly, ethical decisions encompass three specific components which interact together. These include the knowledge of the situation, the dimensions of the decision making process and the value systems that are employed. Typical conflicts that can occur include:

1. A conflict between two ethical principles held by the individual.
2. A conflict between two possible actions in which some reasons favor one course of action and others mitigate against this course. Neither set of reasons is conclusive.
3. A conflict that exists between two unsatisfactory alternatives.
4. A conflict between one's principles and one's perceived role.
5. A conflict between the need to act and the need to consider.

It is helpful to understand the opposing conditions that are present in the ethical decision that must be made. As social workers in nursing homes, the ethical decision may be compounded when the social worker feels inadequate as a result of not being prepared to make such decisions. Reamer (1985) indicts the social work profession for failure to adequately prepare social work students in ethical decision making skills. As opportunities continue to grow for social workers in nursing home facilities, service providers must be knowledgeable and appropriately trained in being able to employ ethical decision making skills.

Interdisciplinary Approach. While the role of a social worker may vary from facility to facility, one commonality that they all share is membership on a health care team. A nursing home social worker is a member of a team that provides a "therapeutic community" to meet the needs of the residents. The team consists of nursing staff, rehabilitation therapists, and social workers. Collaboratively, the team identifies short- and long-term goals, meets on a regular basis to assess progress, and reevaluates or formulates new goals appropriate to client care. One particular contribution that the social worker makes to the team is providing a social history of residents. The social history includes background information about family, medical information and other information relevant in meeting the psychosocial needs of the resident. After the social history is completed, a care plan is developed and short and long-term care goals are established. Care plans are periodically reviewed and updated by team members to ensure that the psychosocial needs are being met.

Future Trends

As social workers in nursing home care look to the future, what changes can be anticipated? As previously indicated, the elderly population, particularly those over age 75, will continue to grow, making it likely for continued growth in nursing home care, particularly in skilled nursing facilities. Although the need for nursing home care will continue to expand into the 1980s and 1990s, several changes arise concerning issues of quality, access and costs of providing care for the elderly.

Quality of Care. Quality care is a difficult term to define. What services, and/or programs can be identified as meeting an acceptable level of quality? Kane and Kane (1987) indicate that quality assurance has three sequential steps. These include: defining quality, assessing programs to identify where quality is deficient, and correcting identified deficiencies. Government approaches to upholding quality have included licensing, certification, inspection of care, the Ombudsman program, and regulation of personnel.

The present federal standards only require that the facility have the capacity to provide for adequate care, rather than ensuring the facility does provide quality care. Recently, The Institute of Medicine (1986) identified a number of issues to establish and enhance the quality of care. These include:

- Regulations should be directed toward assuring that desirable and appropriate outcomes are achieved, leaving providers freer to be creative in their approach but still holding them accountable.

- Facilities house an extremely heterogeneous group of residents. In particular, some residents are severely or moderately cognitively impaired. It is unlikely that quality of life can be assured for both the confused and the mentally intact in the same programs.

- To define quality adequately in facilities, tradeoffs must be made among desirable outcomes--for example, physical well-being, pain control, improvement of functioning, psychological well-being, safety, and social activities. It is unclear who should make those choices (the residents, the staff, the regulators, the payors). Perhaps it is possible to establish specific goals as desired by particular residents, or to develop facilities with differing emphases from which potential residents select.

- Quality assurance has barely been explored for home care and other community long-term care programs. Given the difficulty in guaranteeing adequate care in facilities, the prospect for affording protection in the private settings of dispersed personal homes is daunting, especially when some of the clientele will be vulnerable and unable to report poor care or exploitation.

- Long-term care in facilities and at home depends on a cadre of personnel who tend to be ill trained and paid the minimum wage. Upgrading the quality of care without upgrading the skills and the salary of nursing assistants and homemaker/home health aides seems problematic, yet some argue the cost of any real change would be prohibitive.

- Once a true consensus on the expectations for a long-term care program of adequate quality is reached, the challenge remains to examine the incentives affecting the providers. Incentives should be present that drive the system to that goal, and, at the least, no perverse incentives that encourage negative results should be permitted. Because so much of long-term care is a proprietary industry, the payment system is a candidate for positive incentives and should be examined for lurking disincentives to quality. Incentives are particularly desirable if they encourage providers to strive toward excellence rather than merely to meet minimum standards of acceptability.

Access to Care. In addition to quality of care, access to care will be an issue for the future. Long-term care of the elderly is often viewed as fragmented and uncoordinated. Consumers have difficulty gathering information about existing programs and services. In addition, facilities often avoid residents needing heavy care or exhibiting a behavior problem, or those financed by Medicaid (Kane & Kane, 1987).

Two specific strategies that will improve access to care are preadmission screening and case management. The purpose of preadmission screening is to determine the appropriateness of nursing home placement. In 1985 there were 29 states that had a preadmission program (Iverson, 1986).

The second strategy, case management, consists of a "package" of services to meet an individual's need in allocating resources across a community or catchment area (Kane & Kane, 1987). Case management can be offered by many organizations such as hospitals, Area Agencies on Aging, family service agencies or private case manager agencies. Kane and Kane (1987) point to considerable confusion that exists within the case management system. Issues that go unresolved include:

- Is case management useful without additional services or without additional money to pay for services? The answer to this question depends on whether the major problems of long-term care are getting information about services, finding enough services in the community, or paying for them.

51

- Can case management appropriately be done by organizations that also provide service? Does this introduce a conflict of interest?

- To what extent should case managers build expectations of family care into a plan?

- To what extent should case managers use the client's preferences as the basis for a plan?

Attention to these specific issues will enhance case management as a service method for older clients.

Cost of Care. Another issue that will affect nursing home care in the future is the cost and payment of care. Current tax revenues are not expected to meet increased expenditures. Changes will need to be made in the way health care is financed. Since nursing homes consume a major portion of the health care dollar, policies must be developed to ensure that adequate financing is available for meeting the needs of the residents. Kane and Kane (1987) indicate that future efforts to limit the nursing home sector will include: limiting the supply of nursing home beds, changing the way nursing homes are paid, and substituting less expensive community care for more expensive care in facilities.

As costs continue to grow, there is a danger that adequate health care services will not be available. Society may experience an unwillingness to pay for care since a large portion of health care costs are financed by state and federal governments. If costs are to be controlled, new sources of revenue must be generated. New programs of long-term care insurance provided by private insurers are being proposed, but the risks are substantial to the companies until actuarial data are more complete. Suggested proposals for reform have included: removing prohibitions against reimbursement for preventative care; raising Medicare eligibility to 70 years of age; changing health care from an age-based to a needs-based system; and providing catastrophic insurance for an additional monthly premium (Ball, 1985). Congress passed a version of a catastrophic provision for the elderly in 1988.

Conclusion

The elderly are the fastest growing age group in our society and will continue to show steady growth into the 21st century. The increase in this population group will necessitate the expansion and creation of programs to meet the biopsychosocial needs of the elderly. As the number of those over the age of 75 increases, so will the demand for nursing home care. The changing demographics will provide many challenges for the social work profession. Social workers in nursing homes must be appropriately trained to meet the psychosocial needs of the elderly. This training must include knowledge of social work practice with the elderly, skills for ethical decision making and the ability to advocate for and on behalf of clients. Social workers must also accept the challenge of developing policies that are in the best interests of the elderly.

While no one can predict the future, the outlook for social workers in nursing home care can be viewed with cautious optimism. As the profession of social work continues to increase the knowledge base for practice with elderly in nursing home care, it is expected that additional knowledge, technologies, and instruments will be developed that more effectively meet the psychosocial needs of nursing home residents. Social workers will be called upon to meet these challenges on behalf of the elderly population.

Chapter References

American Association of Retired Persons. (1987). A profile of older Americans: 1987. Washington, DC: U.S. Department of Health and Human Services

Ball, R. (1985). Medicare: A strategy for protecting and improving it. Generations, 14, 9-12.

Beaver, M., & Miller, D. (1985). Clinical social work practice with the elderly. Homewood, IL: Dorsey Press.

Blumenfield, S., & Lowe, J. (1987). A template for analyzing ethical dilemmas in discharge planning. Health and Social Work, 12, 47-56.

Bragg, M. (1986). Ompro appropriateness of discharge study. Paper presented at the Issues in Discharge Planning workshop, Salem, OR.

Brody, E., & Sparks, G. (1966). Institutionalization of the aged. Family Process, 5, 76-90.

Coe, M., Wilkinson, A., & Patterson, P. (1986). Preliminary evidence on the impact of DRGs dependency at discharge study. Portland, OR: Northwest Oregon Health Systems.

Dolenc, D., & Dougherty, C. (1985). DRGs: The counter-revolution in financing health care. Hastings Center Report, 15, 19-29.

Gehrke, J., & Wattenberg, S. (1981). Assessing social services in nursing homes. Health and Social Work, 6, 12-25.

Greene, R. (1982). Families and the nursing home social worker. Social Work in Health Care, 7, 57-67.

Greene, R. (1986). Social work with the aged and their families. Hawthorne, NY: Aldine De Gruyter.

Hancock, B. (1987). Social work with older people. Englewood Cliffs, NJ: Prentice Hall.

Holahan, J., & Cohen, J. (1986). Medicaid: The tradeoff between cost containment and access to health care. Washington, DC: Urban Institute Press.

Hooyman, N., & Kiyak, H. (1988). Social gerontology: A multi-disciplinary perspective. Needham Heights, MA: Allyn & Bacon.

Hooyman, N., & Lustbader, W. (1986). Taking care. New York: The Free Press.

Inglehart, J. (1983). Medicare begins prospective payment of hospitals. New England Journal of Medicine, 308, 1428-32.

Institute of Medicine. (1986). Improving the quality of care in nursing homes. Washington, DC: Academy Press.

Iverson, L. (1986). A description and analysis of state preadmission programs. Minneapolis, MN: Inter-study, Center for Aging and Long-Term Care.

Kane, R. A., & Kane, R. L. (1987). Long-term care: Principles, programs, and policies. New York: Springer.

Lyles, Y. (1986). Impact of medical diagnosis-related groups (DRGs) on nursing homes in the Portland, Oregon metropolitan area. Journal of the American Geriatrics Society, 34, 573-578.

Meadors, A., & Wilson, N. (1985). Prospective payment system for hospital reimbursement. Hospital Administration Currents, 29, 3.

Morreim, H. (1985). The MD and the DRG. Hastings Center Report, 15, 30-39.

National Association of Social Workers. (1981). Standards for social work services in long-term care facilities. Silver Spring, MD: Author.

Pegal, C. (1981). Health care and the elderly. Rockville, MD: Aspen Publications.

Reamer, F. (1985). The emergence of bioethics in social work. Health and Social Work, 10, 271-281.

Schneider, R., & Kropf, N. (1987). Virginia Ombudsman program: Professional certification curriculum. Richmond, VA: Virginia Department for the Aging.

Shanas, E. (1979). The family as social support in old age. The Gerontologist, 19, 169-174.

Silverstone, B., & Burack-Weiss, A. (1983). Social work practice with the frail elderly and their families: The auxiliary function model. Springfield, IL: Charles C. Thomas

Smyer, M. (1980). The differential usage of services by impaired elderly. Journal of Gerontology, 35, 249-255.

Standard and Poor's Industry Surveys. (1987). New York: McGraw Hill.

Strahan, G. (1987). Nursing home characteristics (DHHS Publication No. PHS 87-1250). Hyattsville, MD: National Center for Health Statistics.

U.S. National Center for Health Care Statistics. (1982). Advance data from vital and health statistics. Washington, DC: U.S. Government Printing Office

Vladeck, B. (1980). Unloving care. New York: Basic Books.

Discussion Questions

1. How do social workers incorporate their values and skills into a nursing home setting?

2. Over 70% of nursing homes are owned by profit making enterprises. In what ways might this affect the quality of care?

3. What are the differences between an ICF and SNF facility?

4. What are DRGs and how might they affect the care of the elderly in nursing homes?

5. What are major differences between Medicare and Medicaid policies and programs?

6. Can the public perception of a nursing home ever be changed? How?

7. Mrs. J., a 78 year old resident of an SNF facility, has recently had a feeding tube inserted. She has been in a coma for two weeks. Mrs. J.'s daughter wants the tube removed, but the physician refuses. What ethical issues are present in this scenario?

Learning Activities

Activity #1. Fantasy Exercise

Give students the following instructions:

You are an 80 year old person, and you have come to live in a nursing home. It was difficult for you to leave your home, but you and your doctor, your family and your friends have come to believe that you really need the help you can get from a skilled nursing facility. Your safety, social, nutritional and housekeeping needs are being taken care of in the nursing home.

For the purpose of this exercise, you can only keep seven of the privileges listed below. Place an (X) in front of the seven which are most important to you. If the most important things to your happiness are not listed, you may add two choices by writing them in the space marked "Other." These will be included in your final list of seven. You will have ten minutes to complete this part of the activity. A discussion will follow.

_____ The privilege of taking frequent trips, and visiting with family and/or friends outside the nursing home.

_____ The privilege of engaging in some gainful activity every day, similar to what you did in your home or apartment.

_____ The privilege of keeping pictures of your family and small, treasured momentoes close to you.

_____ The privilege of defining your own schedule, i.e., making noise, staying up late, not getting dressed in the morning, etc.

_____ The privilege of being considered a sexual being and of being able to entertain friends in sufficient space and with privacy.

_____ The privilege of keeping and preparing food any way you please.

_____ The privilege of bringing favorite pieces of furniture from you home or apartment and of having your living space be a reflection of your personality (including not being particularly neat).

_____ The privilege of having a pet.

_____ The privilege of living in a heterogeneous community where you regularly come into contact with people of different ages and races, including children.

_____ The privilege of monitoring your own health; to keep, take, or refuse to take medications.

_____ The privilege of making totally independent decisions, with yourself and your close family and friends as the only people's opinions to consider.

_____ The privilege of choosing how you will spend your time.

_____ The privilege of having space and supplies to work on your hobby.

_____ The privilege of being alone and having absolute peace and quiet.

_____ The privilege of grieving for loss of home and independent living status.

_____ The privilege of receiving considerate, respectful care, with your privacy and need for independence inviolate.

_____ The privilege of living in an environment where it is okay to talk about and discuss your fears and feelings about aging, life and death.

Other: _____

_____

In the discussion after the 10 minute period, the leader should ask students to share their choices and the reasons why those items were so important. During the session, it should be pointed out that placement in a nursing home can often be a major assault on a person's autonomy.

Activity #2. Learned Helplessness

Instructions: Divide the class into four groups of 5-8 members each and give each group a number from one to four. Give each students in Groups 1 and 2 copies of TEST A and give Groups 3 and 4 copies of TEST B. Instruct the students in all groups to fold the TEST in half lengthwise so only COLUMN 1 shows. Tell the students to work as a group to unscramble the words in COLUMN 1 until you tell them to stop. Give the students ten minutes to work on this task. After 10 minutes, have the students flip their sheets to COLUMN B. Instruct them to repeat the unscrambling process for this set of words.

A major difference exists between the scrambled words in TEST A and TEST B. COLUMN 1 of TEST A are not solvable while this column in TEST B can be solved. The purpose of this activity is to demonstrate that Groups 1 and 2 will experience learned helplessness while Groups 3 and 4 will not. The expectation is that Groups 1 and 2 will do poorer on unscrambling the words in COLUMN 2 than Groups 3 and 4. The reason is that Groups 3 and 4 will experience a feeling of competence in unscrambling their first set of words while Groups 1 and 2 would have experienced feelings of helplessness.

After all the groups have unscrambled both columns, read the correct answers. In descending order, the unscrambled words are for Group 3 and 4 (TEST B, COLUMN 1): goals, during, rescue, quite, recently, effects, variety, doing. As stated, the words for Groups 1 and 2 (TEST A, COLUMN 1) cannot be unscrambled. Both TEST A and B have the same words in COLUMN 2 which in descending order are: bawdy, change, faded, heavy, legion, magnet, object, roast. After giving the correct answers, explain how the experiment was set up. The explanation is summarized below.

Explanation:

The purpose of the experiment is to discuss an unsuccessful means of coping with stress called learned helplessness. Learned helplessness is the perception that no matter how hard you try, you can't change your situation (stress.) The individual learns that events are beyond his or her control and therefore does not attempt to "resist" the stress even though he or she could succeed. Learned helplessness can result in loss of motivation, decreased cognitive abilities, and depression.

Let me give you a common example of how learned helplessness can occur in old age. Let's assume that an elderly woman who lives with her children has broken her hip. While recuperating in the hospital, her family tells her that if she is successful with her physical therapy in the nursing home, she can come home. However as time goes on, the family decides it would be better if she remained in the nursing home. What will be this elderly woman's reaction? She will learn that no matter how hard she tries, she will never leave the facility. How much effort do you think she will put into her physical therapy? How much motivation will she have?

The key to understanding, preventing, and treating learned helplessness is the concept of control. Any time you can promote the feeling of control on the part of the elderly, you can prevent learned helplessness. What are ways that control on the part of the elderly can be supported?

After telling the class about the experiment, discuss how Groups 1 and 2 felt after they could not solve the first set of scrambled words. As a class, brainstorm ways of decreasing learned helplessness in nursing home residents.

TEST A

COLUMN 1	COLUMN 2
girfl	wybda
rislon	eganch
digby	fedda
farcle	yaveh
roizza	gonile
sallet	gamten
vandot	jobcet
sumnud	sotar

TEST B

COLUMN 1	COLUMN 2
sgalo	wybda
ridugn	eganch
scerue	fedda
tique	yaveh
clneetry	gonile
cetefts	gamten
iartevy	jobcet
godin	sotar

Activity #3. Decision Rectangles

Directions: Give all students a copy of a blank Decision Rectangle sheet. The instructor should review the copy of the Decision Rectangle sheet that is completed and illustrated with various decisions.

The instructor should inform the students that this learning activity is an exercise that may reflect the range of life decisions over which all of us have or do not have control. The outer rectangle is

Decisions and Adjustments We Make in Controlling Our Lives

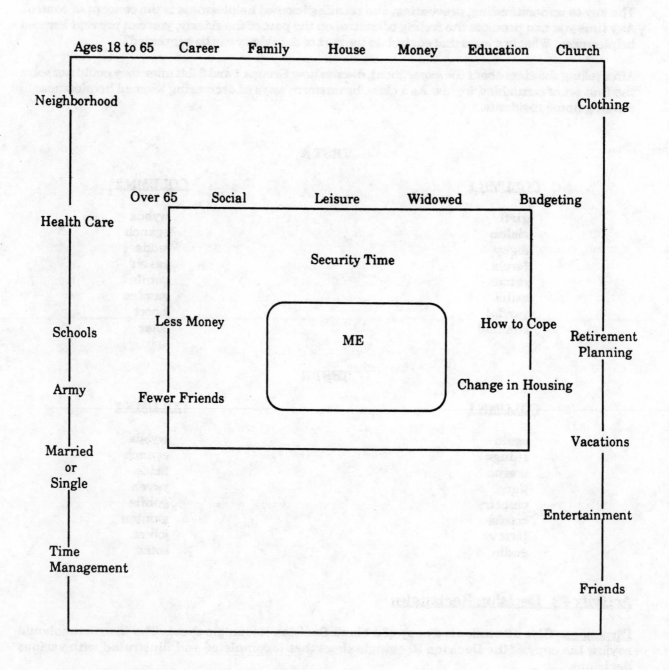

Ages 18 to 65   Career   Family   House   Money   Education   Church

Neighborhood

Clothing

Over 65   Social   Leisure   Widowed   Budgeting

Health Care

Security Time

Schools

Less Money

How to Cope

ME

Retirement Planning

Army

Fewer Friends

Change in Housing

Married
or
Single

Vacations

Entertainment

Time
Management

Friends

Decision Rectangles

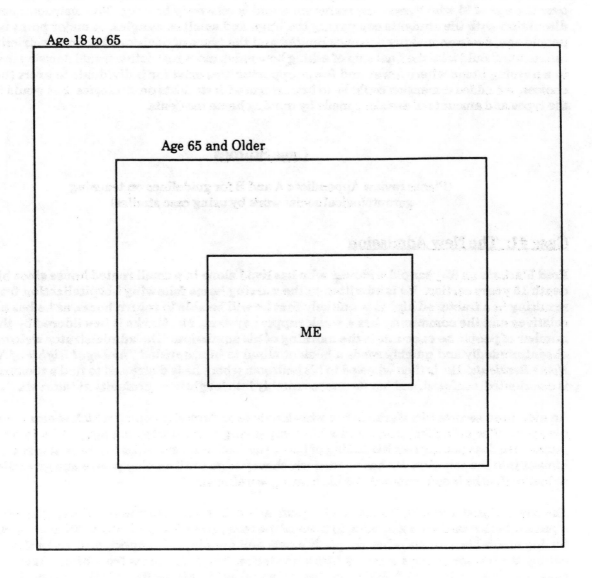

Age 18 to 65

Age 65 and Older

ME

larger than the inner rectangle and it represents all the decisions that we make from age 18 to 65. The smaller rectangle represents the life decisions that we make when we are over the age of 65. Around the rectangle, students should be told to write down all of the important decisions, events, personal choices, roles, plans, or activities that a person from age 18 to 65 might consider throughout this time period. There should be a considerable range of these decisions, e.g., see the completed rectangle.

Students should then begin to identify those decision areas for the smaller rectangle, for a person over the age of 65 who lives in the community and is relatively healthy. The instructor can lead a discussion with the students comparing the large and small rectangles. A major point is that as people age, decision making becomes limited and the types of decisions become restrictive. The instructor should take the final step of asking how much more restrictive would decision making be in a nursing home where fewer and fewer opportunities exist for individuals to exert their own choices. An added dimension could be to brainstorm with students on strategies that would increase the types and amounts of decisions made by nursing home residents.

Case Studies

(Please review Appendices A and B for guidelines on teaching
gerontological social work by using case studies)

Case #1: The New Admission

Fred Marks is an 85-year-old widower who has lived alone in a small rented house since his wife's death 15 years earlier. He is admitted to the nursing home following hospitalization from a fall resulting in a fractured hip. It is unlikely that he will be able to return home, as he has no living relatives and the community has a weak support system. Mr. Marks is bewildered by the sheer number of people he encounters the morning of his admission. The administrator welcomes him absentmindedly and quickly reads a booklet aloud to him, entitled *The Legal Rights of Nursing Home Residents.* He is then wheeled to his bedroom where he is distressed to find a roommate who is disoriented, confused, and bursts unaccountably into laughter or profanity at intervals.

An aide then escorts Mr. Marks in his wheelchair to an "activity room," which seems a mile from his room. The aide disappears and a kind-appearing woman tries to engage him in working a puzzle. He does not express his feeling of being insulted, but as soon as her back is turned, wheels himself into the corridor. He has no idea which way to go until an aide passes and gives directions so loudly that he is embarrassed, for his hearing is unimpaired.

The new resident toys with the food on his plate at lunch. He is accustomed to having lunch, usually a peanut butter sandwich and milk, in front of the television while he looks at the noon news show. Sitting at a table with six other people is a new and unenjoyable experience. Even if he felt like eating, the clamor of trays is giving him a headache. The lady across from him is having trouble chewing. Seeing the food dribble over her chin makes Mr. Marks feel a little queasy. He looks at his watch and sighs, for he is going to miss nearly all of the noon news.

The afternoon is slow. Even the veterans' hospital had more interesting afternoons. He had enjoyed swapping stories with the other veterans. When he was at home he took a walk every afternoon, rain or shine. In nice weather he walked to a park about two miles away. Sometimes he sat on a bench with a couple of old cronies, if they were well enough to be outside. Other times he watched the children. He often took bread to toss to the birds. That seems a long time ago.

A nurse taps his shoulder and announces that it is time for the evening meal. He realizes he had dropped off to sleep, sitting in his chair. He looks closely at the nurse; he has not seen her before, which means the second shift has arrived. He looks at his watch. Dinner at five o'clock. He has been eating his evening meal at seven o'clock ever since he can remember. He isn't hungry, but there is really nothing else to do. Clattering dishes, so many voices, somebody's angry voice. The food looks all right but it tastes so different he can hardly swallow it. He takes a few bites, then quits. He keeps getting lost when he tries to find his way back to his room.

It's now 5:30. Mr. Marks wonders what he will do until 11, his usual bedtime. When he is at home and it's summertime, he weeds the garden in the cool evening air. He smiles, thinking about his neighbor's cat, a feisty gray tom that was forever prowling in his garden, but never did any harm.

The evening seems interminable. He doesn't want to go to the activity room, but the aide insists, saying the "able-bodied" are "supposed" to be in the activity room. He wonders why he is considered able-bodied, until he recalls the rooms he has passed, the inert bodies lying in bed. He is introduced to a large number of people who seem to take little interest in him, with the exception of one woman. She believes she lived next door to him in Louisville. Even though he explains he has never even visited that city, she is not convinced and keeps asking him whether he remembers the corner grocer, the neighborhood soda shop, and so on.

He lies awake that first night for what seems like hours. His roommate wakes up, goes to the bathroom, and then tries to crawl in Mr. Mark's bed. Even though this does not happen again, Mr. Marks finds himself waiting, each time there is a noise on the other side of the room, for the stranger to return. Other noises are also disturbing: rubber soles padding against the floor, doors slamming, a sudden scream, a wail of abandonment. He finally drifts into an uneasy sleep.

Source: Hancock, 1987

Case #2: Socialization for Mrs. Sanders

The Sanders family, two sons and their wives, was upset that their mother, age eighty-five, was becoming increasingly disorganized and confused when they visited her in the nursing home. They were particularly upset because the home wished to move her to a floor where she could receive more protection due to a decrease in her ability to ambulate. The family felt that this segregation would only worsen her condition and she would be depressed by living with "the sick people." The social worker met with the four family members and gave each of them time to ventilate and state their opinion; the social worker pointed out the limitations of the institution in caring for this kind of resident. She noted the fact that the elder Mrs. Sanders would become increasingly isolated on her present floor since she was being rejected by residents and would have more activities and companionship on the new floor.

With the problem outlined, both sons agreed to fill the social gap by visiting more regularly to aid in the care of their mother. They made a commitment to take her to their homes as frequently as possible for visits, take her out on other visits from the home, including other residents when possible, and be helpful to staff in her direct care when they were there. The wives supported their husbands in this commitment. Mrs. Sanders was particularly pleased.

With these commitments, the problem was redefined and the social worker, after talking with staff, agreed to make a tentative commitment to keeping Mrs. Sanders where she was for the time being. The new plan worked well for nine months, at which time the sons felt that their commitment was too much for them since Mrs. Sanders was growing worse, and she was moved to another floor. However, the extension of this time for socialization was a meaningful one for all involved, including the sons and Mrs. Sanders.

Source: Adapted from Silverstone & Burack-Weiss, 1983

Case #3 : A Move for Mrs. Marshall?

Mr. Marshall is a self-referral to the senior center. Mr. Marshall is eighty-three, and is seeking nursing home placement for his seventy-nine-year-old wife, due to the fact that she was becoming increasingly difficult to care for. He learned of the social worker's services through a center newsletter. Clearly in conflict about the move, he had spent a sleepless night following an angry scene with his wife who was reportedly both confused and incontinent.

Mr. and Mrs. Marshall are a black couple, originally from Alabama, and married for sixty years. The husband is a former postal employee now retired for eighteen years. His wife is a former part-time sales clerk who retired with her husband. They are supported adequately by a government pension and Social Security. For the past three years, the couple have lived in a public housing project for seniors after the neighborhood they had resided in all their married years had been razed. Devout Baptists, the Marshalls have not attended church since moving to their new home and have no contact with their neighbors.

The couple have two middle-aged married sons, a lawyer living in Atlanta and a businessman living in Chicago. They visit their parents a few times a year and talk with them weekly on the phone. There are six grandchildren, but no other close family members. Mrs. Marshall's sister, who lived nearby, died one year ago.

One office visit with Mr. Marshall, two home visits with the couple, and one telephone call to each son (with the Marshalls' permission) were conducted for the purpose of assessment and planning. A medical examination was obtained for both Mr. and Mrs. Marshall who had not seen a physician in many years. A psychiatric examination and nursing consultation were also arranged for Mrs. Marshall.

Mr. Marshall appeared quite frail in the interviews. Although he seemed alert and socially appropriate, he was openly distraught that he could no longer manage on his own. In interviews, Mr. Marshall appeared at times angry and at times quite tender toward his wife, who appeared physically well cared for, confused, ingratiating, and inappropriately cheerful and unconcerned about their circumstances.

Source: Silverstone & Burack-Weiss, 1983

Audio Visual Resources

The following AV materials are available through the Virginia Center on Aging, P.O. Box 229, MCV Station, Richmond, VA 23298. Attention: Ruth Finley, 804-786-1526.

Ethical Issues in Casework   20 min., videotape

This film provides the viewer with a variety of ethical issues. An elder abuse case is used as an illustration of an ethical issue involving social workers.

Silent Changes in the Brain   30 min., videotape

This film explores an academic overview of Alzheimer's disease. It describes the biological changes associated with the disease.

The Sixth Sense   27 min., videotape, 1985

This is a useful film that deals with the senses and the aging process. The film discusses the sensory changes which correspond to growing older. The viewer is alerted to the importance of sensory capacities and their changes in individuals.

The following AV materials are available through the Department of Mental Health and Mental Retardation, Office of Geriatric Services, P.O. Box 1797, Richmond, VA 23214, (804) 786-8044.

Psychogeriatrics   30 min., 16mm

Actual patient interviews conducted in a nursing home illustrate the dynamics of chronic brain syndrome and depression. Assessment and care of the elderly are explored.

Someone I Once Knew   30 min., 16mm, 1983

The film explores the medical, emotional and personal aspects of Alzheimer's disease and how this condition affects the family. The film highlights the importance of support for caregivers to Alzheimer's patients.

Annotated Bibliography

Brody, E. (1977). Long-term care of older people: A practical guide. New York: Human Sciences Press.

This source represents one of the first attempts to provide guidelines for the provision of long-term care for the elderly.

Brody, E. (1985). Mental and physical health practices of older people. New York: Springer.

This book provides an excellent source for examining how the elderly utilize the health care delivery system and provides discussion of health practices of older adults.

Dolenc, D., & Dougherty, C. (1985). DRGs: The counterrevolution in financing health care. Hastings Center Report, 15, 19-29.

An excellent overview and discussion of the implementation of the DRGs. The authors provide a discussion of the long-term effects of DRGs.

Greene, R. (1982). Families and the nursing home social worker. Social Work in Health Care, 7, 57-67.

This article provides an excellent discussion about the importance of working with the family in nursing home placement.

Hancock, B. (1987). <u>Social work with older people</u>. Englewood Cliffs, NJ: Prentice Hall.

This book provides a good overview of the physical and mental changes that are characteristic of aging. In addition, there is an excellent chapter that describes the role of the social worker in nursing homes. Good discussion on the use of advocacy in nursing homes.

Herr, J., & Weakland, J. (1979). <u>Counseling elders and their families</u>. New York: Springer.

A practical guide that illustrates some specific counseling approaches in working with the elderly.

Holahan, B., & Cohen, J. (1986). <u>Medicaid: The tradeoff between cost containment and access to health care</u>. Washington, DC: Urban Institute Press.

An excellent overview of the eligibility guidelines for Medicaid and how Medicaid dollars are spent.

Kane, R. A., & Kane, R. L. (1987). <u>Long-term care: Principles, programs, and policies</u>. New York: Springer.

Excellent review and summary of research in long-term care. Good overview of policies and programs and how they affect the elderly.

Kapp, M., Pies, H., & Doudera, E. (Eds.). (1985). <u>Legal and ethical aspects of health care for the elderly</u>. Ann Arbor, MI: Health Administration Press.

Excellent overview of the social, ethical, and political aspects of health care including client self determination, financial aspects, and right to treatment issues.

Lowy, L. (1985). <u>Social work with the aging</u>. New York: Longman.

This book provides an overview of the various problems that confront the elderly population and examines various arenas for social work intervention with the elderly.

Peterson, K. J. (1987). Changing needs of patients and families in long-term care facilities: Implications for social work practice. <u>Social Work in Health Care, 12</u>, 37-49.

With an increase in chronic conditions among the elderly and the creation of DRGs, this article examines how the needs of the elderly have changed in the nursing home setting.

Rabin, D., & Stockton, P. (1987). <u>Long-term care for the elderly</u>. New York: Oxford University Press.

This book provides a wealth of statistical information related to long-term care, including nursing home beds, and Medicare and Medicaid expenditures.

Reamer, F. (1985). The emergence of bioethics in social work. <u>Health and Social Work, 10</u>, 271-281.

A good introduction to the historical and current significance of bioethics in social work practice.

Silverstone, B., & Burack-Weiss, A. (1983). Social work practice with the frail elderly and their families: The auxiliary function model. Springfield, IL: Charles A. Thomas.

Examines the role of the social worker in working with frail elderly and provides discussion of the model for practice.

Vladeck, B., & Alfano, G. (1987). Medicare and extended care: Issues, problems, and prospects. Owings Mills, MD: National Health Publishing.

Excellent description of the historical development of Medicare and discussion of current problems and future directions.

General Bibliography

Blumenfield, S., & Lowe, J. (1987). A template for analyzing ethical dilemmas in discharge planning. Health and Social Work, 12, 47-55.

Brody, E. (1974). A social work guide for long-term care facilities (NIMH Publication No. HSM-73-9106). Washington, DC: U.S. Government Printing Office.

Brody, E. (1977). Long-term care of older people: A practical guide. New York: Human Sciences Press.

Brody, E. (1985). Mental and physical health practices of older people. New York: Springer.

Coe, M., Wilkenson, A., & Patterson, P. (1986). Preliminary evidence on the impact of DRGs dependency at discharge study. Portland, OR: Northwest Oregon Health Systems.

David, S. (1985). Dignity: The search for Medicaid and Medicare. Westport, CT: Greenwood Press.

Dreher, B. (1987). Communication skills for working with elders. New York: Springer.

Elliot, M. (1984). Ethical issues in social work: An annotated bibliography. New York: Council on Social Work Education.

Estes, R. (1984). Health care and the social services. St. Louis, MO: Warren H. Green.

Gehrke, J., & Wattenberg, S. (1981). Assessing social services in nursing homes. Health and Social Work, 6, 12-25.

Greene, R. (1986). Social work with the aged and their families. Hawthorne, NY: Aldine de Gruyter.

Institute of Medicine. (1986). Improving the quality of care in nursing homes. Washington, DC: Academy Press.

Kane, R. A., Kane, R. L., Kleffel, D., Brook, R., Eby, C., Goldberg, R., Rubenstein, L., & VanRyzin, J. (1979). The PSRO and the nursing home. Volume I: An assessment of PSRO long-term review. Santa Monica, CA: The Rand Corporation.

Johnson, C. L., & Grant, L. A. (1985). The nursing home in American society. Baltimore: Johns Hopkins Press.

Kane, R. A. (1985). Health policy and social workers in health: Past, present, and future. Health and Social Work, 10, 258-270.

Kane, R. A. (1985). Minding our PPOs and DRGs. Health and Social Work, 10, 82-84.

Lowenberg, F., & Dolgoff, R. (1982). Ethical decisions for social work practice. Itasca, IL: Peacock.

McKinney, E., & Young, A. (1985). Changing patient populations: Considerations for service delivery. Health and Social Work, 10, 191-298.

Messinger, W. (1981). Residents' legal status and rights in nursing homes. In G. Sarensen (Ed.), Older persons and service providers. New York: Human Sciences Press.

Mitchell, M. (Ed.). (1978). A practical guide to long-term care and health services administration. Greenvale, NY: Panel Publishers.

Mundinger, M. (1983). Home care controversy. Rockville, MD: Aspen Publications.

National Association of Social Workers. (1981). Standards for social work services in long-term care facilities. Silver Spring, MD: Author.

Pegal, C. (1981). Health care and the elderly. Rockville, MD: Aspen Publications.

Reamer, F. (1982). Conflicts of professional duty in social work. Social Casework, 63, 579-585.

Reamer, F. (1985). Facing up to the challenge of DRGs . Health and Social Work, 10, 85-94.

Rehr, H., (Ed.) (1978). Ethical dilemmas in health care. New York: Prodist.

Rehr, H., (1985). Medical care organization and the social service connection. Health and Social Work, 10, 145-257.

Rosenberg, G. & Rehr, H. (Eds.) (1983). Advancing social work practice in the health care field. New York: Haworth Press.

Ross, J. (1982). Ethical conflicts in medical social work: Pediatric cancer care as a prototype. Health and Social Work, 7, 95-102.

Silverstone, B., & Burack-Weiss, A. (1982). The social work function in nursing homes and home care. Journal of Gerontological Social Work, 5, 7-33.

Toseland, R., & Newman, E. (1982). Admitting applicants to skilled nursing facilities: Social worker's role. Health and Social Work, 7, 262-272.

Vladleck, B. (1980). Unloving care. New York: Basic Books.

Wallace, S., Goldberg, R., & Slaby, A. (1984). Clinical social work in health care. New York: Praeger.

CHAPTER 3

CASE MANAGEMENT AND SOCIAL WORK PRACTICE WITH THE ELDERLY

by Patrick Dattalo

Introduction

Although the term "case management" has acquired recognition during the past fifteen years, it can be considered an original and integral component of professional social work practice (Miller, 1983). While case management is fundamentally coordination, it is a concern for providing carefully coordinated services to clients and can be traced to social work's origins in the Charity Organization Society. Case management is a logical extension of social work's unique person-in-environment perspective. Professional social workers are especially qualified to perform case management functions.

Case management, as a social work technique, is an assignment to a single worker or team, the responsibility for ensuring that a client's needs are met (Weil, Karls, & Associates, 1985). The case manager has been termed "the only provider in the human service system who is responsible for being aware of the 'whole client'" (Intagliata, 1982, p. 660). Although case managers may not directly provide services to an older client, they have ultimate responsibility for ensuring that the client's needs are met.

As community service systems become increasingly complex, client needs cannot be met by any single agency. For example, an older client may need financial assistance, housing, nutritional services, care for physical or mental impairments, and social interaction. Coordination has emerged as an essential component of effective service delivery to older people. A knowledgeable and skilled case manager is often a necessary prerequisite to a client's successful passage through the service system.

The case management process is essentially coordinative and includes the following basic components (Vandeberg-Bertche & Horejsi, 1980):

1. Comprehensive Assessment is an appraisal of client needs; informal resources available from family members and friends; the impact of the clients problem on both the clients and family; other related or preexisting problems; the client's values; and, formal (agency) resources available to the client.

2. Case Planning consists of developing an overall service strategy for each client. This plan must be developed with the active participation of the older client. The plan should consist of a list of client goals and objectives, and a detailed description of services that will be provided.

3. Linking Clients to Services involves referring clients to all necessary services. Linking may also require the case manager's assistance in helping a client overcome barriers to utilizing services. These barriers range from the more tangible problem of service inaccessibility because a client lacks transportation to an agency to more subtle forms of practitioner resistance to serving older people (e.g., delay setting an appointment).

4. Service Plan Monitoring is ongoing contact with both the client and service providers. Monitoring allows the case manager to ensure that planned services are being provided, and to assess the client's progress toward achieving service plan objectives.

Learning Outcomes

After completing this unit, the student will be able to:

- **Diagram the generalist case management model**

- **Outline the case manager's functions from a social systems perspective**

- **Define the basic roles of a generalist case manager**

- **Perform a bio-psycho-social assessment of an older client's strengths and weaknesses**

- **Conduct an assessment of a community's service delivery system**

- **Design a case management service plan**

Outline of Key Topics and Content Areas

The Generalist Model of Case Management

Generalist Case Management: Social Systems Management

Generalist Case Management: A Collection of Roles

Case Management Tasks and Skills

Comprehensive Assessments
Assessing An Older Client's Strengths and Weaknesses
Assessing the Service Delivery System

Case Planning

Linking Clients to Services

Service Plan Monitoring

Examples of Case Management Programs

Triage

Access

On Lok Senior Health Services

Summary of Key Topics and Content Areas

The Generalist Model of Case Management

A variety of case management models have been proposed to guide the delivery of human services (Brill, 1976; Frankfather, Smith, & Caro, 1981; Lauffer, 1978; Weil, Karls, & Associates, 1985). Choice of a particular case management model depends upon a variety of factors, such as potential clients, staff capacities, and financial resources (Weil, Karls, & Associates, 1985). The choice of a generalist model for this chapter is based upon two primary assumptions. First, coordination of services to clients is a case manager's fundamental purpose. Second, social workers with BSW degrees will be functioning as the case managers. When the term "case manager" is used, it refers to the generalist case manager. The generalist model closely resembles the traditional social casework model (Levine & Fleming, 1984). In the generalist model, a single professional is responsible for facilitating a client's movement through the service delivery process, including intake/ assessment, case planning, service coordination, and evaluation of client progress. Generalist case managers sometimes are referred to as "service brokers" because they help clients select available services, and arrange for a client to receive them.

Generalist Case Management: Social Systems Management

In order to serve their clients effectively, the generalist case manager must have a broad perspective of human services. This perspective must extend beyond the employee's organization. A useful conceptualization of generalist case management is social systems management. The section below reviews basic social systems concepts that can be applied to the case managers.

A system is a collection of interdependent parts, characterized by wholeness, with the whole being greater than the sum of its parts (Olson, 1968; Von Bertalanffy, 1968). A social systems perspective enlarges the scope of case management beyond a single agency serving a single client. This expanded perspective enables a case manager to focus upon a network of formal helping agencies, supplemented by a network of informal helping resources. Together these networks become potential resources for assisting a client.

Alfred Kuhn (1974) suggests that social systems contain three basic elements--detector, selector, effector. These elements can be used to describe case management functions. The *detector function* involves information gathering. To effectively serve an older client, the case manager first must gather information about the client's problem(s). The detector function also can be described as the "knowing function". The *selector function* involves the screening of information, the processing of information, and deciding which information is useful. The selector function can be described as the "wanting function", since this function involves deciding which information will be used (i.e., How the problem will be solved). For example, after gathering information about an older client's problems, the case manager decides that ongoing services will be needed for the client to remain in her home. The selector function may involve choosing chore or homemaker services as opposed to adult day care services. The *effector function* is the "doing function." After deciding what the older client's problem is and how the problem will be solved, the case manager takes whatever action is necessary to assist the client (e.g., referral, arranging for transportation). Figure 1 summarizes Kuhn's three elements of systems.

Kuhn's detector/selector/effector scheme can be used to guide the case manager as he or she works with a client (see Ms. Gray, Example 2, pp. 76-78). The assessment form is a structured device used to detect information. This assessment form allows the case manager to systematically gather

Figure 1.
Kuhn's Social System Model

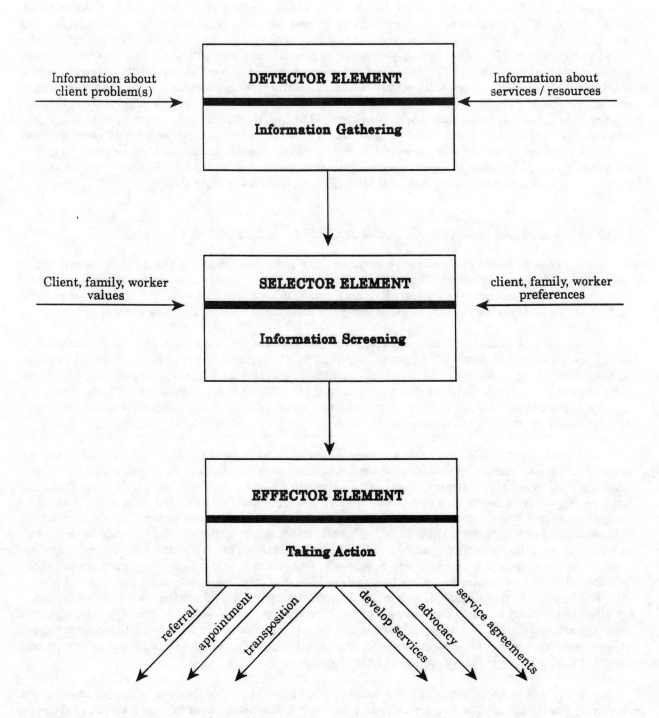

information about Ms. Gray and any problems she may be experiencing. Required information important to the detector function includes: income; independent living skills; other persons living in her home; current medical problems; and, specific needs.

Once the detector function is completed, the case manager can begin to perform the selector function. This function entails the assessment of Ms. Gray's strengths, resources, and needs. Ms. Gray's daughter is available to provide some assistance, but Ms. Gray will need assistance in bathing and dressing. These may need to be provided by a paid professional.

After Ms. Gray's strengths and needs are identified, the case manager can begin to perform the effector function. The case manager may contact a home health aide service and arrange to have Ms. Gray's personal care needs met. The case manager may contact Ms. Gray's daughter to establish a schedule for her to provide general housekeeping assistance.

In summary, a perspective of generalist case management as social systems management allows a social worker to identify three basic functions--detector, selector, and effector. These elements can serve as a framework for describing and analyzing the case management process.

Generalist Case Management: A Collection of Roles

Another framework for discussing generalist case management is role theory. From this perspective, case management can be viewed as a collection of social work roles. A role can be defined as, "the class of one or more norms that applies to a person's behavior with regard to some specific external problems or in relation to a specific class of other persons" (Thibault & Kelly, 1959, pp. 142-143). This definition contains two important role theory principles. First, roles are expected sets of behaviors (norms). Second, roles are context specific. In other words, the roles people perform are determined by where and when they are performed (i.e., a father at home). A case manager working with older people will perform different roles based upon the nature of a client's problems and upon available resources.

Usually, case managers serving older people perform multiple roles. Case manager roles can be placed into three basic categories--service coordinator, advocate, and counselor (Steinberg & Carter, 1983). Each of these categories contains several discrete responsibilities. Figure 2 summarizes these roles, the responsibilities associated with them, and the relationship of these roles to the case management process.

Consistent with the generalist model, the *coordinator role* is represented in Figure 2 as the fundamental role. As the coordinator of a client's services, the case manager must ensure that a client's needs are met. To accomplish this, the case manager scans the environment to gather information about the client, and the resource network (boundary spanner). The case manager then arranges for and ensures the delivery of appropriate services (broker). In the case of Ms. Gray, the case manager may arrange for Ms. Gray to be visited by a home health aide.

If the coordinator role is fundamental to achieving client goals, and is represented as the basic role, the advocacy and the counselor roles are instrumental to achieving coordination. The *counselor role* is mainly client-focused. As counselor, the case manager is an educator and provides information to the client about the resource network and about the problem-solving process. The enabler responsibility is also related to the counselor role. Enabling provides general emotional support, and can help the client to accept and use services, e.g., Ms. Gray may need support as she adjusts to her increased dependence on others to perform some activities of daily living.

Figure 2.
Case Management Roles

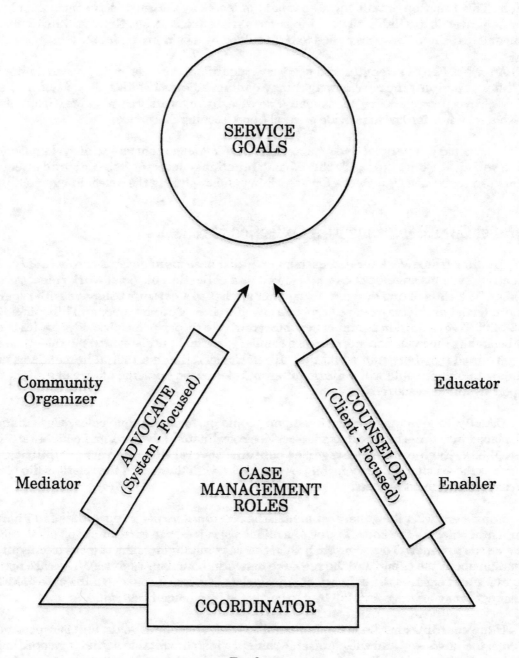

The *advocate role* is the second role instrumental to coordination. If a case manager is to coordinate services successfully, clients must be willing and capable of using services. Needed services must be available and accessible. As advocate, the case manager may need to mediate between a client and potential service providers to remove barriers to services. Mediation may involve clarifying a client's eligibility for services and ensuring that responsive and effective services are provided. For example, Ms. Gray's home health aide may not be keeping appointments. Ms. Gray may prefer that the case manager intervene in order to arrange for another aide or to explore ways to ensure regular visits. The advocate role includes the identification of needed services and the development of new services. This process often requires organizing or reorganizing community resources.

Describing and analyzing case management as a collection of roles clarifies the relative importance of these roles and their relationship to each other. The coordinator role is fundamental in generalist case management. The counselor and advocate roles are instrumental in accomplishing coordination and ultimately achieving a client's goals. If coordination is to be performed effectively, the client must be capable of using services (counselor) and needed services must be available and accessible (advocacy).

The case manager's basic responsibility as coordinator is to arrange for the needed services and ensure their delivery. The case manager as counselor should discuss with the client how services will help. In the example of older clients requiring homemaker assistance, the case manager would discuss the benefits of this in-home service. The case manager may also need to support the clients as they adjust to the idea of having a "stranger" in their home doing what they once were able to do for themselves. As advocate, the case manager may need to intervene with the agency that provides homemaker services if the service is not delivered adequately.

Case Management Tasks and Skills

The previous sections reviewed the roles and functions of the generalist case manager from social systems and role theory perspectives. The following section examines specific tasks and skills that enable the case manager to perform these roles and functions. Tasks and skills performed by the case manager are organized into four categories: comprehensive assessment; case planning; linking clients to services; and service plan monitoring and evaluation.

Comprehensive Assessment

Case management assessment differs from most clinical assessment because its primary purpose is appropriate referral and coordination and not direct treatment. This assessment provides the information which guides the coordination process. In case management, assessment has a dual purpose: one task is to analyze and describe an older client's strengths and weaknesses and another task is to analyze and describe formal resources (agencies, institutions) which may assist the older client.

Assessing An Older Client's Strengths and Weaknesses. Case management requires a multi-dimensional or comprehensive assessment of an older client. Most authorities on assessment of older clients agree that the main task is to determine the client's "functional status". Burton, Eggert, Bowlyow, & Nichols (1983) describes functional status as "a general measure of overall well-being; a picture of how the client is doing in a variety of areas, which is defined by assessing a variety of dimensions" (p. 78). Functional status is a client's strengths and coping abilities, in addition to impairments and service needs. In other words, it is a summary of both strengths and weaknesses. Describing illnesses and problems alone is not an accurate indicator of a client's coping capacity or functional status.

Assessment should be viewed as a means to formulating the client's service goals, and not an end in itself. Therefore, effective assessment approaches must be sensitive to individual client differences, practical to use, and repeated over time as changes occur during an older client's life. Assessment can be performed by a team or by a single practitioner. Kane and Kane (1981) refer to team assessment as the "Cadillac of professional assessment" (p. 212). Team assessment allows a variety of professionals to participate in the process, such as social workers, psychologists, physicians, nurses, and occupational therapists. By combining the skills of each professional, a complete assessment of an older client's functioning can be developed.

Information relating to a functional assessment of older clients can be obtained from many sources. In addition to the client and family, other sources of information include physician's reports and existing case records. Moreover, during the assessment process the case manager may request a supplemental assessment or advice from a specialist. The case manager, however, should begin with the older client as the primary source of information. With the permission of the client, the case manager may use supplemental sources, if necessary. Privacy and self-determination of the client must also guide the assessment process.

A case management process should seek to answer some or all of the following questions:

1. Which problem(s) places the client at risk?

2. Which problem(s) is the client willing to begin to solve?

3. Which solutions best fit the client's values and belief systems?

4. What, if any, resources are the client's friends and relatives willing to contribute?

To answer these questions the case manager must collect a variety of information. There is general agreement that the information collected should attempt to balance physical and psychosocial perspectives. Both perspectives are necessary since physical and psychosocial factors are interrelated in their impact on client well-being (Beaver & Miller, 1985). Standard categories of information to be collected include:

1. Physical health
2. Cognitive status (i.e., memory, orientation to time and place)
3. Emotional status (e.g., morale)
4. Self-care capacities (e.g., impairments in activities of daily living)
5. Economic/financial status
6. Values and interpersonal style
7. Availability of support from family and friends
8. Housing status
9. Capacity and willingness for self-help
10. Current services being used
11. Satisfaction with current services

Information from clients using these categories can be collected through observation, informal conversation, and structured approaches. A standardized interview is an example of a structured approach. These interviews contain a pre-established list of questions. This organized approach helps ensure that all relevant areas are covered and helps to organize answers for easy access later. The ideal interviewing approach has pre-planned content but permits the interviewer (case manager) some flexibility during the interview. For example, the case manager can adjust the sequence of questions.

Two examples of standardized assessment instruments are provided. These instruments can be used separately or conjointly by a case manager to collect information about a client.

Example 1.
Mental Status Questionnaire

1. Where are we now?
2. Where is this place (located)?
3. What is today's date - day of month?
4. What month is it?
5. What year is it?
6. How old are you?
7. When is your birthday?
8. What year were you born?
9. Who is President of the U.S.?
10. Who was President before him?

Scoring:
0-2 errors:	chronic brain syndrome -	absent or mild
3-8 errors:	chronic brain syndrome -	moderate
9-10 errors:	chronic brain syndrome -	severe
nontestable:	chronic brain syndrome -	severe

Source: Kahn, Goldfarb, & Pollack, 1964

Example 2.
Assessment for Ongoing Services to Elderly Clients

(Review Example 2, pp. 76-78, and the information about Mrs. Gray)

Once such a form is completed, the case manager can use the information to assess Ms. Gray's strengths and needs. For example, what monetary and personal resources are available to her? What problems have been identified? What, if anything, is being done by Ms. Gray to address these problems? What can be done?

Assessing the Service Delivery System. The previous section focused on assessing the older client's strengths and weaknesses. To coordinate services effectively for older clients, the generalist case manager also must be familiar with available services. This familiarity requires ongoing assessment of a community's service delivery system. As a result, the case manager should be able to answer the following questions.

1. *What services are available for older clients?*

   Case managers working with older clients require knowledge about two types of services available to the elderly. The first type is general services based upon needs. Need-specific services are provided by numerous community agencies, such as medical clinics, departments of social services and community mental health agencies. Low income elderly, for example, may be eligible for food stamps in the same way as other adults.

Example 2.
Assessment for Ongoing Services to Elderly Clients

NAME: _____ _Gray_ _____ _Jane_ _____ _Ann_ ____
                    (Last)   **(First)**   **(Middle)**

ADDRESS: _____ _123 Oak Street_ _____ _23223_ ____
                                                     (Zip Code)

TELEPHONE: _____ _804-234-1234_ _____ LOCALITY: _____ _Richmond, Virginia_ __

March 8, 1910 _____ _Widowed_ _____
(Date of Birth)   **(Marital Status)**   **M**   **S**   **W**   **D**   **SEP**

OTHERS IN THE HOME/RELATIONSHIP:
_____ _None_ _____

REFERRAL BY: _____ _Alice Smith_ _____
                    (Name)   **(Agency)**

March 24, 19-- _____ _804-234-0011_ ___
(Date)   **(Phone)**

INTERESTED PERSONS (Physician, Relatives, Friends and Designated Emergency Contact):

Name	Relationship	Address	Phone
Alice Smith	_Daughter_	_12 Main Street_	_804-234-0011_

INCOME/BENEFITS:

Social Security	_$432_	**Food Stamps**	_0_
Supplemental Security Income (SSI)	_0_		
Pension	_$175_	**Fuel Assistance**	_0_
Other Income	_0_	**Medicaid**	_No_
Medicare	_Yes_	**Other Health Insurance**	_No_

76

INDEPENDENT LIVING SKILLS

CLIENT IS:		Yes	No
1. Capable of preparing or obtaining nourishing meals			x

2. Needs assistance with:

	Yes	No
• walking		x
• rising from chair		x
• wheelchair		x
• bathing	x	
• eating		x
• using toilet or bedside toilet		x
• dressing	x	

	Yes	No
3. Is aware of time, place and date	x	
4. Has good memory of past events		
a. recent (several days ago)	x	
b. remote (years ago)		x

MEDICAL INFORMATION

1. **Current Medical Problems** _Diabetes, Long-term memory difficulties, mobility somewhat limited (uses cane)._

2. **Medications (prescribed by doctor and over the counter)**
Insulin

3. **Impairments**

			Corrected	Yes	No
a.	Visual	_Good_	(Glasses)		x
b.	Hearing	_Fair_	(Hearing Aid)		x
c.	Speech	_Good_			

Comments _____

SPECIFIC NEEDS

1. **Personal Grooming Assistance** _____ _Bathing, dressing_ _____

   - Bathing, hair care, shaving, foot care (except nail clipping of diabetic clients), mouth care, dressing, assistance with toilet, supervision of medication

2. **Housekeeping** _____ _General assistance needed_ _____

   - Vacuuming, dusting of client's room, personal laundry, meal preparation, sweeping

3. **Assistance with Obtaining Services** _____

   - Food stamps _____ _Should be explored_ _____
   - Medicaid _____ _Should be explored_ _____
   - Supplemental Security Income _____
   - Fuel assistance _____ _Should be explored_ _____
   - Other _____
   - _____
   - _____

4. **Recordkeeping Assistance** _____

   - Banking _____
   - Insurance claims _____
   - Other _____
   - _____

5. **A Friendly "Check" and Companionship** _____

Comments _____ _Daughter will provide general housekeeping_ _____

_____

_____

Date of Home Visit _____ _March 29, 19--_ _____

Source: Assessment Form used by Family and Children's Services of Richmond
         Richmond, Virginia, 1988

The second type of services available to older people is based upon age eligibility. These programs provide services to all people meeting a certain age criterion. Examples of these programs are the congregate meals and public transportation discounts. Anyone over a certain age limit can take advantage of these services. Case managers with elderly clients need to be familiar with these special programs for older people, along with general community services.

2. *How accessible are these services?*

Although community services exist, barriers often prohibit older clients from using them. A major potential barrier is transportation to a service site. Since many older people do not drive, inadequate transportation will decrease the chance that older people will use services. Ways to assist older people with transportation issues are to have agency sites on major public transportation routes, offer agency transportation services for older clients or offer home visits by staff.

A second accessibility issue is scheduling services for the older client. Appointments with older clients can be made around public transportation schedules so these clients need to be scheduled within day time hours since many people have impairments which inhibit travelling in the dark. This situation is compounded by a fear of some elderly of going out after dark.

A third access barrier is the physical characteristics of the service site. Older clients with impairments may be unable to access certain buildings. For example, people with severe arthritis, gait impairments or wheelchair users will not be able to climb stairs. Agencies with architectural boundaries may need to think of alternative sites to serve the older clients.

3. *Are services available but not used by older clients?*

In addition to physical barriers, attitudinal barriers may prohibit older clients from using services. Service providers can discourage elderly from using agency programs. Studies of perceptions of older clients by professionals report that the elderly are viewed as unglamorous clients, unable to master new skills or behaviors, and a drain on agency resources (Gatz, Popkin, Pino, & Vanden Bos, 1984). Although programs may be available for older clients, providers often resist including this group in the delivery of services.

Besides negative attitudes by professionals, older clients themselves may also resist using services. Older clients who are uneducated about or misunderstand services may view these programs as charity or "hand-outs." For example, one study on food stamp use reported that the elderly are an underrepresented group in these programs (Hollenbeck & Ohls, 1984). Although they may be eligible, the elderly feel their independence is threatened by taking advantage of these services. Case managers often need to begin with educating the older client about available services and decreasing their perception of stigma in using programs.

4. *What needs are unmet by available services?*

Although many programs are available for the elderly, many older clients do not receive the assistance they require. Since part of the case managers' role is to be knowledgeable about available services, they are good resources in discovering what additional services are needed. For example, a case manager in a rural setting begins noticing that greater numbers of families require day care for their older members. Caregivers are having to decide between quitting a job or admitting their family member in a nursing home. Case managers who recognize this pattern of unmet needs can make these needs public. After establishing that community elderly do not have adequate day care options, efforts can be initiated to fill this gap in services.

5. *Who are potential providers of needed but unmet services?*

When services are not available to meet the needs of older clients, case managers can fill vital roles in identifying how needs can be met. One possibility is to help create a new system to address a particular need. For example, if no adult day care centers exist, an agency of this kind could be established in the community. Case managers are beneficial in deciding how these new services should be structured and identifying possible agencies to administer the new day care.

A second option in meeting needs is to modify existing services to fill gaps. Case managers can assist in deciding how programs can adapt for the clients not currently served. One possibility in modifying services for day care is to identify possible nursing homes which can incorporate a day care center within their facility. A second kind of modification in current services is aligning existing programs with needs. For example, although day care is available, the hours of the centers may not be meeting needs of families. Case managers are resources in deciding how programs can be expanded to accommodate caregivers, such as evening or weekend hours.

Lauffer (1982) suggests that an effective approach to describing and analyzing "the web of relationships" (p. 21) between organizations is an interagency linkage map. (See Figure 3). The case manager can use this diagram to list programs and services available for older clients. The diagram also can help the case manager to develop a list of service gaps and potential providers of needed but unavailable services.

Case Planning

The case plan is a detailed description of steps to be taken by the client, the case manager, and the service delivery network to resolve a client's problems (Kemp, 1981). Case planning is the process of translating assessment information into intervention strategies (Intagliata, 1982). During the case planning process, it is essential that the client be involved, and desirable that the client's family be involved (Salzberger, 1979). The ultimate purpose or goal of the service plan should not be simply to provide services but to develop a client's capacities. Long-term case management should not be a case plan's purpose.

Case plan formats vary from agency to agency but should address the following issues (Maluccio & Marlow, 1984):

1. *Statement of the client's problem(s).*

This section is a statement of the difficulties the client is experiencing. Some clients may present only one problem while others face multiple difficulties. Summarizing the clients' major problem areas is an important first step in formulating a case plan to minimize the difficulties.

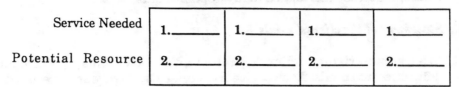

Needed, But Unavailable Services

Service Needed	1._____	1._____	1._____	1._____
Potential Resource	2._____	2._____	2._____	2._____

Figure 3.
Interagency Linkage Map

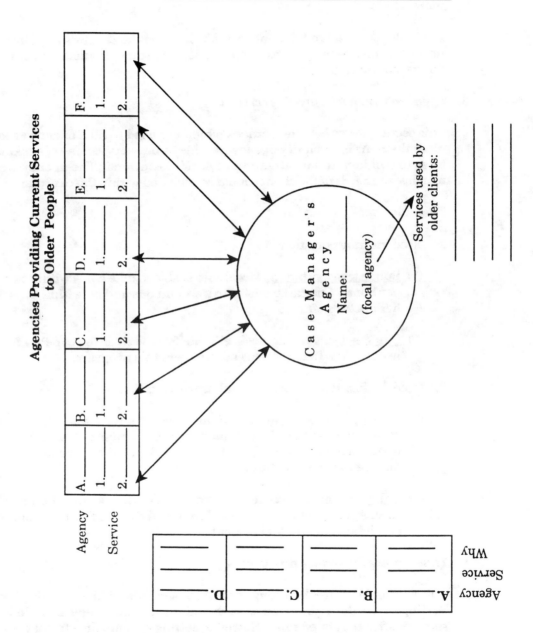

Example: Mrs. Jones lives alone in the community. She has high blood pressure and takes medication prescribed by a physician. Her problem is that she does not drive and cannot afford public transportation to her doctor's office. As a consequence, she has missed many appointments.

2. *Statement of the clients' needs.*

After summarizing a client's problem, the case manager translates these difficulties into needs. Each problem expressed by the client corresponds to one or more needs.

Example: To resolve Mrs. Jones' inability to make doctor's appointments she needs (a) some form of transportation, and (b) some financial assistance to pay for transportation.

3. *Agencies which will provide services.*

This section describes the methods which are used to fill a client's needs. Since more than one community agency provides some services, a case manager may have to conduct an investigation of possible options. The agency which best matches the needs of the client should be included within the case plan.

Example:

a. Need for transportation

   (1) Public transportation. Mrs. Jones is able to take a bus within two blocks of her home. She can transfer to a second bus and be within three blocks of her doctor's office.

   (2) Cab service. Mrs. Jones is eligible for a waiver for cab fees for medical needs. City Taxi Services administers this program.

b. Need for financial assistance with transportation

   (1) Public transportation. Mrs. Jones is eligible for a senior citizen discount card. This card can be obtained from the senior center in her neighborhood, located on Main Street. This card will allow her to ride city buses for one-half normal fare.

   (2) Cab service. Assistance program eligibility is administered through Area Agency on Aging. Mrs. Jones will fill out financial aid forms for receiving a monthly allotment.

4. *Time frames for service provision.*

This section identifies how long each of the services will be provided for a client. Setting limits does not mean that the client will no longer be able to receive services after the stated time. However, setting specific time frames does ensure that case progress will be monitored. If services need to be modified or extended, the case plan can be reformulated and new time limits established.

Example:

a. Public transportation. Mrs. Jones will have a valid discount card for one year. After one year, she will need to have her card revalidated. She can have this procedure done at the Senior Center.

b. Cab service. Mrs. Jones will not be eligible for the cab service program until her application has been fully processed. Until that time, she will use public transportation. Once eligibility is determined, Mrs. Jones will be able to use City Taxi once a month for transportation to and from her physician's office.

5. *Problems/barriers which may be encountered during implementation of the case plan.*

a. Transportation service: The City Taxi

(1) City Taxi only allots certain days and times for this transporting service. These times are listed below:

Monday	10 AM - 2 PM
Wednesday	10 AM - 2 PM
Friday	8 AM - Noon

In order for Mrs. Jones to have her fare covered, she must be transported during one of these slots.

(2) City Taxi requires pre-arranged scheduling for this service. Mrs. Jones needs to schedule her transportation needs at least one week prior to her appointment. Medical emergencies are not handled by City Taxi.

These five issues are used to generate a case plan for the older client. Case plans should contain three basic elements (Steinberg & Carter, 1983). Goals are long-term, general statements of outcome for a client. Goals describe the ideal state which a client will be helped to achieve. Using the example of Mrs. Jones, a goal statement is: Assist Mrs. Jones in making doctor's appointment.

Goals are accomplished by meeting one or more objectives. Objectives have a measurable result and include a time frame for completion. The completion of the objectives will lead to accomplishing the clients' goals. An example of one objective in the case of Mrs. Jones is: Arrange for Mrs. Jones to receive a senior discount card for the public transportation system. This task will be accomplished by April 10.

Just as goals are broken into the measurable units, objectives are accomplished by undertaking certain tasks. The list of tasks necessary to accomplish an objective are activities. An example of an activity in getting Mrs. Jones a transportation card is having her complete paperwork to determine eligibility.

Example 4. is an example of a complete service plan for Mrs. Jones.

Linking Clients to Services

Case planning is the process of transforming client assessment into a service strategy or linking clients to required services (Gambrill, 1983). During the linking phase, the generalist case manager is primarily responsible for arranging delivery of services to the client. A critical

Example 4.
Client Service Plan

NAME: _____Esther Jones_____

DATE: _____March 29, 1989_____

BACKGROUND INFORMATION/SERVICE NEEDS: _Mrs. Jones is unable to make doctor's appointment. She does not have adequate transportation currently and requires financial assistance in paying for transportation services._

OBJECTIVES AND SERVICE ACTIVITIES (include projected dates if applicable):

Goal: _To help Mrs. Jones obtain transportation to her doctor's office._

1. **Objective:** _Arrange for Mrs. Jones to receive a senior discount card for public transportation services. Completed by: April 10._

    Activities: _Assist Mrs. Jones in completing forms for card, transport Mrs. Jones to senior center to have picture taken for card._

2. **Objective:** _Arrange for Mrs. Jones to receive cab assistance benefits._
    Completed by: May 30.

    Activities: _Contact Area Office on Aging to receive eligibility forms; contact City Taxi Company and receive packet of information about the program; discuss with Mrs. Jones the method for using this service including possible limitations; contact Mrs. Jones' physician and explain the services she will use to make appointments, including necessity of having appointments scheduled during certain hours. Completed between: April 1 & May 30._

I hereby declare that I am in agreement with the service plan outlined above. I understand that the plan may be modified to better meet my needs. I understand that services depend upon the availability of funding.

_____   _____
Signature of Case Manager   **Date**

_____   _____
Signature of Client   **Date**

component is allowing the client and family to maintain as much responsibility as possible for implementation. The case manager's ultimate task is to promote client independence. Some related skills and tasks are:

1. <u>Modeling behavior</u>. The case manager may assist clients and their families in obtaining needed services by demonstrating how to take appropriate and effective action. This instructional strategy is useful in keeping the clients active and independent in decisions that affect them. By showing the older person(s) and other family members how to obtain a service, the case manager is also serving as a model for future behavior and decisions. For example, the case manager may "model" the various steps to be taken in order to obtain an appointment with a medical specialist. The manager will show clients how to locate names and phone numbers, how to speak to the receptionist, how to choose among various times and dates for the appointment, how to confirm a specific date and how to arrange for transportation to the medical office. The case manager may gradually increase the involvement of the client in the steps and supervise the behavior and actions in order to ensure proper follow through. The clients should become more independent and participate in decisions due to the careful instructions of the case manager.

2. <u>Providing support or helping a client obtain services</u>. The case manager may pride emotional or physical support to an older person who seeks assistance or service. This support may be in the form of encouragement or it may be actually doing some task that enables the older person to request and receive the desired services. For example, a case manager encouraged an eighty year old woman with a recently fractured arm to contact a neighbor to accompany her to the doctor's office. Another case manager went to the bank with an older client and assisted him in setting up a direct deposit account for Social Security checks and automatic bill payment.

3. <u>Confronting a client about how he or she may be exacerbating problems or helping to create barriers to receiving services</u>. A case manager must be skilled in promoting effective communication between older persons and others, including the case manager. Usually, case managers are empathetic and open in their exchanges with a client. On occasion, it is necessary to be direct and to challenge the client's behavior in order to overcome barriers to obtaining services. This challenge does not imply abusive language or a meanness of spirit on the part of the case manager. For example, an older woman who could shop independently if she could get to the supermarket, continually stretched her shopping beyond the time limit agreed upon by the volunteer driver and herself. The driver was increasingly annoyed and no longer wanted to assist this woman. The case manager spoke frankly with the older woman and told her how her tardiness was going to cause the termination of this opportunity to shop.

4. <u>Mediating conflicts between service providers and older clients</u>. Misunderstandings and conflicts over major and minor issues frequently occur between an older person and some service providers. The occurrence of this conflict is not any more surprising than conflict among younger persons. Nevertheless, the case manager may need to step into a conflict and mediate a solution before other negative side effects take place. For example, an older man who was hearing-impaired and wheelchair bound argued weekly with an aide who placed him in the rear of the chapel where there was room for wheelchairs, but a spot from which he could hear nothing. It was apparent that the man was not going to continue to come to chapel much longer. The case manager intervened and brought the aide and older man together for a problem solving session.

5. <u>Identifying and reporting service system barriers</u>. The case manager may identify a problem within the service delivery system itself and attempt to get the appropriate authorities to correct the situation. The older client may not be familiar with bureaucratic or complex organizational structure and be unable to arrange a resolution to the problem. For example, an older woman who never ate meat products discovered, upon admission to a personal care unit, that she did not have a meat-free menu choice for every evening meal. The kitchen said that it was too difficult to provide such a choice everyday. The case manager discussed the situation with the Director of Nursing and the facility administrator. Within two days, the kitchen began providing a meatless choice for each evening menu.

6. <u>Helping to develop new services</u>. The case manager may discover that there are gaps in the available services to older clients. Communities may not be large enough to support a service or an institution, like a home for adults, or may not have sufficient numbers of residents to justify a service. In these instances, the case manager may devise new approaches to service provision that a client requires. For example, in one medium-sized town, there was no low cost housing available to elderly persons. The case manager knew that federal programs included housing for low income elderly and he obtained a copy of the regulations and application. Together with the assistance of the mayor and town council, a planning committee was formed by the case manager and an appropriate sponsor, a local Quaker congregation, was identified to submit a proposal for housing for low income elderly in the town.

During the linking process, the client and case manager may encounter barriers to services. These barriers can range from the more tangible problem of geographic inaccessibility (i.e., no transportation is readily available to and from the service providing agency) to more subtle forms of practitioner resistance (e.g., delay setting an appointment). To overcome these barriers, a case manager must have sound advocacy skills.

Case managers must be able to move from thinking about barriers to services for a particular client (case advocacy) to a concern about how barriers can affect groups (class advocacy). Saul Alinsky (1979) helps clarify the distinction between case and class advocacy by relating a story about saving drowning people. According to Alinsky, social workers can remain down stream and continue to pull drowned or nearly drowned people from a river. On the other hand, social workers can venture upstream to see why people are falling in the river. By "going upstream" social workers can address the causes of problems. Class advocacy is one way to address these causes.

McGowan (1978, p. 280) suggests that effective advocacy requires answering the following questions:

1. What is the source or cause of the access problem?
2. What change(s) must occur to resolve the problem?
3. What is the level of resistance to these changes?
4. How best can these changes be made to occur?

McGowan's last question concerns intervention strategies. Brager and Specht (1973) suggest that advocacy be guided by a "least-contest" principle. Advocacy strategies range from education, to campaign, to confrontation. But, as Weisman, Epstein, and Savage (1983) state, "If you can persuade someone, then why mediate? If you can mediate, then why fight" (p. 105).

In the case of Ms. Gray, advocacy by a case manager may help to clarify concerns. If the aide assigned to Ms. Gray misses half of her appointments during the first month, advocacy efforts by the case manager are needed. Contact with the aide's supervisor may be necessary to explore the absences. Other options may include a meeting with the aide, or the assignment of a new aide to Ms. Gray.

Service Plan Monitoring

Service plan monitoring requires ongoing contact with both the client and service providers (Boone, Coulton, & Keller, 1981; Mittenthal, 1976). Monitoring enables the case manager to ensure that planned services are being provided and is also necessary to assess client progress toward achieving service goals and objectives. Monitoring may include face-to-face visits with the client and service providers.

In the process of monitoring, the case manager must maintain accurate and current files of each client. The forms and case plans are usually the primary sources for evaluation an assessment. The plans usually contain dates by which a certain action will take place. Monthly bi-weekly review of these plans will permit a timely assessment of progress towards certain goa For example, a case manager in a home health agency reviews the files of clients every month order to compare planning objectives with activities. Every quarter, the agency review tea composed of a social worker, nurse, physical therapist and agency director do an in-depth asses ment of the case plan and modify the goals and/or activities as needed. This continuous monitoring with different levels of review provides the ongoing evaluation of each client and ensures a high quality of care.

Monitoring requires reassessment, in order to determine if the service plan should be modified. For example, should some services be substituted for current services? Do some services need to be provided more or less often? Is the client satisfied with these services? Are there additional problems being experienced by the client? Should or can case management services be terminated? An ongoing review of a service plan keeps services to date with the changing needs of older clients.

Examples of Case Management Programs

Kane (1985) uses the following examples of case management programs to illustrate the range of variations and emphases.

Triage

Begun in 1974, the Triage program was targeted at the Medicare population in a small, seven-town area in central Connecticut that includes urban, suburban, and rural districts. Triage was a single-entry, service coordination organization that used teams composed of a nurse clinician and social worker to assess clients and arrange for services from a well-established provider network. Section 222 waivers enabled Triage to authorize payment for ancillary services not usually included in Medicare and to waive Medicare copayments, deductibles, and restrictions on home health care. The services available beyond traditional Medicare benefits were home health aides, homemakers, nursing and physician visits, psychological and family counseling, home-delivered meals, chore services, companion services, and dental care.

Triage differed from many other demonstrations. In this project, care was prescribed according to need rather than according to third-party payer restrictions. Additionally, it used highly skilled teams for assessment and case management. A team's caseload numbered about 200 with care plans monitored carefully. All Medicare beneficiaries over age sixty-five were eligible, and referrals were accepted from any individual or agency. When fully operational, Triage had seven case management teams serving about 1,500 clients. After referral, clients were put on a waiting list, and some clients waited a year to get to the top of the list and be seen by the team.

Access

Operational since 1977, Access is centered in Rochester, New York (Monroe County), with a single-entry model for all long-term care services in the county. A freestanding, nonprofit organization was developed to authorize services under 115 Medicaid waivers; these waivered services include friendly visiting, home maintenance, transportation, and respite care. All persons aged eighteen and over requesting long-term care are eligible, but the leverage over private-pay patients is minimal. In 1981, Access was expanded to offer service to Medicare beneficiaries over age sixty-five (using 222 waivers).

Access uses a preadmission assessment form (PAF) containing medical data, a nursing assessment, and a psychosocial assessment, which forms the basis for judgments. Assessments are done by community health nurses from the health department or visiting nurse associations if the client is in the community. A discharge planning nurse and a social worker provide the assessment information on hospitalized clients. The psychosocial assessment is a series of judgments on client status rather than responses to direct questions. If home care is judged feasible, the assessor develops a care plan. The case manager then calculates whether the estimated cost of that plan is less than the costs of a nursing home placement. If those costs are 75% or less than those of institutionalization, the plan is implemented. Sometimes a special home assessment is authorized to determine whether architectural barriers need attention. Negotiations are conducted with the client and the family to develop an optimum plan. Access separates the assessment function from the responsibility for authorizing a care plan. All clients are followed up through a formal review system. Waiting periods are minimal for assessment under Access, and case aides handle the details of implementing the service plan. In contrast to Triage, Access is a high-volume program that has saturated an urban area, but the case manager's direct relationship to the client is quite minimal.

On Lok Senior Health Services

On Lok Senior Health Services is a single-entry organization serving about 400 disabled elderly clients in San Francisco's Chinatown. The project evolved from a day health program funded by the Administration on Aging to an Health Care Finance Administration demonstration of the feasibility of a capitation system of reimbursement under 222 waivers. Unlike the previous examples, On Lok delivers many services directly, including physician, nursing, pharmaceutical, occupational, speech, and recreational services; social work services; transportation; personal care; escort and interpreting services; meals; home health care; and homemaker services. Much of the direct service is organized around two day health centers and one social center. In addition, On Lok may purchase or otherwise arrange additional services, including acute hospital care; skilled and intermediate nursing home care; dental, optometric, and prosthetic services; ambulance, medication, podiatry, and laboratory services; psychiatry; medical equipment; and attendant care. Presently all services are provided on a cost basis under Medicare waivers, but data are being gathered to predict costs and set capitation fees.

Assessments and case management are done by a team that includes a staff physician, a social worker, a nurse, physical and occupational therapists, and a dietitian. Each team member sees all patients, and the team meets weekly to discuss findings and to refine treatment plans. When a plan for a client is first developed, the social worker reviews it with the client and his or her family and incorporates any changes. The final care plan is written up as an agreement, signed by the client and On Lok, and a copy is sent to the client's personal physician. Clients are reevaluated at predetermined intervals, and the plan is updated as needed.

Summary

Case management is a social work technique which has the responsibility for ensuring that a client's needs are met. Case management functions can either be performed by a single worker or a team. This chapter provides an overview of case management as essentially a coordinative process. The generalist model is presented and described as both systems management and as a collection of roles. The basic tasks and skills needed for case management are then discussed. These are: comprehensive assessment; case planning; linking clients to services; and service monitoring. Finally, examples of case management programs are offered as methods of coordinating services to community elderly.

Chapter References

Alinsky, S. D. (1979). Of means and ends. In F. M. Cox, J. L. Erlick, J. R. Rothman, & J. E. Tropman (Eds.), Strategies of community organization (pp. 426-437). Itasca, IL: Peacock.

Beaver, M. L., & Miller, D. (1985). Clinical social work practice with the elderly. Homewood, IL: Dorsey.

Boone, C. R., Coulton, C. J., & Keller, S. M. (1981). The impact of early and comprehensive social work services on length of stay. Social Work in Health Care, 7, 65-73.

Brager, G., & Specht, H. (1973). Community organizing. New York: Columbia University Press.

Brill, N. I. (1976). Team work: Working together in the human services. Philadelphia: Lippincott.

Brubaker, E. (1987). Working with the elderly: A social systems approach. Newbury Park, CA: Sage.

Burton, B., Eggert, G. M., Bowlyow, J. M., & Nichols, C. W. (1983). Functional assessment inventory training manual. Tampa: Suncoast Gerontology Center, University of South Florida.

Frankfather, D. L., Smith, M. J., & Caro, F. G. (1981) Family care of the elderly. Lexington, MA: Health, Lexington Books.

Gambrill, E. (1983). Casework: A competency based approach. Englewood Cliffs, NJ: Prentice-Hall.

Gatz, M., Popkin, S. J., Pino, C. D., & Vanden Bos, G. R. (1984). Psychological interventions with older adults. In J. E. Birren & K. W. Schaie (Eds.), Handbook of the psychology of aging (2nd ed.). New York: Van Nostrand Reinhold.

Hollenbeck, D, & Ohls, J. C. (1984). Participation among the elderly in a food stamp program. Gerontologist, 24(6), 616-621.

Intagliata, J. (1982). Improving the quality of community care for the chronically mentally disabled: The role of case management. Schizophrenia Bulletin, 8, 655-674.

Kahn, R. L., Goldfarb, A. I., & Pollack, M. (1964). The evaluation of geriatric patients following treatment. In P. H. Hoch & J. Zuben (Eds.), Evaluation of psychiatric treatment (pp. 187-209). New York: Grune & Stratton.

Kane, R. A. (1985). Case management in health care settings. In M. Weil, J. M Karls, & Associates, <u>Case management in human service practice</u>. Washington, DC: Jossey-Bass.

Kane, R. L., & Kane, R. A. (1981). <u>Assessing the older client: A practical guide to management</u>. Lexington, MA: D.C. Heath.

Katz, S., Ford, A. B., Moskowitz, R. W., Jackson, B. A., & Jaffee, M. W. (1963). Studies of illness in the aged. The index of activities of daily living: A standardized measure of biological and psychosocial function. <u>Journal of the American Medical Association, 185</u>, 89-101.

Kemp, B. (1981). The case management model in human service delivery. In E. Pan, T. E. Backer, & C. L. Vash (Eds.), <u>Annual review of rehabilitation</u>, (Vol. 2, pp. 66-83). New York: Springer.

Kuhn, A. J. (1974). <u>The logic of social systems: A unified, deductive, system-based approach to social science</u>. San Francisco: Jossey-Bass.

Lauffer, A. (1978). <u>Social planning at the community level</u>. Englewood Cliffs, NJ.: Prentice-Hall.

Lauffer, A. (1982). <u>Assessment tools</u>. Beverly Hills, CA: Sage.

Levine, I. S., & Fleming, M. (1984). <u>Human resource development: Issues in case management</u>. Baltimore: Center of Rehabilitation and Manpower Services, University of Maryland.

Maluccio, A. N., & Marlow, W. D. (1984). The case for the contract. In B. Compton & B. Galaway (Eds.), <u>Social work processes</u> (3rd ed., pp. 407-414). Homewood, IL: Dorsey Press.

McGowan, B. G. (1978). The case advocacy function in child welfare practice. <u>Child Welfare, 57</u>, 275-284.

Miller, G. (1983). Case management: The essential services. In C. J. Sanborn (Ed.), <u>Case management in mental health service</u> (pp.3-16). New York: Haworth Press.

Mittenthal, S. (1976). Evaluation overview: A system approach to services integration. <u>Evaluation, 3</u>, 142-148.

Olson, M. (1968). <u>The process of social organization</u>. New York: Holt, Rinehart, & Winston.

Salzberger, R. (1979). Casework and the client's right to self-determination. <u>Social Work, 24</u>, 398-400.

Steinberg, R. M., & Carter, G. W. (1983). <u>Case management and the elderly</u>. Lexington, MA: Lexington Books.

Thibault, J. W., & Kelly, H. H. (1959). <u>The social psychology of groups</u>. New York: Wiley.

Vandeberg-Bertsche, A., & Horejsi, C. R. (1980). Coordination of client services. <u>Social Work, 25</u>(1), 94-98.

Von Bertalanffy, L. (1968). <u>General systems theory: Foundations, development, applications</u>. New York: Braziller.

Weil, M., Karls, J. M., & Associates. (1985). Case management in human service practice. San Francisco: Jossey-Bass.

Weisman, H., Epstein, I., & Savage, B. (1983). Agency-based social work: Neglected aspects of clinical practice. Philadelphia: Temple University Press.

Discussion Questions

1. Discuss the advantages and disadvantages of having one person, i.e., the case manager, being responsible for coordinating services to elderly clients.

2. What risks exist if the case manager stresses the advocate role over the coordinator or counselor roles?

3. Which is more important for a case manager: knowing the resources and agencies in the community or being able to assess the strengths and weaknesses of an individual client?

4. Discuss the phrase, "A case plan is only as good as its statement of goals and objectives."

5. How much responsibility should the case manager give to the client(s) and familie(s) in order to ensure services?

6. Is coordination of services the same thing as case management? What dimensions are present or missing?

Learning Activities

Activity #1: The Case of Mrs. Peabody

Mrs. Alma Peabody lives alone in a rural part of the county. The Area Agency on Aging has been informed of her case by a nephew, Tim Elliott. Tim is the only relative who lives near "Aunt Alma" and he has started to worry about how she's getting along. "She's 78 now," says Tim, "and I don't think she's doing all she used to." A social worker from the AAA visited Mrs. Peabody in her house. Mrs. Peabody was interviewed and her environment was assessed. The worker had some concerns that perhaps Mrs. Peabody was not functioning at an independent level. Mrs. Peabody agreed to be re-interviewed at a later time. This second interview included an assessment of her functioning status. The instrument used was "Katz Index of Activities of Daily Living." The completed assessment form for Mrs. Peabody is attached.

Instructions: Have the students break into small groups of five or six members. Give each group one or two copies of the case summary above and the Katz Index on pp. 92-93. Have the group discuss each of the following questions about Mrs. Peabody:

1. How would you assess her overall functioning level?
2. Which of the activities of daily living do you think are especially problematic in her case?
3. What services do you think she requires?
4. What about her living situation may be barriers to receiving needed services?
5. How would a case manager begin working on this case?

Katz Index of Activities of Daily Living

Evaluation Form

For each area listed below, check the description that applies. (The word "assistance" means supervision, direction, or personal assistance.)

BATHING – either sponge bath, tub bath, or shower.

_____ Receives no assistance (gets in and out of the tub by self if tub is usual means of bathing).

_____ Receives assistance in bathing only one part of the body (such as back or leg).

_____ Receives assistance in bathing more than one part of the body.

__X__ Unable to bathe without assistance.

DRESSING – gets clothes from closets and drawers.

_____ Gets clothes and gets completely dressed without assistance.

_____ Gets clothes and gets dressed without assistance except for assistance in tying shoes.

__X__ Receives assistance in getting clothes or in getting dressed or <u>stays partly or completely undressed</u>.

TOILETING -- going to the "toilet room" for bowel and urine elimination; cleaning self after elimination and arranging clothes.

_____ Goes to "toilet room", cleans self, and arranges clothes without assistance (may use object for support such as cane, walker, or wheelchair and may manage night bedpan or commode, emptying same in morning).

_____ Receives assistance in going to "toilet room" or in cleansing self or in arranging clothes after elimination or in use of night bedpan or commode.

__X__ Doesn't go to "toilet room" for the elimination process.

TRANSFER

__X__ Moves in and out of bed, and in and out of chair without assistance (may be using object for support such as cane or walker).

_____ Moves in or out of bed or chair with assistance.

_____ Doesn't get out of bed.

CONTINENCE

_____ Controls urination and bowel movement completely by self.

__X__ Has occasional "accidents".

_____ Catheter is used or is incontinent.

FEEDING

_____ Feeds self without assistance.

__X__ Feeds self except for getting assistance in cutting meat or buttering bread.

_____ Received assistance in feeding or is fed partly or completely by using tubes or intravenous fluids.

92

Katz Index of Activities of Daily Living

<u>Scoring Form</u>

For each area assessed earlier indicate (by placing a check mark) whether the client's functioning is "independent" or "dependent".

BATHING

    _____ Independent: assistance only in bathing a single part (as back or disabled extremity) or bathes self completely.

    __X__ Dependent: assistance in bathing more than one part of body; assistance in getting in or out of tub or does not bathe self.

DRESSING

    _____ Independent: gets cloths from closets and drawers; puts on clothes, outer garments, braces; manages fasteners; act of tying shoes is excluded.

    __X__ Dependent: does not dress self or remains partly undressed.

GOING TO TOILET

    _____ Independent: gets to toilet; gets on and off toilet; arranges clothes, cleans self.

    __X__ Dependent: uses bedpan or commode or receives assistance in getting to and using toilet.

TRANSFER

    __X__ Independent: moves in and out of bed independently and moves in and out of chair independently (may or may not be using mechanical supports).

    _____ Dependent: assistance in moving in or out of bed and/or chair.

CONTINENCE

    _____ Independent: urination and defecation entirely self-controlled.

    __X__ Dependent: partial or total incontinence in urination or defecation; partial or total control by enemas, catheters, or regulated use of urinals and/or bedpans.

FEEDING

    _____ Independent: gets food from plate into mouth.

    __X__ Dependent: assistance needed to eat; does not eat at all.

Source: Katz et al., 1963

Activity #2. Interagency Linking Map

Instructions: Distribute a blank copy of the "Interagency Linking Map" (Figure 3., p. 81) to all students.

1. Have the students choose a social service agency in which they have worked, volunteered or had a field placement. Have them write the agency name in the focal agency circle. Next have them identify any services within their agency which are used by older clients. Students will list those services on the lines beside the agency name.

2. Ask the students to think of other agencies with which their agency has contacts. Have them identify those agencies which do provide services to older clients. Have students write the names of those agencies at the top of the map and identify the services which the older client can use.

3. Next have students think of services which are available in the community that older clients do not use. Have them identify the services which are not used and the agency which offers that service. This column is on the left side of the map. Have the students postulate why those services are not used and write the reasons under each.

4. In the final right-hand column, have students think about which services are needed by older clients but are currently not available. Have them identify some of these services and list a resource for each which could be a possible service provider.

5. Use this map as a discussion about the service delivery system for elderly clients in the community. Ask questions like:

    *   Where are the service gaps for older clients?
    *   How could certain services be modified so older clients would use them?
    *   Why is this type of map helpful for case managers who work with older clients?

Case Studies

(Please review Appendices A and B for guidelines on teaching
gerontological social work by using case studied)

Case #1: How Long Can the Neighbors Help?

Mr. Jacobs is a social worker employed by the county Department of Human Services. He has met with his 75-year-old client, Miss Winley, on several occasions. Having gathered background information concerning her needs, Mr. Jacobs and Miss Winley are currently in the process of assessing her situation and establishing service delivery goals.

Miss Winley was referred to Mr. Jacobs because she recently had a stroke and was partially paralyzed. Miss Winley's niece, who lived in a distant city, had called Mr. Jacobs' agency and expressed concern about her aunt living alone. Mr. Jacobs had met with Miss Winley, spoken with the niece over the telephone, and talked with several of Miss Winley's neighbors who had been providing some help to her.

Mr. Jacobs established a trusting relationship with Miss Winley and she expressed her anger about having a stroke and being unable to care for herself. When the two met to review the information that had been gathered and to establish service priorities, Miss Winley stated that she believed she

94

could continue to live on her own and did not want services from formal agencies. She said the help provided by her neighbors was adequate for her needs. Mr. Jacobs felt that this was inappropriate for several reasons. First, the neighbors had indicated that they could not continue to help Miss Winley indefinitely as they had other obligations. Second, the help they were able to provide was insufficient. Miss Winley was only eating one meal a day. She had developed bed sores and her personal hygiene was inadequate for her health.

Mr. Jacobs shared with Miss Winley the concerns of her neighbors and expressed his own about nutrition and hygiene. Together, they then reassessed her situation and attempted to establish service priorities. These priorities were based upon Miss Winley's desires for service and the actual needs she experienced.

Source: Brubaker, 1987

Case #2: Follow Up and Follow Through

Mrs. Lipman's physician referred her to a local social service agency following her annual physical examination. Mrs. Lipman had told her physician that she lived alone and was having some difficulty in cooking her meals and in meeting some of her other household needs. In addition, the physician thought that Mrs. Lipman seemed disoriented at times during the examination. Mrs. Lipman agreed to call the social worker to whom she had been referred but was unsure why her physician wanted her to call.

She did call the agency, however, and spoke with Mrs. Smith, a social worker. Mrs. Smith asked Mrs. Lipman why her physician had referred her. When Mrs. Lipman responded that she did not know, Mrs. Smith outlined the services her agency could provide and suggested that Mrs. Lipman might want to consider whether those services were appropriate for her needs. Mrs. Lipman said that she would do that and call back if she wanted to use the agency's services.

Mrs. Lipman did not call back. When the social worker followed up on Mrs. Lipman's call the following week, she found that Mrs. Lipman was not talkative and did not provide much information. Mrs. Lipman stated that she preferred to have her neighbors help her, although she did not know if they would be able to do so.

Source: Brubaker, 1987

Case #3: Decision to Move or Stay at Home

Miss Landers contacted a retirement village about the possibility of becoming a resident. She was given an appointment with a social worker employed by the facility. The administrator questioned Miss Landers about why she wanted to move to the village and Miss Landers responded that she needed increasing amounts of help in order to continue living in her own home. Thorough questioning revealed that she did receive a good deal of help from her two nephews and a cousin who lived near her. However, Miss Landers was concerned that she was imposing on these individuals and was uncomfortable in asking them to continue to help. Miss Landers stated that she currently was not receiving services from any formal helping agencies.

Miss Landers related that she and her cousin had a friendship that extended over the years. Also, she and her nephews had always been fond of one another. The administrator requested Miss Landers' permission to contact the relatives who had been involved in helping her in order to determine their feelings about meeting some of her needs. Miss Landers agreed to this and also gave the administrator permission to contact various social service agencies in the area to determine whether they had available resources that would allow her to remain in her own home. Miss Landers indicated that her wish was to stay in her home but that she felt it was too much of an imposition on others.

As a result of contacting Miss Landers' nephews and cousin, it was discovered that they were unaware of her concerns about imposing on them. The administrator suggested a meeting with Miss Landers and her relatives in which each individual expressed his or her feeling regarding their relationship. It was agreed that if Miss Landers remained in her home, formal services would be needed. However, Miss Lander's relatives clearly stated their desire to share in care-giving and their feeling that she was not an unwanted burden to them.

Source: Brubaker, 1987

Audio-Visual Resources

Let's Keep Mrs. Gordon In Her Home   15 min., slides with audio tape, 1980

Presents the case of an older woman who is able to remain at home because in-home services are provided.

CONTACT: Dr. Sherry L. Berkman, School of Social Work, California State University at Long Beach, 1250 Bellflower Blvd., Long Beach, CA 90840.

The Rights of Age   28 min., 16mm

The film shows how coordinated efforts of professionals attempt to keep older people from accidents, injuries and losing touch with the world. A doctor, psychiatrist, social worker and others consult on the best ways to help an older woman without taking away her independence.

CONTACT: Department of Mental Health and Mental Retardation, Office of Geriatric Services, P.O. Box 1797, Richmond, VA 23214 (804-786-3909).

Project Open   3/4" video cassette, 1981

Depicts a model program of services that uses a team approach to help elderly maintain their independence.

CONTACT: Dr. Lawrence Weiss, Mt. Zion Hospital and Medical Center, 1600 Divisadero St., San Francisco, CA 94115 (414-563-7001).

Living in a Nightmare   25 min., 16 mm., 1984

Two families share their stories and heartaches about Alzheimer's disease and their daily struggles.

CONTACT: Dr. Lawrence Weiss, Mt. Zion Hospital and Medical Center, 1600 Divisadero St., San Francisco, CA 94115 (414-563-7001).

Annotated Bibliography

Austin, C. (1983). Case management in long-term care: Options and opportunities. Social Work, 8, 16-30.

The author proposes case management as a strategy for reforming long-term care delivery systems. Discussion relies on resource dependency theory for a theoretical base.

Capitman, J. A., Haskens, B. & Bernstein, J. (1986). Case management approaches in coordinated community oriented long-term care demonstrations. Gerontologist, 26, 398-404.

Describes design and costs of twelve federal long-term care projects. Reviews basic components of general case management model, and discusses the relative impacts of various client identification strategies, and intervention approaches. Essentially, an analysis of case management as one component of long-term care.

Emlet, C. A. (1984). Coordinating county based services for the frail-elderly: A tri-departmental approach. Journal of Gerontological Social Work, 8, 5-13.

Results of a cooperative project to respond to the more complex cases involving the frail elderly. Discusses benefits of coordinated case management approach to both clients and providers of service.

Goldmeier, J. (1985). Helping the elderly in times of stress. Social Casework, 66, 323-332.

Discusses the importance of the timing of interventions in social casework with the elderly. A framework is proposed for time-limited, ongoing intervention. Case examples are provided. Discusses skills needed for effective case management.

Greene, V. L., & Monahan, D. J. (1984). Comparative utilization of community based long-term care services by Hispanic and Anglo elderly in a case management system. Journal of Gerontology, 39, 730-735.

An exploration of ethnicity as a factor in service utilization by older clients. Comparison of the use of formal and informal supports by Hispanic and White older clients in a comprehensive case management system in Tucson, Arizona.

Kane, R. L., & Kane, R. A. (1981). Assessing the older client: A practical guide to management. Lexington, MA: D.C. Health.

Focus is on areas of measurement important to long-term care. Detailed criteria for selecting assessment instruments are provided.

Koff, T. H. (1981). Case management in long term care: Assessment, service coordination. Hospital Progress, 62, 54-57.

Overview, with case examples, of experiences in case management with older clients. Focus is on case management goals, the first contact, assessment, and service access.

Lamb, H. R. (1980). Therapist-case managers: More than brokers of services. Hospital and Community Psychiatry, 31, 762-764.

Argues that case management is a normal responsibility of the conscientious therapist. Suggests that the case manager should be not simply a broker of services, but the patient's primary therapist. Well-articulated rebuttal to the generalist model.

Milloy, M. (1964). Casework with the older person and his family. Social Casework, 45, 450-456.

Sound introductory overview for bachelor level students. Discusses diagnostic considerations when working with older people and their families.

Moore, S. T. (1987). Capacity to care: A family focused approach to social work practice with the disabled elderly. Journal of Gerontological Social Work, 10, 79-97.

The role of social work practice in community based care is discussed which has many parallels to the case management function. Family is analyzed as an informal resource and factor in practice .

National Association of Social Workers. (1985). NASW standards and guidelines for social work case management for the functionally impaired. Washington, DC: NASW.

Standards and guidelines for social workers who function as case managers. Stresses case management as a process within the traditional framework of generic social work practice.

Preston, C. E., & Gudiksen, K. S. (1966). A measure of self-perception among older people. Journal of Gerontology, 21, 63-71.

Discusses techniques to explore the ways in which older people see themselves and their world. Includes assessment approaches that can be used by generalist case managers.

Seltzer, M. M., Simmons, K., Ivy, J., & Litchfield, L. (1984). Agency-family partnership: Case management services for the elderly. Journal of Gerontological Social Work, 7, 57-73.

Describes a demonstration project in which partnerships are formed between social workers and family members of older clients. Family members are taught to assume responsibility for some case management functions.

Steinberg, R. M., & Carter, G. W. (1983). Case management and the elderly. Lexington, MA: Lexington Books.

Overview of case management primarily from the perspective of the planner, administrator, and evaluator. Discussion of various case management program designs, together with guidelines for development, implementation, and evaluation.

Stroller, E., & Earl, L. (1983). Help with activities of everyday life: Sources of support for the noninstitutionalized elderly. Gerontologist, 23, 152-165.

An exploration of various levels of functional capacity and appropriate patterns of assistance for noninstitutionalized older persons. Focus is on the potential and limitations of informal helping networks.

Weil, M., Karls, J. M., & Associates. (1985). <u>Case management in human service practice</u>. San Francisco, CA: Jossey-Bass.

Discussion of case management from both the perspectives of clinicians and administrators. Provides suggestions for a variety of theoretical frameworks which can be used to structure discussions of case management.

<u>General Bibliography</u>

American Health Planning Association. (1982). <u>A guide for planning long-term care health services for the elderly</u>. Washington, DC: Author.

Blazyk, S., Crawford, C., & Wimberley, E. T. (1987). The ombudsman and the case manager. <u>Social Work</u>, <u>32</u>(5), 451-453.

Gottesman, L., & Schneider, B. (1983). Case management variations on a theme. In <u>Final report, Community care system project</u>. Philadelphia: Temple University.

Greenberg, J. J., Doth, D. S., Austin, C. D. (1981). <u>Comparative study of long-term care demonstrations: Project summaries</u>. Rockville, MD: Aspen Systems Corporation.

Intagliata, J. (1982). Improving the quality of community care for the chronically mentally disabled: The role of case management. <u>Schizophrenia Bulletin</u>, <u>8</u>, 655-674.

Kane, R. A. (1985). Case management in health care settings. In Weil, M., Karls, J. M., & Associates, <u>Case management in human service practice</u>. Washington, DC: Jossey-Bass.

Kemp, B. (1981). The case management model in human service delivery. In E. Pan, T. E. Backer, & C. L. Vash (Eds.), <u>Annual review of rehabilitation</u> (Vol. 2, pp. 66-83). New York: Springer.

Levine, I. S., & Fleming, M. (1984). <u>Human resource development: Issues in case management</u>. Baltimore: Center for Rehabilitation and Manpower Services, University of Maryland.

Miller, G. (1983). Case management: The essential services. In C. J. Sanborn (Ed.), <u>Case management in mental health services</u> (pp. 3-16). New York: Haworth Press.

O'Connor, C. G. (1988). Case management: System and practice. <u>Social Casework</u>, <u>69</u>(2), 97-106.

Quinn, J., Segal, J., Raisz, H., & Johnson, C. (1982). <u>Coordinating community services for the elderly</u>. New York: Springer.

Vandeberg-Bertsche, A., & Horejsi, C. R. (1980). Coordination of client services. <u>Social Work</u>, <u>25</u>(1), 94-98.

Wan, T. T. H. (1982). <u>Stressful life events: Social support networks and gerontological health</u>. Lexington, MA: Heath, Lexington Books.

Zimmer, A. H., & Mellor, M. J. (1981). <u>Caregivers make the difference: Group services for those caring for older persons in the community</u>. New York: Community Service Society of New York.

CHAPTER 4

DISCHARGE PLANNING: THE SOCIAL WORKER AND THE ELDERLY

by Debbie Costigan

Introduction

Hospitals provide much of the acute health care of the elderly and over a third of all nursing home admissions originate from hospitals. Consequently, decisions made in hospitals often determine whether older people are institutionalized prematurely or unnecessarily (Kulys, 1983). Because older persons enter the hospital more often and stay longer than those under age 65, the hospital social worker inevitably becomes involved in discharge planning for elderly patients. The sheer numbers, complexity of their problems, and their vulnerability make older persons highly visible in the hospital setting (Berkman, Campion, Swagerty, & Goldman, 1983). With the current emphasis toward community rather than institutional care, effective discharge processes are becoming increasingly more important in providing a high quality level of care (Waters, 1987).

The discharge planning role was once viewed as a nonprofessional task and considered a "stepchild" function of the hospital social worker (Davidson, 1978). Recently, concerns about cost containment in health care have brought about a rediscovery of discharge planning "as a truly professional role that demands the highest abilities of assessment and intervention" (Blumenfield, 1986, p. 52). Discharge planning requires basic social work knowledge of crisis intervention, interviewing, community resources, advocacy, family system functioning, geriatrics, death and dying, and systems theory (Foster & Brown, 1978).

Care provided by health care professionals is usually oriented toward the individual patient. Social workers must be prepared to assist individual patients and their families within institutions, communities, and with many different professionals. Social workers provide leadership in interdisciplinary collaboration and the coordination of services and linkages for the patient to services both within and outside of the hospital setting (Rehr, 1986). The hospital is often a point of access to other services and serves as a vital component of the long-term health care of the elderly and as a primary setting for social work practice with older persons (Blumenfield, 1982).

Learning Outcomes

After completing this learning unit, students will be able to:

- Define discharge planning, using a social work perspective.

- Identify those factors that place older patients at high risk and in the greatest need of discharge planning.

- Conduct a discharge planning interview.

- Identify information and community resources needed to develop an effective discharge plan.

- Analyze ethical and legal issues faced by social workers who are responsible for discharge planning.

Outline of Key Topics and Content Areas

Overview of Discharge Planning

Definition
Three Recurring Themes
Process
Multidisciplinary Collaboration
Continuity of Care
Aims and Objectives of Discharge Planning

Basic Principles of Discharge Planning

Patient and Problem-Centered Approach
Coordination and Linkage
Advocacy

Components of Discharge Planning

Working with Staff
Access to Patients
Access to Medical Staff

Working with the Patient and Family
Goals
The Discharge Planning Interview

Working with Facts (Assessment)
About the Patient
Environmental and Community Resources

Considerations for Effective Discharge Planning

Barriers to Timely Discharge
Ethical Issues
Legal Issues

Summary of Key Topics and Content Areas

Overview of Discharge Planning

Definition

There are many possible answers to the question, "What is discharge planning?" A hospital administrator may say that discharge planning is a service that helps protect the organization's solvency (Davidson, 1978). Hospital accrediting organizations and governmental agencies emphasize discharge planning as a mechanism for containing costs and assuring quality (Jessee & Doyle, 1984). Patients and families may view discharge planning as a right (DeRienzo, 1985), or as an unnecessary intrusion (Crittenden, 1983).

Discharge planning can be defined from the viewpoint of the different professionals involved in the process. For the social worker, discharge planning is viewed as casework which "encompasses the whole scope of hospital social work, from psychosocial diagnosis to termination" (Holden, 1987, p. 7). The social worker uses various clinically demonstrated methods to assist patients and their families in adjusting to issues such as illness, impairment, hospitalization, role changes and losses, and in returning to the community with the appropriate level of assistance (Holden, 1987). From a broad perspective, discharge planning may be defined as "a multidisciplinary approach to providing coordinated services to patients and their families in order to ensure continuity of care for the patient from hospital to home, from hospital to another facility, or from service to service within the hospital" (Shields, 1987, pp. 1-2). The Hospital Discharge Planners Association adds the importance of addressing the patient's nonmedical as well as medical needs during the discharge planning process (cited in Crittenden, 1983).

Three Recurring Themes

Definitions of discharge planning are abundant, and within these definitions are three recurring themes: discharge planning as a process, as a multidisciplinary activity, and as a mechanism for ensuring continuity of care.

Process. Discharge planning, as a special form of social casework, is a systematic, problem-solving process. The tasks involved in this process are (Blumenfield, 1986):

- identifying people who need discharge planning;
- assessing their needs;
- identifying resources available to meet those needs;
- collaborating with the patient, family, and health care team;
- developing and implementing a plan of action.

The discharge planning process should begin early, ideally, upon the patient's admission to the hospital. It is not a one-time process, but one of periodic reevaluation of the patient's current state (Hochbaum & Galkin, 1982). The process does not end with the patient's discharge from the hospital. Follow-up is an important component (Rossen, 1984) to monitor and evaluate how effective the discharge planning process has been (Society for Hospital Social Work Directors of the American Hospital Association, 1986).

To illustrate this problem-solving process, consider the case of Mr. Sykes, an 83-year-old widower who enters the hospital with a severe respiratory infection. Due to his age and the fact that he lives alone, the social worker considers Mr. Sykes at high risk. An assessment soon after Mr. Sykes' admission reveals that he has two sons and a daughter who have been "seeing about" their father. Mr. Sykes wants to go home when he is well enough, and his children are willing to care for him in his home. For Mr. Sykes, his "problem" is his illness and hospitalization. His financial situation, living environment, and social support system do not need social work intervention. For the social worker, Mr. Sykes' case is a relatively uncomplicated one. He was screened as a high-risk, but assessed as having resources available to meet his needs. He, his family, and his health care team agree that he should return home after discharge. After his discharge, the social worker will follow up on Mr. Sykes' medical condition, and the extent to which his adult children are able to continue their care as he needs them.

Multidisciplinary Collaboration. Historically, discharge planning has been a role for hospital social workers. Entry of nurses into the role is a relatively new phenomenon. According to the guidelines of the Joint Commission of Accreditation of Hospitals (JCAH), both nursing and social services are to be involved in the process (Crittenden, 1983). It is no wonder that "turf" has become an issue in the field of discharge planning.

Social workers involved in discharge planning are members of a health care team. The team may be composed of all or some of the following: primary physician, nurse, utilization review coordinator, patient educator, dietician, pharmacist, and physical, occupational, respiratory, and speech therapists. The social worker is responsible for coordinating the contributions of the team (Society for Hospital Social Work Directors of the American Hospital Association, 1986) so that patients and their families will receive coordinated services (Shields, 1987).

No one can be schooled in every area pertinent to a patient's situation. If discharge planning is to have a holistic approach, collaboration with health care professionals from a variety of disciplines is essential. The patient and the patient's support system are important members of the collaborative effort, the very heart of discharge planning (Crittenden, 1983), because they are the ones who must carry out the plan. Discharge planning is not something done to or for a patient but a collaboration of professionals and informal supports.

Continuity of Care. Few patients are discharged from the hospital without needing some continuation of treatment. They may require as little as a special diet and rest. But for many older patients who often have several chronic health problems, continuity of care after hospitalization may mean the difference between returning to their level of functioning prior to illness, or returning to the hospital.

As illustrated in Figure 1, everyone who enters an acute care setting is discharged in one of four ways: returning home without supports, returning home with assistance from the family or community services, going to an alternative care facility, or through death (Zarle, 1987). Besides leaving due to death, the discharge planner uses his or her expertise to help structure a plan to meet the needs of the patient after leaving the hospital.

Patient-centered discharge planning must involve both patient and family in decision-making to incorporate their needs and expectations. This type of collaborative decision-making is very important. The discharge plan is designed to ensure the patient's safety, well-being and continuing care (Davidson, 1978). The expectation of reasonable continuity of care is so important to the discharge planning process that it is included in the American Hospital Association's (AHA) (1975) patient's bill of rights.

Aims and Objectives of Discharge Planning

Despite differences among hospitals in staffing, policies, and procedures of discharge planning, several objectives are common to all. In each case, the social worker needs to (Jupp & Sims, 1986; Raitt & Wilson, 1984):

- identify at an early stage those patients who will require discharge planning;

- develop a patient assessment program that coordinates the judgments of the physician, patient, family, and other members of the health care team;

- develop a plan for the continuing care of the patient;

- prepare the patient and family physiologically and psychologically for transfer;

- promote the highest level of independence possible for patient and family;

- develop and maintain effective liaison within the hospital and out in the community.

Figure 1.
Continuing Care Planning Continuum

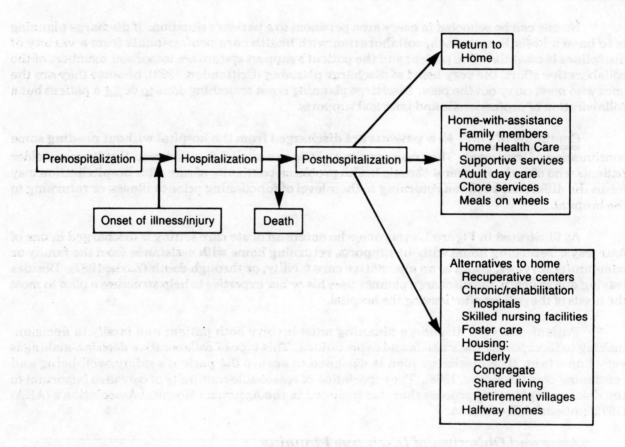

Source: Zarle, 1987, p. 3

Basic Principles of Discharge Planning

All discharge planning efforts should be guided by four general principles:

Patient and Problem-Centered Approach

What may be practical for one person or family may be counterproductive or useless for another. Developing a discharge plan that the patient is able and willing to implement requires patient and family input. Lack of involvement may lead to feelings of helplessness, hopelessness, and despair (Coulton, Dunkle, Goode, & MacKintosh, 1982; Crittenden, 1983).

Using this patient-centered approach, the social worker also needs to focus on the anticipated consequences of the medical problems. For example, will the patient be able to resume normal activities? If not, how will the patient and family be affected mentally, physically, and socially? By anticipating these effects, the social worker can help the patient learn to cope effectively with the inherent problems of his or her situation.

Coordination and Linkage

Social workers have an important role in coordinating different professionals within a hospital and linking community resources to a patient. Discharge planning involves input from a variety of sources, such as patients, families, and professionals. Often, the social worker is the only professional talking with all of these sources so is in a perfect position to assume the role as "director" or coordinator of their input. The goal of the social worker is to then "channel the information into a workable discharge plan" (Crittenden, 1983, p. 10).

Unlike many other health care professionals whose work is done primarily within the hospital setting, the social worker also must function within the community as it relates to the patient. He or she serves as a bridge between the hospital and the community. One tool that is helpful to physicians, patients, families, and staff in planning for continuing care after hospitalization, is a list of community resources. Social workers provide a vital link for the patient between hospital and community through appropriate referral and use of these community resources (Crittenden, 1983).

Advocacy

Advocacy is fundamental to the social work role in discharge planning. First and foremost, the social worker is an advocate of the patient. Patients need to understand and cooperate with the medical care system to receive the full benefit of hospitalization, and to be informed of their rights. The social worker also serves to communicate the patient's expectations and needs to the health care professionals involved (Crittenden, 1983).

Case advocacy goes beyond the hospital. Discharged patients may have difficulty obtaining the governmental or community programs they need. Through personal contacts and linkages, the social worker can help patients and their families to gain access to services (Lurie, 1982).

Social workers must be knowledgeable about community resources to develop effective discharge plans. As they work with patients and their families, they may discover gaps in those resources such as transportation or nutritional services. Meeting unmet needs through resource development is another important social work advocacy role (Lurie, 1982).

Components of Discharge Planning

Working with Staff

Discharge planners need to know which patients should receive discharge planning, and which staff members are to be involved in the process. They need access to patients, and access to other staff members.

Access to Patients. Traditionally, discharge planners have had access to patients by a referral from a physician who requests discharge planning intervention. Currently, an automatic access system or case-finding technique is often incorporated into discharge planning policies. This newer system directs staff energies towards patients who require earlier intervention and intensive attention from discharge planners (Rossen, 1984; "Strategies Given," 1984). Using this case-finding technique, the social worker often sees the patient before a diagnosis has been reached. High-risk patients are identified early in their hospital stay through established high-risk screening criteria (Cunningham, 1984). Some factors that place patients at high risk include (Crittenden, 1983; Cunningham, 1984):

- age 80 or over, or age 70 or over with a disability;
- living alone or without a residence;
- multiple illnesses;
- limited social and/or physical functioning;
- limited ability to perform activities of daily living;
- depression, confusion, and slowness of comprehension;
- poor appetite or nutritional status;
- incontinence;
- a history of repeat admissions;
- lack of a readily available social support network;
- limited financial resources;
- admission from an intermediate care or skilled nursing facility;
- victim of a severe accident.

Generally, any combination of two or more of these factors justifies an early assessment of the patient's situation.

Timeliness is essential to meet the demands for better utilization of the medical system. Discharge planning should begin on the day of admission to a hospital. In addition, the discharge planner must have a consistent and reliable system for finding patients so that all patients who meet established discharge planning criteria have access to the same services and benefits (Crittenden, 1983).

Finally, a system of access to patients should include the premise that biological and psychosocial needs are interrelated. Resources and limitations in both of these areas should be assessed and addressed together. The discharge planner needs to understand the interrelationship of the medical problem and the patient's and family's psychological relationships and social situation (Crittenden, 1983).

Access to Medical Staff. Initial responsibility for a discharge plan rests with the patient's primary physician (Rehr, 1986). One of the discharge planner's tasks is to facilitate the relationship between patients and their physicians while being tactful and respectful of the physician's authority. Occasionally, it may be necessary to advocate the patient's position to the physician when there is disagreement about the discharge plan (Crittenden, 1983).

106

The discharge planner also needs to work closely with the physician as part of an interprofessional collaborative team. Older people frequently have multiple and complex social and psychological needs. The team approach has been shown to be an effective discharge service delivery model for serving this patient population (Berkman et al., 1983).

Each profession represented in the collaborative team has different responsibilities to fulfill and priorities to meet in serving hospital patients. The discharge planner needs to facilitate the collaboration of the team by minimizing problems of territoriality. After all, the professions share a common goal: excellent patient care and the patient's return to optimum health (Crittenden, 1983).

Working with the Patient and Family

The heart of discharge planning is working with the patient and family to identify discharge problems, then formulate and implement a discharge plan. "Family" may be those who have no blood ties with the patient but who provide support and are trusted by the patient. The family relationship is so important to the discharge planning process because it influences the extent of the role that staff need to play during hospitalization and the discharge process (Bennett & Beckerman, 1986).

Goals. The discharge planning process is designed to meet the many needs of the patient and family, and consists of six primary goals (Crittenden, 1983):

Goal 1: Educating the patient and family about the functions of discharge planning.

Many patients and families are unfamiliar with the concept of discharge planning. During the first visit, the discharge planner needs to explain the process, and emphasize the patient's and family's importance as members of a problem identification and problem solving team. The helping relationship is reinforced by assuring the patient and family that a discharge plan will not be done to or for them but with them.

The patient and family need to understand that discharge planning means thinking about leaving the hospital and convalescing as the physician orders. They need to be informed that physicians, not discharge planners, decide when patients leave the hospital. They also should be oriented to the idea that discharge planners work as a part of a team that includes the physician, other hospital staff, and the patient and family.

Goal 2: Assisting the patient and family to identify practical and psychosocial problems for discharge.

After understanding the function of discharge planning, the patient and family need to focus on the practical problems created by illness. What needs must be met after the patient leaves the hospital in order to continue prescribed medical care in an appropriate setting? The medical diagnosis and prognosis create a framework for establishing needs. Through a process called partialization, that is, focusing on particular problems in a time-limited situation, the discharge planner discusses with the patient and family their practical needs related to the medical problem.

The discharge planner must sort out what the patient and family need and want, and what the physician and medical staff consider necessary. Practical problems of how, where, and by whom a patient's needs will be met can then be addressed. One of the most difficult tasks of this stage of discharge planning is to hear the "possible" from patients and staff, and to weigh that against the "probable" based on available resources.

Once practical problems such as patient education, equipment, and home or institutional planning have been addressed, the discharge planner needs to move into psychosocial issues. Sudden or chronic illness alters the perception of the patient and family and influences their thoughts, feelings, and behaviors. If psychosocial issues are not addressed, patient and family may feel overwhelmed by the experience of illness, hospitalization, and readjustment. They may freeze when confronted with the task of making plans. Another common reaction is to deny their situation and proceed with unrealistic plans.

Goal 3: Assisting the patient and family to meet practical and psychosocial problems for discharge.

Once the patient and family and the discharge planner have identified the practical problems which must be faced, alternative resources need to be presented. Ideally, the patient and family contact resources and make arrangements as much as possible, and the discharge planner provides direction and support about where to call or go, whom to see, and what to request.

Often patients and families are so caught up in illness that they do not realize that their feelings of anger, fear, or anxiety are normal. The discharge planner can provide psychosocial support by (Crittenden, 1983):

- listening;
- encouraging verbalization;
- reassuring the patient and family of those behaviors that are normal and helpful;
- educating the patient and family about the facts of their situation and helping them understand how to work on it;
- observing actions, reactions of patient and family as they work on the problems;
- identifying ego strengths and coping mechanisms and reinforcing them.

Goal 4: Formulating the discharge plan.

The next step of discharge planning is to formulate the actual discharge plan (see Table 1). This step involves the coordinated effort of the medical staff and patient and family. Formulation of the plan moves from consideration of problems and potential solutions to specifying where, when, and what is going to happen upon discharge. The discharge planner assumes the role of coordinator of the plan and documents the complete plan on the patient's record.

Goal 5: Implementing the discharge plan.

Implementing the discharge plan requires flexibility on the part of the discharge planner and the patient and family. Problems often arise during actual implementation of the plan that require creative problem-solving and changes or substitutions. Discharge planners must expect problems during implementation. A familiarity with community resources is a valuable tool for rescuing a discharge plan that goes awry. If substituting resources is not possible, the patient and family, discharge planner, and physician must consider the consequences to the patient of postponing some details of the discharge plan.

Goal 6: Monitoring the discharge plan through follow-up.

Some hospitals do not believe they have the time or resources to devote to follow-up activities ("Strategies Given," 1984). But follow-up, whether by telephone, by questionnaire, or in person, is essential to the continuation of high-quality care. Follow-up assures that changing needs are

Table 1.
Sample Discharge Plan

Patient's Name: _____

History #: _____

Discharge Date: _____ Floor: _____

Closed Case: Yes ( ) No ( )

I. *Patient Information Prior to Admission*

Address: _____

_____

Responsible Relative: _____

Telephone: _____

II. *Patient was discharged to:*

Home	Institution
( ) Own	( ) Acute Hospital
( ) Relative	( ) Chronic Hospital
( ) Foster Care	( ) Rehab. Hospital
( ) Boarding Home	( ) Residential
( ) Group Home	Treatment
( ) Other	( ) Nursing Home
	( ) 1/2 way, 1/4 way
	( ) State Mental
	Hospital
	( ) Other

Name: _____

Address: _____

_____Telephone: _____

III. *Referrals to Community Resources completed:*

1. ( ) Home Health
2. ( ) Financial/Environmental Support
3. ( ) Counseling Agencies
4. ( ) Training/Rehab. Agencies
5. ( ) Residential/Day Care
6. ( ) Equipment
7. ( ) Other

Agency Information

Name: _____

Address: _____

_____

Service Requested: _____

Name: _____

Address: _____

_____

Service Requested: _____

_____

Source: Lawrance, 1988, p. 148

Social Worker: _____

History #: _____

IV. *Pending Placement:* Yes ( ) No ( )

If this is a temporary arrangement state final plan including approximate date of placement: _____

_____

V. *Factors Complicating Discharge Planning:* (Explain)

1. ( ) Patient Condition: _____

_____

2. ( ) Community Resources: _____

_____

3. ( ) Patient/Family: _____

_____

4. ( ) Hospital: _____

_____

5. ( ) Other:

_____

_____

VI. *Anticipated Problems with this Case Postdischarge:* Yes ( ) No ( ), *if yes, explain:*

_____

_____

_____

_____

_____

Plan to Address Potential Problem:

_____

_____

_____

_____

VII. *Other Interventions Planned:*

_____

_____

_____

_____

_____

_____

identified and actions implemented, and allows the hospital to express a continued interest in the patient and family (Rehr, 1986). In fact, social work departments are required to have a system for monitoring and evaluating the quality and appropriateness of patient care (Coulton, 1986). A method to monitor the effectiveness of discharge planning needs to include internal program evaluation and effectiveness at the community level, and the patient's and family's perception of the usefulness of the discharge planning process (Kaye & Leadley, 1985). As the current economic climate in health care has resulted in shorter lengths of stay, patients and families are apt to feel new stresses, frightened, angry, abandoned, or unprepared for self-care. Follow-up can ease these feelings and provide much-needed support (Rossen, 1984).

The Discharge Planning Interview.
An essential tool for working with the patient and family is the discharge planning interview. Discharge planner should have a course in basic interviewing skills as part of their professional preparation. The discharge planner acts as a facilitator in the interview, moving the conversation while extracting and channeling information.

Characteristics of the Interview.
There are time limits, often time pressure, on discharge planning. Much needs to be accomplished in a short time. In an emergency, discharge planning may need to take place within an hour, and often, must be accomplished within two or three days. The interview must be structured to get the necessary information and give adequate assistance within the available time.

Interviews can take place in various locations and have a variety of forms. Interviews are often held at bedside and with minimal privacy. The discharge planner must be able to interview under distracting conditions and focus attention on the patient and family. Much interviewing, particularly with families, occurs over the telephone. The discharge planner needs telephone courtesy while obtaining information and giving assistance and support. The discharge planner needs to have courtesy, persistence, and patience when having to interview when not invited or wanted. If the patient and family are resistant, the physician may help to stress the importance for planning to leave the hospital.

Consistent with the six goals for working with the patient and family, the interview needs to be both problem-oriented and person-oriented. The discharge planner must listen for concerns of the persons with the needs, as well as identify those needs and problems. An active and accurate listening process within a problem-solving orientation is a critical method in obtaining information from an interview.

Framework of the Interview.
Interviewing is both a method and a process. The method is the framework or steps you follow in obtaining information you need. The process is the dynamics: what happens between people and between you and those people during the interview? How do the facts emerge? How do things develop? How do they "feel"? In an interview, the discharge planner is a facilitator moving the conversation and extracting and channeling information.

The discharge planner's interviewing method should include the following (Crittenden, 1983):

Opening: Introduce yourself and your function. Indicate to patient and family awareness of their problem and desire to help the patient not only leave the hospital but also do well at home and return to some normalcy in daily living. State needs commensurate with this goal as seen by staff, physician, and yourself.

110

Development: Ask for patient and family input and reaction. Restate their perceptions in concrete terms in a mutually agreeable way.

Assessment: Notice patient and family dynamics and interaction with you and one another. What feelings or reactions are expressed overtly or covertly? Where do conflicts occur in perception, opinion, or communication? What issues are avoided or downplayed or overstated? Where is there uncertainty, anxiety, or insecurity? Where is there lack of knowledge or understanding?

Reaction: Channel conversation, advise or structure, guide with facts and relevant information. Encourage support and communication between patient, family, and the hospital. Suggest and reinforce ways of dealing with practical problems.

Construction: Lead the patient and family into stating a plan for discharge needs and ongoing care. Introduce them to wellness as a goal for their living.

Close: Summarize, agree on the next meeting or telephone call, and the details that will be finalized or ready by then.

Working with Facts (Assessment)

Discharge planning is an excellent example of social work's distinctive focus on the person in transaction with the environment (Rauch & Schreiber, 1985). The assessment factors that need to be considered before a discharge plan can be formulated (Figure 2) include characteristics and abilities of the patient as well as characteristics and resources of the environment to which the patient will return.

About the Patient. Good discharge planning needs to be both patient- and problem-centered, so information must be gathered from the patient as well as about the patient. The initial interview with the patient and family can be more sensitive and productive if the discharge planner is already acquainted with the patient's medical problems and treatment plan.

Information to Obtain from the Hospital Chart. As summarized in Table 2, the hospital chart can provide valuable information about the patient's medical history, current problems, treatment, and progress of the patient.

Medical Team Members to Consult. An important function of discharge planners is to coordinate the contributions to the discharge planning process by the members of the multidisciplinary team. Table 3 summarizes the kind of information that each team member can provide about the patient.

Environmental and Community Resources. In addition to knowing the patient, the discharge planner needs to know the environment to which the patient will be returning and the resources that are available in the community. An essential tool for the discharge planner is a list of community resources. Table 4 summarizes potential patient needs upon discharge and the types of agencies and organizations that may be available to fulfill those needs.

Because agencies, personnel, and guidelines change periodically, an important task for the discharge planner is to update available resources every few months. In addition to referring a patient to resources appropriate for the patient's age, financial, social, and medical condition, and specific need, the discharge planner needs to assure that the existence and guidelines of an agency are current.

Figure 2.
Assessment Factors to be Considered before Discharge Planning

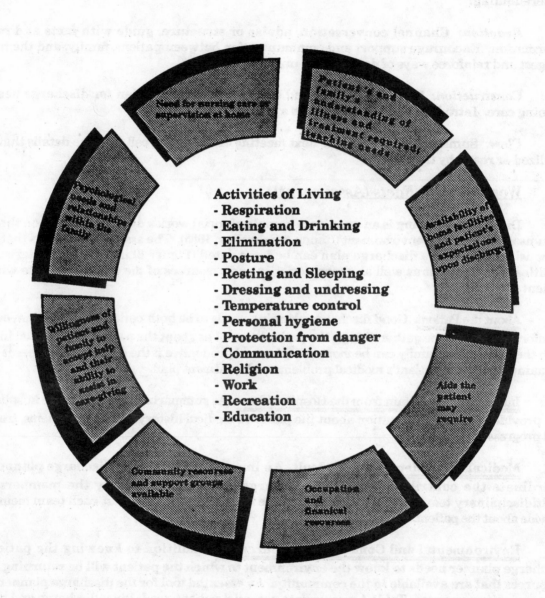

Activities of Living
- **Respiration**
- **Eating and Drinking**
- **Elimination**
- **Posture**
- **Resting and Sleeping**
- **Dressing and undressing**
- **Temperature control**
- **Personal hygiene**
- **Protection from danger**
- **Communication**
- **Religion**
- **Work**
- **Recreation**
- **Education**

Source: Jupp & Sims, 1986

Table 2. Information to Obtain From the Hospital Chart

History and Physical	A resumé of patient's medical history and current medical problem with anticipated goals to be accomplished by hospitalization
Physician's Orders	Treatment and activity ordered for the patient, usually on daily basis; includes orders for diet, medication
Physician's Progress Notes	Daily notation of medical progress of patient with note of special problems; anticipated discharge may be noted
Nursing Notes	A record of daily care of patient with any significant problems or reactions indicated
Vital Signs Sheet	Usually included near nursing notes: indicates progress of patient's temperature and blood pressure; deviations from average, such as a drop in blood pressure or a rise in temperature, usually indicate complications
Pharmacy Sheet	Included in many hospital charts; lists patient's medications along with frequency and dosage; a good indicator of what patient will need at home
Consultation Sheets	Communication from one physician to another indicating problems and a diagnosis and prognosis, and usually recommendations for treatment
Paramedical Progress	One or several sheets from services and therapists, such as social services; physical, speech, or occupational therapy citing patient's treatment and progress
Face Sheet	Includes admitting data and specific information about the patient: age, sex, marital status, address; employer or job; source of insurance; primary attending physician; room assignment and diagnosis. Other information may be included also.
Other Information	Included at the end of many hospital charts: gives information sent from another hospital or emergency room, a nursing home, a home care program. Any of this may have valuable information for the discharge planner; for example, a patient returning to a nursing home will probably return to the same one. Name, address, and phone number are available if there are transfer records.

Source: Crittenden, 1983

Table 3. Medical Team Members to Consult for Information about the Patient

Team Member	Information About
Primary Physician	Synopsis of the case and patient's history; present diagnosis and anticipated treatment; probable discharge date; discharge order and followup care (including medications, activity limits, self-care, and return visits or out-patient referrals or therapy); social information relevant to case
Nurse	In-hospital progress and treatment; patient functional ability; attitudes, emotions, and adjustment of patient and family; family support and notable problems; anticipated medical problems on discharge; education needed by or given to the patient for continuing care and treatment
Utilization Review Coordinator	For Medicare/Medicaid patients, adequacy of documentation of patient's progress and appropriateness of stay; anticipated barriers to discharge; and termination of federally or state-funded benefits; expected letters of denial; avenues of appeal of denial and procedures for same
Physical Therapist	Physical limitations; anticipated rehabilitation potential; progress in therapy; anticipated length of therapy and out-patient needs; medical equipment needed for outpatient use including specifications for same; education or training needed by family; home care therapy visits, if needed and how often
Occupational Therapist	Progress in activities of daily living (ADL) training and special assistive devices needed; rehabilitation potential; need for out-patient care or home care services; family training needs
Respiratory Therapist	Anticipated breathing difficulties and degree ADL is affected; training and education needed by patients or family; equipment needed for outpatient use; rehabilitation potential and outpatient or home care followup
Speech Therapist	Rehabilitation potential and prognosis for adequate communication with others; special devices or equipment needed; family training needs; outpatient or home care followup
Social Services	Emotional, intellectual assessment; counseling needs of patient and family; family and patient problems such as socialization, emotional support, community resources
Patient Educator	Status of patient's ability to perform self-care and treatment; understanding of medical situation and convalescent needs (diet, activity level, medication and medication use, self-understanding about depression, stress, and role of emotions in illness)
Dietitian	Plan for patient's diet; special restrictions for salt, calories, or other factors; instruction given, materials given
Pharmacist	Information on medications; reactions to medications

Source: Crittenden, 1983

114

Table 4. Environmental and Community Resources

Need	Agencies and Organizations
Physician services	Local medical society
Nursing services	Home health agencies; professional registries for in-home care; nursing homes; psychiatric care centers
Rehabilitation services	Organizations and societies by specific diagnosis (American Cancer Society, for example); county and state medical and paramedical societies; state vocational rehabilitation department
Clinical laboratory and Radiology services	County and state medical or paramedical societies
Nutrition	Meals on Wheels or Meals to Homebound program; senior citizen centers
Social services	County Department of Public Social Services
Education	Organizations and societies by specific illness (American Heart Association, Arthritis Foundation); public library; federal Department of Health, Education and Welfare; local colleges, universities; local hospitals or clinics for educational programs or groups
Transportation	Local transit programs; taxis; local organizations that provide service to the handicapped; senior centers; programs such as Dial-A-Ride, Medi-ride; local ambulance companies
Financial assistance	State and federal benefits programs (Medicare, Medicaid, Social Security); local unemployment and welfare offices for general relief; specific societies such as American Cancer or Eastern Seals that may make short loans or grants
Pharmaceutical services	Local pharmaceutical society; special senior programs at chain pharmacies such as Rexall; American Assn. of Retired Persons (AARP)
Equipment or prosthetic needs	Local businesses in hospital equipment, oxygen service, prosthetics; local medical society; specific organizations such as Arthritis Foundation, American Cancer Society, or Easter Seals; equipment provided by Medicare and Medicaid
Domestic assistance	Local employment agencies; home health agencies; the Homemaker Chore Program or similar Medicaid programs; societies for specific diseases that may help train, locate, or finance help, such as ALS (amyotrophic lateral sclerosis) Society, American Cancer Society; day-care centers or programs at county or state level or sponsored by community organizations
Housing	Local or county organization that lists housing resources such as senior helplines or hotlines, renters' association, aid to handicapped agencies or Easter Seals, HUD local office, and real estate organizations; state licensing agencies for list of licensed retirement hotels and board/care facilities; local churches may have church housing; the American Red Cross and Salvation Army sometimes aid with emergency housing
Legal services	Local or county bar association
Employment	Employment agencies; human resources development (unemployment) offices; state or federal programs for retraining; vocational rehabilitation office of state; local senior programs that may have employment possibility listings

Source: Crittenden, 1983

There is certain information that patients and families need for each referral in order to get the kind of help they need (Crittenden, 1983):

    a. the proper name of the resource or agency;
    b. a correct phone number;
    c. the times when the resource may be called or visited;
    d. the name of a contact person;
    e. the type of information that the agency will need;
    f. the limits of services the agency or resource can provide;
    g. cost of service.

As a consequence of updating the resource list and working with patients and families to fill their needs, the discharge planner is likely to discover gaps in services in the community. Unfortunately, the patient and family may ascribe the limitation of resources to the social worker (Bennett, 1984). The discharge planner needs to be involved in documenting and working to eliminate real service gaps (Blumenfield, 1986).

A major area of work with older patients is helping them to obtain financial assistance. The discharge planner must be familiar with entitlement programs for older people and spend a large amount of time giving entitlement information (Blumenfield, 1982). Providing written information to the patient and family can be helpful in reducing the repetition of information. The information must be kept current, however, and the discharge planner must have a sound grasp of current entitlement information (Bennett, 1984).

Considerations for Effective Discharge Planning

Barriers to Timely Discharge

New pressures for cost-containment provide hospitals with incentives to shorten patients' lengths of stay. One cost-containment measure which has affected discharge planning is Medicare's prospective pricing system under which hospital rates are predetermined by the patient's diagnostic category (diagnosis-related groups or "DRGs"). This system permits less time to work with patients in the hospital, and underscores timely discharge as an important task for social workers. However, there are several kinds of barriers that may prevent timely discharge (Crittenden, 1983; Schrager, Halman, Myers, Nichols, & Rosenblum, 1978).

Patient Problems
- unable to manage own affairs
- change in medical condition
- no insurance coverage

Communication Problems
- communication breakdown between staff and patient
- patient or family refuses to leave the hospital
- physician declines to discharge the patient

Internal Hospital Problems
- treatment not completed due to personnel or equipment failure
- inadequate or confusing documentation
- inaccessibility of personnel (i.e., physician unavailable)
- poor preparation or coordination of details by discharge planner

Community Resource Problems
- lack of family or support group to care for patient
- unavailable beds in intermediate care or skilled nursing facilities
- lack of resources to hire personal care or to obtain equipment such as oxygen or medication
- lack of transportation

Freak-of-Nature Problems
- natural phenomena (i.e., blizzards, fires, flood, etc.) that make implementing discharge plans impossible.

In some cases, such as with freak-of-nature problems, there is little the discharge planner can do to predict or prevent delay in discharge. But other obstacles can be targets for intervention. Educating staff on the importance of necessary paperwork, the proper completion of forms, and on the limitations of community resources can minimize certain factors that delay patients' discharge most often (Schrager et al., 1978).

Ethical Issues

Discharge planning was met with ambivalence during the time that hospitals received payment at a per diem rate under cost-based reimbursement (Rossen, 1984). Keeping patients meant more money to the hospital. Now the emphasis is on cutting costs. Those who pay the greatest percentage of the nation's hospital bill, private insurance companies and the government, have taken steps to reduce hospital costs and to monitor care (Foster & Brown, 1978). The prospective pricing system and other regulatory requirements have been designed to reduce unnecessary hospital days (Cunningham, 1984). Discharge planning can promote the efficient use of hospital resources and enhance continuity of care (Rossen, 1984). This hospital service has begun to receive renewed attention (Jessee & Doyle, 1984).

Within this environment, discharge planners will face role and value dilemmas. For example, is the role of the social worker one of service to the institution or to the patient? Blumenfield (1982) argues that "discharge planning must not be allowed to become a euphemism for cost containment" (p. 52). The professional value of self-determination and the patient's right to quality health care are fundamental to sound discharge planning.

In addition to this "crisis of ethics" (Davidson, 1978), created when the interest of the institution and that of the client are in conflict, social workers in the hospital setting will be faced with patients who become known as "disposition problems." These patients are generally very physically or mentally frail, and need a great deal of nursing care. Often they are just above Medicaid eligibility levels, but do not have the personal resources to pay for the high cost of nursing home care. These patients will remain in the hospital beyond the time they are medically ready to leave because of bed shortages and selection of "easier to care for" patients by skilled nursing facilities (Blumenfield, 1982).

Hospital social workers face these and other quandaries that present moral conflicts for those practitioners involved in the discharge planning process (Abramson, 1983). Even adhering strictly to the profession's code of ethics does not give the social worker pat answers for the daily confrontation with ethical and value dilemmas (Abramson, 1981). In the presence of these difficult questions, the social worker needs to develop a way of analyzing ethical dilemmas. One model begins by having the social worker establish the morally relevant facts and persons. After determining a decision-making process, possible alternatives are selected, and relevant value issues and ethical principles for each alternative are identified (Abramson, 1983).

The social worker's professional values--respect for the patient's individual dignity, maximum self-determination, and capacity for change --are an important underpinning to the analysis of ethical dilemmas (Blumenfield, 1986). The model described above provides a mechanism for reaching one of the basic goals of the discharge planning process: "making the best use of increasingly scarce resources for those who need them most" (Abramson, 1983, p. 50).

Legal Issues

Professional social workers involved in discharge planning often find themselves between "a rock and a hard place." They are employees of the hospital and are responsible for performing their jobs in accord with the profession's code of ethics. They are often pressed between the patient and the patient's family, and by a health care system that emphasizes cost control (Mullaney & Andrews, 1983). Social workers must also address release of information, competency, financial liability, family and hospital responsibility, and placement considerations, all of which vary from jurisdiction to jurisdiction (Mullaney & Andrews, 1983).

There are aspects regarding release of information that concern social workers differently than other hospital professionals. Within the hospital, charts are strictly confidential, and are for use by the medical team providing the patient's care. But social workers involved in the discharge planning process are often involved in transferring patients to agencies or facilities in the community. Generally, the hospital will have a policy requiring the patient to sign a Release of Medical Information form so that the social workers can supply medical and psychosocial information to professionals outside of the hospital. Sharing information with the spouse or next-of-kin usually is not a problem but should be checked with the patient. Medical records are liable to subpoena if the patient initiates a lawsuit against the hospital or any members of the medical team (Crittenden, 1983).

The presumption that adults are legally "competent" to carry out their activities and responsibilities is often lost in the environment of the acute care hospital. Older patients, in particular, are assumed to be unable to participate in the discharge planning process based on their physical illness, even in the absence of cognitive impairment. The social worker needs to assess the patient's capabilities for participating in decision-making, and involve the patient based on the assessed level of capability (Zuckerman, 1987).

Some patients are clearly unable to be involved in the discharge planning process. In these cases, a surrogate such as a close relative or appointed guardian works with the health care team to develop a discharge plan that is sensitive to the patient's desires and can be implemented by the surrogate (Zuckerman, 1987). Cases in which the older person is fully capable of participating in the discharge planning process, and those in which a surrogate is involved, are more clear-cut. Those cases in which the older individual's decision-making capacity is questionable, fluctuating, or diminished, raise difficult legal questions (Zuckerman, 1987).

The social worker is faced with two equally unattractive options when confronted with a patient of diminished capacity who consistently presents a preference for discharge that is different than the health care team's notions of what the patient needs. The first option is to accept the patient's "spoken choice." Acceptance puts the social worker in the position of sanctioning a plan that may be inadequate to meet the patient's assessed needs. In some states, this option is unavailable to social workers as hospital professionals are required to create a "safe" discharge plan. The second option is to disregard the patient's choice, devise a plan that the health care team deems adequate, and transfer the patient to the recommended site. This option abrogates the patient's right to choose (Dubler, 1987).

In formulating a discharge plan, the social worker must take a number of facts and systems into account. In addition to balancing the wishes of the patient and family, the recommendations of the health care team, and the resources available to the patient outside the hospital, the social worker must consider the potential risk to others if an impaired older person is allowed to return home. If the discharged patient forgets to turn off the gas stove or has poor hygiene that leads to infestation of the surrounding apartments, who is responsible? (Zuckerman, 1987) Another important issue is that to date, due process safeguards are not applied to hospitalized older persons who are on the threshold of nursing home placement. Should they have the same legal protection as psychiatric patients entering mental hospitals (Spring, 1987)?

The many legal issues faced during the discharge planning process create a need for social workers to utilize the hospital attorney as a resource for the discharge planning team (Mullaney & Andrews, 1983). The hospital attorney may prove useful in several situations:

- clarifying the legal principles involved in aspects of patient care that require a determination of the patient's right to choose a less than optimal discharge plan, family responsibility, transfer to a nursing home, and financial assets to pay for care;

- clarifying the responsibilities of the social worker to the patient and to the hospital regarding these patient care situations;

- developing a good quality discharge plan for patients with whom it is nearly impossible to plan because of their mental, physical, or social deficits;

- advocating for the discharge planner and the hospital in cases where a patient is competent but uncooperative, by enforcing the need for decision-making; and advocating for patients by insuring appropriate representation and protection of their individual rights.

Discharge planning provides social workers with a challenging opportunity to integrate their knowledge and skills. Social work education is ideal preparation for the discharge planning process. In order to be effective discharge planners, social workers must be skilled in assessment, interviewing, collaboration, and advocacy. A thorough knowledge of community resources as well as a good working relationship with these resources are also essential. These skills are an integral part of social work education. In order to be effective discharge planners with older patients, in addition to the skills acquired in an undergraduate social work program, social workers need to become knowledgeable about the field of gerontology. What are the realities of aging? What are the special needs of older patients? What special considerations for effective discharge planning are posed by older patients? What are the legal and ethical issues involved in working with older patients?

As the population continues to age, gerontological education will become an increasingly important partner to social work education. Hospital social workers will be faced with more and more older persons who need discharge planning and other social work services. Social workers who are well-grounded in aging will be vital to the delivery of high quality care of older persons.

Chapter References

Abramson, M. (1981). Ethical dilemmas for social workers in discharge planning. Social Work in Health Care, 6(4), 33-42.

Abramson, M. (1983). A model for organizing an ethical analysis of the discharge planning process of the chronically impaired older person from an acute care hospital to the community or an institution. Social Work in Health Care, 9(1), 45-52.

American Hospital Association. (1975). A patient's bill of rights. Chicago: Author.

Bennett, C. (1984). Testing the value of written information for patients and families in discharge planning. Social Work in Health Care, 9(3), 95-100.

Bennett, C., & Beckerman, N. (1986). The drama of discharge: Worker/supervisor perspectives. Social Work in Health Care, 11(3), 1-12.

Berkman, B., Campion, G. W., Swagerty, E., & Goldman, M. (1983). Geriatric consultation team: Alternate approach to social work discharge planning. Journal of Gerontological Social Work, 5(3), 77-88.

Blumenfield, S. (1982). The hospital center and aging: A challenge for the social worker. Journal of Gerontological Social Work, 5, 1-2 & 35-60.

Blumenfield, S. (1986). Discharge planning: Changes for hospital social work in a new health care climate. Quality Review Bulletin, 12(2), 51-54.

Coulton, C. J. (1986). Implementing monitoring and evaluation systems in social work. Quality Review Bulletin, 12(2), 72-75.

Coulton, C. J., Dunkle, R. E., Goode, R. A., & MacKintosh, J. (1982). Discharge planning and decision making. Health and Social Work, 7(4), 253-261.

Crittenden, F. J. (1983). Discharge planning for health care facilities. Bowie, MD: Robert J. Brady.

Cunningham, L. S. (1984). Early assessment for discharge planning: Adopting a high risk screening program. Quality Review Bulletin, 10(12), 561-565.

Davidson, K. W. (1978). Evolving social work roles in health care: The case of discharge planning. Social Work in Health Care, 4(1), 43-54.

DeRienzo, B. (1985). Discharge planning. Rehabilitation Nursing, 10(4), 34-36.

Dubler, N. N. (1987, Summer). Introduction. Generations, 6-8.

Foster, Z., & Brown, D. L. (1978). The social work role in hospital discharge planning: An administrative case history. Social Work in Health Care, 4(1), 55-63.

Hochbaum, M., & Galkin, F. (1982). Discharge planning: No deposit, no return. Society, 2(136), 58-61.

Holden, M. O. (1987). The effect of social work intervention and other variables on meeting diagnostic related groups goals for hospitalized elderly patients. Doctoral dissertation, Catholic University of America, Washington, DC.

Jessee, W. F., & Doyle, B. J. (1984). Discharge planning: Using audit to identify areas that need improvement. Quarterly Review Bulletin, 10(12), 552-555.

Jupp, M., & Sims, S. (1986). Discharge planning: Going home. Nursing Times, 82(40), 40-42.

Kaye, C., & Leadley, V. (1985). QA and discharge planning: Ongoing process at Niagra General. Dimensional Health Services, 62(6), 35-36.

Kulys, R. (1983). Future crisis and the very old: Implications for discharge planning. Health and Social Work, 8, 182-195.

Lawrance, F. P. (1988). Discharge planning: Social work focus. In P. J. Volland (Ed.), Discharge planning: An interdisciplinary approach to continuity of care (pp. 119-152). Owings Mills, MD: National Health Publishing.

Lurie, A. (1982). The social work advocacy role in discharge planning. Social Work in Health Care, 8(2), 75-85.

Mullaney, J. W., & Andrews, B. F. (1983). Legal problems and principles in discharge planning: Implications for social work. Social Work in Health Care, 9(1), 53-62.

Raitt, J., & Wilson, B. (1984). Manual helps formalize discharge planning services. Dimensional Health Services, 61(4), 29-30.

Rauch, J. B., & Schreiber, H. (1985). Discharge planning as a teaching mechanism. Health and Social Work, 10(3), 208-216.

Rehr, H. (1986). Discharge planning: An ongoing function of quality care. Quality Review Bulletin, 12(2), 47-50.

Rossen, S. (1984). Adapting discharge planning to prospective pricing. Hospitals, 58(5), 71, 75, 79.

Schrager, J., Halman, M., Myers, D., Nichols, R., & Rosenblum, L. (1978). Impediments to the course and effectiveness of discharge planning. Social Work in Health Care, 4(1), 65-79.

Shields, L. (1987). A training and resource handbook for hospital discharge planners. Richmond: Virginia Department for the Aging.

Society for Hospital Social Work Directors of the American Hospital Association. (1986). The role of the social worker in discharge planning. Quality Review Bulletin, 12(2), 76.

Spring, J. (1987, Summer). Applying due process safeguards. Generations, 32-39.

Strategies given for discharge planning activities. (1984). Hospitals, 58(14), 72, 76.

Waters, K. (1987). Discharge planning: An exploratory study of the process of discharge planning on geriatric wards. Journal of Advanced Nursing, 12, 71-83.

Zarle. (1987). Continuing care: The process and practice of discharge planning. Rockville, MD: Aspen Publications.

Zuckerman, C. (1987, Summer). Conclusions and guidelines for practice. Generations, 67-73.

Discussion Questions

1. The guidelines of the Joint Commission of Accreditation of Hospitals (JCAH) state that both nursing and social work are to be involved in the discharge planning process. Why should both professions have responsibility for the discharge plan? What problems does joint responsibility pose?

2. The American Hospital Association includes 'continuity of care' in its patients' Bill of Rights. Why is continuity of care so important to the patient? To the hospital?

3. What should the social worker do if the patient, the patient's family, and the primary physician all disagree about the plan for patient care after discharge from the hospital?

4. What type of information is needed about each community resource in order for the social worker to provide an accurate and appropriate referral?

5. How is the discharge planning interview the same or different from other interviews conducted by social workers?

Learning Activities

Activity #1. Identifying Medical and Psychosocial Problems

Study the following list of patients:

A. a 13-year-old girl with a broken leg in a waist-to-ankle body cast

B. a 35-year-old postman, father of four, who has a severe gastric ulcer probably related to nervous stress

C. a 57-year-old female school teacher, living alone, with chest pains diagnosed as angina (coronary artery disease)

D. a 92-year-old man with fever, dehydration, and malnutrition, who lives in an apartment on skid row

E. a 23-year-old welfare mother with a seventh newborn child

F. a 67-year-old man, retired banker, with a slight stroke leaving a residual slight weakness in the left arm and leg

G. a 47-year-old single parent with a recent diagnosis of acute leukemia

H. a 72-year-old lady, married, with two broken toes

1. Construct a table using the following headings: patient, medical problem, medical needs, social needs, psychological needs. Then fill in the table for each patient. (One has been done for you.) Please be creative and draw from your own experiences and common sense to infer possible medical, psychological, and social needs. You may find it helpful to consult a medical dictionary, such as *Taber's Medical Cyclopedia*.

PATIENT	MEDICAL PROBLEM	MEDICAL NEEDS	SOCIAL NEEDS	PSYCHOLOGICAL NEEDS
A	broken leg with waist-to-ankle cast	cast care, x-rays cast changes, visits to physician for followup, wheelchair and bed rest, pain relief	care for all daily needs: food, bath, toilet, dressing, companionship and recreation	help with anxiety, anger, and depression relating to illness, especially isolation from friends and school

NOTE: The object of this exercise is not to make you a medical diagnostician. It is to help you think about needs other than the medical problem--needs arising from the medical problem that may affect discharge planning.

2. Assume you were the hospital social worker involved in making discharge plans for each patient in the table. You would need to "prioritize" your work. In other words, you would have to decide which cases needed the most immediate attention and organize your work accordingly. You would need to consider questions such as these (please answer):

    a. Which case would be most likely to need a lot of medical care once the patient left the hospital?

    b. Which case would be of most concern to utilization review?

    c. Which case(s) might need a visiting nurse?

    d. Which cases might need nursing home care?

    e. Which cases have the greatest social need for a support group or help from community agencies?

    f. Which case would be most likely to need a lot of patient education to deal with illness?

    g. Which case would be most likely to need ongoing counseling help to deal with illness?

    h. Which cases do you think would be likely to be discharged from the hospital after a short stay?

    i. Having answered the above questions, which case would you, as a discharge planner, work on first?

Suggested Answers to Learning Activity #1

1.

PATIENT	MEDICAL PROBLEM	MEDICAL NEEDS	SOCIAL NEEDS	PSYCHOLOGICAL NEEDS
B	severe gastric ulcer	treatment and observation for ulcer, good diet; stress reduction and pain control, appropriate medication; rest	disability insurance as other income help for family during illness	help with tension, fear, or depression; reassurance
C	angina, mild	medicines for cardiac problems; special diet; rest; education about illness and how to manage it	a less demanding workload	help with fear of heart attacks; stress-reduction techniques
D	fever, dehydration, and malnutrition	diagnosis of cause of fever; fluids and food to restore body to optimum health	adequate shelter and personal care; a support group; financial aid possible facility placement	assessment of mental status; emotional support to discontinue drinking; help with possible depression
E	childbirth	postpartum care for baby and mother; medical supervision, diet, rest for both; education in birth control	assessment of personal living situation and family history, including financial, housing, diet and nutrition, education, health, work situation; support groups in community and family	emotional support; assessment of basic behavior, mother-child relationships, adult social relationships
F	stroke	physical therapy; medication for circulatory system; education about illness, diet; cane or walker	support group or family help in recovery	help with fear or concern of body failure or image change; anger or depression over illness and loss
G	acute leukemia	chemotherapy, diet, rest and long-term doctor supervision and possibly hospitalization for symptoms of disease including fever, weakness; education about illness for self as well as family	good support group: help with children; adult to care for domestic details; financial assistance	help to cope with life-threatening disease and prolonged hospitalization and illness; probable fear, anger, depression, stress; lot of reassurance and emotional support

2. a. G, A, D
    b. D
    c. A, D, G, F
    d. D, G
    e. D, G, C
    f. G, F
    g. G, F
    h. H, E
    i. D (due to Medicare/utilization pressures and probable short-term acute treatment needs)

Source: Crittenden, 1983, pp. 47-49.

Activity #2. Using Medical Resources

1. Sallie Woeful is a 92-year-old patient who has been admitted to the hospital and appears on your roster to be evaluated and helped with discharge planning. Indicate what part or parts of her hospital chart you would consult to find the following information (use Table 1):

    a. why she has been admitted to the hospital
    b. how she behaved and acted last night
    c. what treatments are planned today
    d. what professionals will work with Sallie
    e. Sallie's family and her present address
    f. what problems Sallie has in addition to the one which resulted in this hospitalization

2. Indicate which professionals could supply the following information about Sally Woeful (use Table II):

    a. when she may leave the hospital and what care she will need for her present illness after the hospital stay
    b. how well Sallie can walk and how well she can feed herself, bathe herself, and take care of her bathroom needs
    c. whether Sallie will need an IPPB breathing machine at home
    d. whether Sallie knows how to take care of her diabetes
    e. how Sallie's financial needs are being met by her stepdaughter, and whether Sallie is depressed seriously enough to require medication
    f. whether Sallie knows about following a high-protein diet

Suggested Answers to Learning Activity #2

1. a. history and physical
    b. nursing notes, possibly physician's progress notes
    c. physician's order sheet
    d. physician's order sheet, consultation sheets
    e. face sheet or admitting sheet
    f. history and physical

2. a. physician, nurse, physical therapy
    b. nurse, physical therapist, occupational therapist
    c. physician, respiratory therapist
    d. nurse, nurse educator, physician
    e. social worker
    f. dietitian

Source: Crittenden, 1983, pp. 63-64.

Activity #3. What We Need to Know

Consider the following information about Sallie Woeful, our 92-year-old patient from the previous learning activity. Sallie has a medical history of diabetes, indigestion, constipation, a hysterectomy some years ago, and congestive heart failure for the past two years. Sallie lives in her own apartment with a dog and bird and goes out little. Her stepdaughter, the only relative except for a grandniece in Phoenix, manages Sallie's finances and is her landlady. Sallie's deceased husband was a minister. Her income needs have been met through a small pension and Social Security. Sallie does not see or hear well and gets around poorly due to "old age"; her stepdaughter lives across town but comes by frequently and provides groceries and a bath. Sallie has had the "flu" for a week with high fever, poor liquid intake and dehydration, and vomiting.

Look back over the information you have about Sallie and fill in the worksheet with information we need to know about her. Indicate what else we need to know and whom we will contact for the information. (Do not include the patient as a person to ask.) You will certainly need to consult Table II.

Please note that your worksheet is not a prototype for a form. It is to help you organize your thinking for *this* exercise. Discharge planners must learn to assess problems and work them through in their heads. Difficult as this may seem to the novice, such assessment becomes routine and is done easily by the professional with some practice. Forms *are* appropriate in some cases--when they are necessary as a matter of record. This is an important point to think about.

Worksheet for Learning Activity #3

Sallie Woeful

diagnosis/prognosis

other problems and illnesses

psychological problems and/or
altered mental status

care/treatment plan

professionals involved in case

patient/family awareness of
diagnosis, prognosis, and
treatment plan

time or length of treatment and
anticipated discharge date

special problems now or post-
discharge

any supplies or medications

known resources available

Worksheet for Learning Activity #3

Sallie Woeful

Suggested Answers to Learning Activity #3

diagnosis/prognosis	flu: fever, dehydration, vomiting; prognosis apparently "fair" but not specifically mentioned
other problems and illnesses	diabetes, indigestion, constipation, congestive heart failure, poor vision and hearing, old hysterectomy

psychological problems and/or altered mental status	not indicated	need to know: if any significant confusion, senility or diagnosis of organic brain syndrome, or depression exists. Ask MD, psychiatrist if active in case, social worker, or RN working with patient
care/treatment plan	not indicated	need to know: plan for medical workup; medications, procedures, or therapies. Consult MD, nursing care plan, RN

professionals involved in case	MD, RN, RN educator, respiratory therapist, dietitian, social worker (implied in previous learning experience)

patient/family awareness of diagnosis, prognosis, and treatment plan	not indicated	need to know: ask MD, RN, or family if anyone has discussed the patient's plan of care with them
time or length of treatment and anticipated discharge date	not indicated	need to know: anticipated length of stay. Check with MD, also with UR coordinator for guidelines for length of stay for current illness

special problems now or post-discharge	possibly more help at home due to visual and auditory handicaps and weakness from illness. Supervision of diet and medication. Implied is need for compliance with ongoing medical care such as return trips to physician

	need to know: functional ability of patient for activities of daily living such as walking, dressing, bathing, bowel/bladder function. Need for equipment such as cane/walk-aid

any supplies or medications	not indicated	need to know, continued from above: consult with MD, RN, patient care plan, PT, OT

known resources available	stepdaughter for support group; own apartment; Social Security and pension from life work

Source: Crittenden, 1983, pp. 67-69.

Case Studies

(Please review Appendices A and B for guidelines on teaching gerontological social work by using case studies)

Case #1. Balancing Patient's Rights and Needs with Family Responsibility and Limitations

The hospital admission of Mr. D., 70, was precipitated by a fire in the patient's bedroom; smoke inhalation exacerbated his condition of chronic obstructive pulmonary disease. At the time of admission, Mr. D. was ambulatory with the aid of a cane, and required some assistance with activities of daily living. Social work intervention was initiated within two days of admission. The referral source was a community health agency whose staff had some knowledge of the patient and questioned the safety of the home environment.

The hospital social worker assessed Mr. D. as oriented but mildly confused. He provided conflicting information at times, and became argumentative and hostile with little provocation. Mr. D. refused to follow directions, presenting management problems for nursing and physician staff. Efforts by the social worker to plan for his discharge and continuing care were met with indifference by Mr. D. He did not acknowledge any need for care after discharge, and seemed not to understand his medical condition. Mr. D. maintained that he would return to his daughter's home, with his daughter assuming the role of primary caretaker.

Miss D., the daughter, did not visit or call during the first two weeks of the patient's hospitalization. The social worker secured Mr. D.'s permission to contact his daughter. Although when contacted she agreed to a meeting and discussion of discharge plans for Mr. D., she failed to keep this scheduled appointment as well as four subsequent ones. In her telephone talks with Miss D., the social worker observed signs of alcohol abuse. Miss D. was unaware of times and dates, speech was slurred at times, nonsensical. Miss D. did not visit her father, and blamed this on transportation difficulties.

Mr. D.'s medical and mental status improved; discharge would be possible in the near future. With her permission, a home visit was made to Miss D. The home was in disarray; Miss D. was noticeably intoxicated; empty liquor bottles were evidence. Miss D. maintained that she was able to care for her father but would honor his decision if he chose not to return to her home. She refused an offer of intervention for her alcohol problem.

The social worker assessed the home situation as unsafe for Mr. D. Although greatly improved, Mr. D. still required assistance with activities of daily living. Alternatives for discharge were presented to the patient; he was insistent on discharge to the home of his daughter.

The social worker questioned his ability to make decisions. Mr. D. had demonstrated impaired reasoning and judgement throughout the hospital stay. He continued to disregard medical information and instruction without exhibiting comprehension of the information.

The question of Mr. D.'s ability to represent himself became the deciding factor in planning. The psychiatric consultation requested by the social worker dictated acceptance of Mr. D.'s decision for discharge albeit to a situation which seemed unsafe. Discharge alternatives were again presented by the social worker and refused by Mr. D. He was discharged to his daughter's home with a referral for visiting nurse services.

As Mr. D. was found able to represent himself, his decision had to be honored. Consultation with the hospital attorney confirmed this; the attorney stressed the importance of documenting efforts to offer Mr. D. other alternatives. However, as a competent adult, his choice could not be challenged.

Following discharge, Mr. D. was home with his daughter for four months. The patient's physical condition and the home situation deteriorated. Mr. D. was readmitted with a diagnosis of chronic pulmonary insufficiency. His mental status was impaired. During the third week of hospitalization, Mr. D. was declared incompetent following the procedures described earlier. Mr. D. 's grandson was appointed guardian. Mr. D. was discharged to his home.

Source: Mullaney & Andrews, 1983, pp. 57-59

Case #2. Working with Families

Mrs. M. is an 87-year-old, Orthodox Jewish widow, admitted to the hospital for internal bleeding and anemia. Mrs. M. had been living at home, suffering from a variety of chronic conditions. She had been cared for by an 8 hour/day home attendant. Overseeing her care was her 57-year-old, married son, who lived nearby.

During the patient's hospitalization, her son stayed at the hospital all day, everyday. Mrs. M. suffered one medical crisis after another with the physician needing to do a variety of procedures and nursing staff being particularly attentive. The patient was quite ill and inaccessible to interview. Mr. M. spent most of the time reading religious books, but would jump up to meet an physician or nurse entering his mother's room to ask questions, suggest changes in procedures or discuss the merits of particular foods for his mother. Staff began to avoid entering Mrs. M.'s room unless absolutely necessary. They also had problems restraining Mr. M. from feeding his mother. Staff had warned Mr. M. of risks in trying to give his mother food since she was restricted to a special diet. However, he persisted in trying to urge her to eat ice cream or soup brought from outside. Staff became frustrated and angry in trying to deal with the son both because of his behavior in the hospital and their belief that he was acting out of guilt for having let his mother become so ill before being brought to the hospital.

The unit social worker was asked to see Mr. M. to help staff deal with the problems. Mr. M. was difficult to get to know. His orthodoxy contributed to the discomfort he had speaking with women and the social worker needed to respect such feelings. He was eventually able to respond to discussion about his concerns and needs and explained how fearful he was of the discomfort his mother was having, and his anger that the doctors couldn't seem to do more for her. He felt that no one was talking to him and that he was helpless in the situation, for he never knew when the physician would be around or when something new would happen. Mr. M. was almost frantic in his need to do something. Praying in the hall outside his mother's room was one thing he felt he could do, as was trying to force her to eat in order to regain strength.

The social worker met with staff and was able to reframe Mr. M.'s behavior to the staff, from that of inscrutable, angry and ungrateful, to frightened, overwhelmed, and lacking direction. House staff and nurses were engaged in considering ways to help Mr. M. with his problems while attempting to do the most they could for the patient. It was agreed that the intern in charge of Mrs. M.'s care would schedule a specific time each day to meet with Mr. M. Setting limits on Mr. M.'s demands, yet attempting to give him information and support appropriately was suggested by the social worker as a way of providing structure that would help the patient's son.

The social worker also suggested that they attempt to find some roles for Mr. M. to fill his need to do something. It was suggested that Mr. M. read to his mother and help feed her the specific diet provided by the hospital.

By providing more understanding of the patient's son and how meeting his needs could help in caring for the patient, the social worker was able to engage the staff in thinking creatively together. Providing structure in which to work with this family member and some role for him to play helped him to cope with the hospitalization of his mother and be ready to actively help in planning for his mother's eventual discharge.

Source: Blumenfield, 1983, pp. 47-48

Case #3. Balancing Conflicting Demands and Pressures

Mr. G. came to the hospital quite confused, weak, and unable to walk. He was a 72-year-old, Hispanic man whose wife had died eights years before and who had been living since that time with one of his married daughters. Upon his admission to the hospital, the daughter spoke to the social worker and discussed her feelings of being overwhelmed with his care and her inability to go on providing such care. Her own children aged 4, 8, and 10 needed her attention, the space in her apartment was cramped and tensions had increased between her and her husband.

Throughout Mr. G.'s hospitalization, his daughter's plaintive cry ran in counterpoint to his continuing improvement. Mr. G. proved a rewarding patient for staff. With medication changes, and improvement in the heart problems, Mr. G.'s mental status improved. He remained with moderate disorientation and confusion, but was able to respond appropriately in general and evidenced an engaging personality. He was cheerful, optimistic and amusing. With a great deal of nursing input, Mr. G. started to walk and provide his self-care with minimal assistance.

With the dramatic improvement, everyone was hopeful that Mr. G. could return to live with his daughter. All staff, including the unit social worker, began to press for such a discharge plan. However, the daughter, while guilty and most unhappy, remained adamant that Mr. G. could not continue to live in her apartment. The social worker began to receive calls from another daughter and son of the patient and was able to arrange a meeting with all the patient's children who were clearly at odds around the planning.

Mr. G. expected to return to his daughter's, although he acknowledged that his grandchildren were sometimes loud and bothersome. He also thrived on the attention given him by staff and responded to the interchange with the other patients in his room.

The social worker needed to help the family sort out their conflicting needs in regard to the patient. All three adult children were unhappy about sending their father to a nursing home, yet the brother and single sister could not agree to provide either a home or more aid for their father. The daughter who had been caring for him was still viewed as the logical person to continue such care, but her plight became clearer as they met together. Finding Mr. G. an apartment of his own and providing help there was ruled out as something not only difficult to do but something he had been unable to adjust to even years earlier. The fact that now, although appealing, Mr. G. needed direction, assistance, and help in orientation 24 hours-a-day made such a plan quite unrealistic.

The family agreed to apply for admission to a nursing facility near them so they could visit frequently. They found it difficult to discuss these plans with Mr. G. and needed help in including him in the planning.

The social worker was pressured by the family to "go ahead and make the arrangements." She was also pressured by the staff who were invested in this patient and who felt nursing home placement was inappropriate. The patient, himself, while speaking of returning to his daughter's was also somewhat aware of his comfort in the hospital. The social worker, herself, was not without bias and wanted this patient, who had improved so much, to return to the community.

However, the role of the social worker in planning discharge is to help to effect what is possible once the needs of the patient and resources at his disposal are known. The social worker had to work with the family to help them come to a plan of action. At the same time she helped them discuss this plan directly with the patient. Mr. G. was initially unhappy with the thought of not returning to his daughter's home. Because of the chance she had had to work through some of her ambivalent feelings with the social worker, the daughter was able to cope with Mr. G.'s disappointment and to help him see some positives in the proposal. The possibility of this being a temporary plan was discussed.

The social worker also had to work with staff who were angry at this plan, and therefore at her for "allowing" it. The fact that families cannot be "told" what to do, as well as the ramifications of this particular family's interactions, were shared with staff. The feelings of investment in this patient and the fears that his improvement was "wasted" had to be acknowledged and dealt with. The hospital experiences that had been so positive for Mr. G. were features that would continue in a long-term institution.

Source: Blumenfield, 1983, pp. 49-51

Audio Visual Resources

My Mother. My Father   33 min., 16mm, color, 1984

This excellent documentary looks at four families as they deal with caring for their aging parents. The film reveals deep-seated emotions associated with stresses related to caregiving and emphasizes the necessity of individualized decision-making processes, as well as caregiver support. Recommended for viewing by hospital discharge planners and caregivers.

CONTACT: Terra Nova Films, Inc., 9848 S Winchester Avenue, Chicago, IL 60643.

Beware: The Gaps in Medical Care for Older People   20 min., 16mm, color, 1982

Details the experiences of Beatrice, a 78-year-old woman living alone, as depression and disorientation result in her hospitalization and subsequent return to her daughter's home. Following unsuccessful attempts to locate a physician who specializes in medical care for the elderly, a severe emotional episode leads again to hospitalization. Ultimately, she is examined by a geriatrician who uses the hand-face test, the mental status exam, and other assessment methods to diagnose pseudodementia due to overmedication. With a reduction in medication and home health services, Beatrice is able to return to her home and to an independent life.

CONTACT: University Film & Video, University of Minnesota, 1313 Fifth Street S.E., Suite 108, Minneapolis, MN 55414 (800-847-8151).

The Last of Life: A Positive Look at Aging   28 min., 16mm, color, 1979

The thrust of the presentation is that aging is not a disease, but a normal part of human development. Of particular interest is the case study of an elderly couple diagnosed as "irreversibly demented" while under the stress of hospitalization. When reunited in a nursing facility, they recovered their senses and were able to return home. A recurring theme is that health care professionals should value the individuality of the elderly patient. Older people should be encouraged to lead independent lives, and wherever possible, should be offered health care on an out-patient basis.

CONTACT: Filmakers Library, 133 East 58th Street, New York, NY 10022.

"Will Medicare Really Pay the Bill?"   41 min., video

This consumer-oriented work addresses Medicare benefits in general and Part A benefits specifically. Emphasis is placed on understanding and utilizing the appeal process, with attention to "rigged" denials resulting from waiver of liability provisions regulating skilled nursing facilities and home health care coverage. Also addressed are concepts such as: "medical necessity," DRGs and reimbursement structures including "reasonable charges" and "assignment."

CONTACT: Center for the Public Interest, Inc., 1800 N. Highland Avenue, Suite 719, Los Angeles, CA 90028.

A Family Decision   25 min., video

Placing an elderly family member in a nursing home can be a traumatic experience. Complex emotions collide with rational thought. Guilt and anger mix with love and concern. In this video, people openly discuss the experiences and feelings that made up their own decision making process.

CONTACT: Terra Nova Films, Inc., 9848 S. Winchester Avenue, Chicago, IL 60643 (312-881-8491).

No Heroic Measure!   23 min., video, 1986

This film, based on a New Jersey Supreme Court decision, deals with the issue of whether or not life support measures should be terminated for elderly incompetent patients.

CONTACT: Carle Medical Communications, 510 W. Main Street, Urbana, IL 61801 (217-384-4838).

Caregivers: Showing the Hard Times, Too   4 videotapes

This series of videotapes was designed to increase the understanding and responsiveness to caregivers by human service specialists. Topics include: (1) demands of caregiving and caregiver contributions, (2) information on available support services and programs (e.g., home, respite), (3) place of care issues and options, and (4) financial and legal issues of caregiving.

CONTACT: The Brookdale Center on Aging, Hunter College/CUNY, 425 E. 25th Street, New York, NY 10010.

Annotated Bibliography

Abramson, M. (1981). Ethical dilemmas for social workers in discharge planning. Social Work in Health Care, 6(4), 33-42.

This article examines the conflicting values inherent in the discharge planning process, and proposes a framework for analyzing an ethical dilemma. The framework will not resolve dilemmas, but offers the social worker ways of structuring and clarifying them.

Bennett, C., & Beckerman, N. (1986). The drama of discharge: Worker/supervisor perspectives. Social Work in Health Care, 11(3), 1-12.

Using drama as a framework, the authors examine the thoughts and actions of the social worker and social work supervisor during the process of discharge planning for Mr. W., an 89-year-old patient in a large urban teaching university.

Berkman, B., Campion, E. W., Swagerty, E., & Goldman, M. (1983). Geriatric consultation team: Alternate approach to social work discharge planning. Journal of Gerontological Social Work, 5(3), 77-88.

This article reinforces the importance of the multidisciplinary nature of discharge planning. The authors compare social work discharge planning services as part of a geriatric consultation team to those offered by the social worker alone. The consultation team's comprehensive view of the elderly results in utilization of more social-health services and reduces early recurrent readmissions.

Blumenfield, S. (1982). The hospital center and aging: A challenge for the social worker. Journal of Gerontological Social Work, 5, 1-2 & 35-60.

The author uses case studies to illustrate how the social worker in a hospital setting can help older patients and their families adjust to hospitalization and illness, balance conflicting demands and pressures faced during discharge planning, help patients to obtain entitlements, work with confused patients who have no family or supportive network, and provide support for other hospital staff working with older people.

Crittenden, F. J. (1983). Discharge planning for health care facilities. Bowie, MD: Robert J. Brady.

This book is designed for social work students who wish to become discharge planners, and for seasoned discharge planners who wish to reassess their goals, objectives, and abilities as well as their philosophy toward their work. Each topic concludes with a learning experience and activities for personal enrichment.

Dubler, N., & Zuckerman, C. (Eds.). (1987, Summer). Coercive placement of elders: Protection or choice? Generations.

The entire issue of this journal is devoted to the problems of planning for the discharge of older patients from hospitals. Topics include ethical dilemmas and due process, as well as guidelines for practice and recommendations for new policies and procedures. Two extensive case studies are analyzed from the perspectives of an attorney, a medical anthropologist, a social worker, and a philosopher. A set of curriculum materials including cases, commentaries, and study questions for social work, medicine, law, and nursing were produced by the project upon which this issue is based.

Lurie, A. (1983). The social work advocacy role in discharge planning. <u>Social Work in Health Care</u>, <u>8</u>, 75-85.

The author stresses that social workers involved in discharge planning also must serve as advocates in three areas: improving governmental programs, developing resources to meet unmet needs, and ensuring that programs are accessible and appropriate for eligible patients and families. The social work skills that contribute to taking an activist role in working with the voluntary, private and public sectors in order to achieve high quality discharge planning are discussed.

Mullaney, J. W., & Andrews, B. F. (1983). Legal problems and principles in discharge planning: Implications for social work. <u>Social Work in Health Care</u>, <u>9</u>(1), 53-62.

The authors stress the importance of hospital social workers being knowledgeable of the legal principles related to placement, competency, release of information, financial liability, hospital responsibility, and family responsibility. Case examples are used to illustrate the types of situations which require legal counsel.

Rauch, J. B., & Schreiber, H. (1985). Discharge planning as a teaching mechanism. <u>Health and Social Work</u>, 10(3), 208-216.

This article highlights the social work knowledge and skills inherent in discharge planning, and presents a framework that organizes content into performance objectives for planning field instruction and in-service education.

General Bibliography

Abramson, J. (1988). Participation of elderly patients in discharge planning: Is self-determination a reality? <u>Social Work</u>, <u>33</u>, 443-448.

Baker, F. (1986). Legal issues afflicting the older patient. <u>Hospital and Community Psychiatry</u>, <u>37</u>, 1091-1093.

Blumenfield, S., & Lowe, J. I. (1987). A template for analyzing ethical dilemmas in discharge planning. <u>Health and Social Work</u>, <u>12</u>, 47-56.

Coulton, C., Dunkle, R., Chow, J., Haug, M., & Vielhaber, D. (1988). Dimensions of post-hospital care decision making: A factor analytic study. <u>The Gerontologist</u>, <u>28</u>, 218-223.

Coulton, C. J., Dunkle, R. E., Goode, R. A., & MacKintosh, J. (1982). Discharge planning and decision-making. <u>Health and Social Work</u>, <u>7</u>(4), 253-261.

Gambel, J. A., Heilbronn, M., & Reamer, F. (1980). Hospital social workers become "decision makers" in nursing home placement. <u>Journal of the American Health Care Association</u>, <u>6</u>, 19-23.

Hubbard, R., Santos, J., & Wiora, M. (1978). A community-based model for discharge planning and after care for hospitalized older adults. <u>Journal of Gerontological Social Work</u>, <u>1</u>, 63-68.

Kane, R. (1980). Discharge planning: An undischarged responsibility. <u>Health and Social Work</u>, <u>5</u>, 2-3.

Ledbetter, J., & Batey, S. (1981). Consumer education in discharge planning for continuity of care. International Journal of Social Psychiatry, 27, 283-288.

Lurie, A. (1984). The social work advocacy role in discharge planning. In A. Lurie & G. Rosenberg (Eds.), Social work administration in health care (pp. 293-303). New York: The Haworth Press.

Lurie, A., Pinskey, A., & Tuzman, L. (1981). Training social workers in discharge planning. Health and Social Work, 6, 12-18.

Lurie, A., Robinson, B., & Barbaccia, J. (1984). Helping hospitalized elderly: Discharge planning and informal support. Home Health Care Services Quarterly, 5, 25-43.

Marcus, L. G. (1987). Discharge planning: An organizational perspective. Health and Social Work, 12, 39-46.

Markey, B., & Igou, J. (1987). Medication discharge planning for the elderly. Patient Education Counseling, 9, 141-249.

Office of General Counsel. (1987). Discharging hospital patients: Legal implications for institutional providers and health care professionals. American Hospital Association.

Sandman, G. (1981). Discharge planning: A social worker's perspective. In E. McKeehan (Ed.), Continuing care: A multidisciplinary approach to discharge planning (pp. 107-118). St. Louis: C.V. Mosby.

Shamansky, S., Boase, J., & Horn, B. (1984). Discharge planning: Yesterday, today, and tomorrow. Home Healthcare Nurse, 2, 14-17, 20-21.

Shulman, L., & Tuzman, L. (1980). Discharge planning - A social work perspective. Quality Review Bulletin, 6, 3-8.

Smeltzer, C., & Flores, S. (1986). Preadmission discharge planning: Organization of concept. Journal of Nursing Administration, 16, 18-24.

Volland, P. J. (Ed.) (1988). Discharge planning: An interdisciplinary approach to continuity of care. Owings Mills, MD: National Health Publishing.

CHAPTER 5

OLDER MINORITIES: SOCIAL WORK PERSPECTIVE

by Joyce O. Beckett
and Delores Dungee-Anderson

Introduction

The term "old people" is used categorically to describe individuals at a certain age or beyond. Typically implied is that all persons who meet this criterion are alike. In reality, however, the elderly are a highly diverse population group in which heterogeneity cannot be overemphasized. When the combination of ethnicity and minority status is added, being elderly is, at best, a unique life-stage experience and often results in oppression. This chapter will examine the dual membership status of individuals who are both elderly and belong to minority groups in the United States.

There are many oppressed groups which comprise the elderly population, however, discussion in this chapter is limited to ethnic minorities of color:

     1. Asian Americans
     2. Black Americans
     3. Hispanic Americans
     4. Native Americans

Though each of these groups has a distinct history, they share the common experience of oppression in the United States. They have customs, values, traditions, and sometimes, languages that differ from dominant society and from each other. They have identifiable physical characteristics which make them easy targets for discrimination and exclusion from mainstream America.

The Aging Process

Senescence, or aging, is a cultural, behavioral, psychological, chronological, social and biological process. No matter what definition is used, the aging process is highly individual. Definitions of aging shape the perceptions, preferences, beliefs, and behavior of all persons and, frequently, the treatment of older persons. In America, being "old" is associated with certain culturally unpleasant occurrences such as physical decline and death, and as a result, elderly persons may be treated with less than respect. White elderly men, for example, may experience discrimination for the first time in their lives simply because they have become "old." For minorities of color, the negative conditions and reactions associated with aging may be the last stage in a life history of oppression, powerlessness and low status. Minority elderly tend to lead a more difficult life as aging itself may compound or intensify discriminatory treatment. In addition, the stresses associated with being a minority group member can accelerate the aging process so that minorities may be faced with aging concerns at a much earlier point in life than majority persons.

Individual characteristics and the nature of the aging process itself make it difficult to define or measure when a person is considered "old" or "elderly." For example, when chronic ailments and disabilities are considered, many Native Americans are old at age 45. Because definitions and measures vary with circumstances, this chapter relies on the data sources' definition of "aged" which range from 45 years and over to 65 years and over.

Learning Outcomes

After completing this chapter, students will be able to:

- compare and contrast the life situations of Asian Americans, Black Americans, Hispanic Americans and Native Americans

- identify strengths and problem areas for each minority group

- demonstrate self awareness through analyses of personal attitudes, biases and behavioral patterns with minority elderly

- exhibit an appreciation of the complexity of human diversity among the elderly

- demonstrate appreciation of the socio-cultural variables in understanding, planning, and intervention with minority elderly

Outline of Key Topics and Content Areas

Overview of Minority Elderly
    Asian Americans
    Black Americans
    Hispanic Americans
    Native Americans

Demographics
    Size and Growth
    Education
    Heterogeneity

Economics
    Income and Poverty
    Sources of Income
        Employment
        Social Security and Pensions

Living Arrangements and Social Support
    Housing
    Marital Status
    Family Life

Health
    Physical and Mental Well-Being
    Utilization of Services
    Participation in Medicaid and Medicare Programs

Working with Minority Elderly
    Assessment
    Intervention

Overview of Minority Elderly

To understand the present status of minority elderly groups requires an appreciation for the context in which these individuals matured. Those who are 62 or older in 1988 were born in 1926 or earlier, almost 40 years before the civil rights era of the sixties. They are one generation, and in some cases, a few generations removed from immigration, slavery, conquest and/or forced labor. Each group has a history of a hostile induction into American society. The world of the minority elderly often has been limited to the ghetto, barrios, reservations and enclaves.

Minority elderly were oppressed in almost every aspect of life. They grew up in an historical period when resources, roles and status were determined almost exclusively by race and ethnicity. Discrimination and segregation were sanctioned, and in some cases, upheld by laws. These experiences have influenced their orientation to life, perception of the world, and yet continue to influence the relationship they have with each other and the Anglo majority.

That the minority elderly have coped and survived despite the overwhelming barriers is a testament to their strengths. They have learned to live with and overcome adversity and scarcity. They have developed coping strategies such as reliance on the extended family and the development of community networks that have buffered them from the harsh Anglo world.

Demographic and socio-economic characteristics provide a snapshot of the current experiences of the minority elderly and are compared and contrasted in this section.

Asian Americans

Asian-American elderly have received little attention in social work literature and as consumers of social services. Several factors help to explain this occurrence. First, the designation Asian Americans includes several culturally distinct and diverse groups. There is little agreement, even among governmental institutions, about which groups to designate as Asian American. The discussion in this section will rely primarily on the definition of the U.S. Census Bureau which is congruent with that of the Council on Social Work Education and National Association of Social Workers. However, the general literature often does not specify which groups are defined as Asian Americans.

A second reason is that, unlike the other minorities of color, Asian Americans are not a protected minority under the definition of "socially and economically disadvantaged" persons. Public Law 95-507 specifically excludes Asian Americans from this category (U.S. Commission on Civil Rights, 1979). This results in the exclusion of Asian Americans from programs that are specifically targeted toward the poor minority elderly.

A related third factor is the prevalence of referring to Asian Americans as the "model minority." This label suggests Asian Americans have been able to overcome prejudice and oppression, the proof being that as a group their socio-economic characteristics are similar to or exceed those of White Americans. This stereotype has become the basis for several unfounded assumptions including that Asian Americans do not have problems, are able to care for their own and do not need or desire social services. The socio-economic situation and the history of elderly Asian Americans in this country do not support this myth. Like other minorities of color, they have been and continue to be victims of discrimination and oppression. For example, unlike European immigrants, Asian Americans faced quotas which for decades (1882 to 1965), limited their entry into the United States. Furthermore, once in America, prejudice and racism not only continued but escalated for some groups of Asians. Among elderly Japanese Americans, for example, the climax of this discrimination was their internment from 1941 to 1946. During those years, all persons with as little as one-eighth Japanese blood, whether American citizens or not, were evacuated from their homes and herded into "relocation camps" or concentration camps. They lost millions in property and income (Lum, 1984; Lum, 1986; Weeks, 1984).

Fourth, the perceived positive situation of Asian Americans rests to some extent on the erroneous use of data for all Asian Americans. When treated as a homogeneous group, important differences are masked such as bimodal distribution on most social characteristic indicators. For example, when one looks at occupation or income, Asian Americans concentrate at the top and the bottom levels. An arithmetic average camouflages these extreme scores and perpetrates the myth of "average" or "above average" achievement on social indicators. Once the data are disaggregated, the elderly are one group that emerges as having some special concerns.

A fifth factor is the scarcity of historical and contemporary national data. Statistics from the Census, for instance, do not report on Asians as a separate group until 1980 (Kim, 1983). Even in 1988, there is no consistent effort to include Asians as a separate group when national or local data are considered. Therefore, it is extremely difficult to find statistical information on elderly Asian Americans.

Black Americans

Blacks have received relatively little attention in the gerontological literature, despite the fact that they constitute America's largest and most underprivileged minority group. The history of their immigration to this country is necessary for understanding their place in contemporary American society. Blacks began coming to the United States in the early 1600s along with the first White settlers. While many were free or indentured servants similar to a number of whites, a large majority came involuntarily as slaves. As the need for labor increased, especially in agriculture, fewer Blacks were free and laws were erected to support the institution of slavery (Watson, 1983).

There are at least two immigration patterns for Black Americans. One is that they came directly to the United States from Africa. The other is that they went from an African country to another country--frequently the Caribbean Islands or South America--and later migrated or were brought to the United States.

All Black Americans can trace their roots to Africa. They represent a number of African countries which have had and continue to have distinct cultures and languages. Even in the same country, Africans lived in tribes with different dialects. Currently, African countries reflect their own indigenous historical culture and the culture of the European countries which colonialized them. Thus, variant customs and dialectical vestiges remain today among Black population subgroups that have been relatively isolated from the majority population.

In the United States, many of the current elderly Blacks grew up in the rural, agricultural south where they had few rights and privileges. Laws as well as customs prevented them from actively participating in and receiving rewards from the larger society. The majority (59%) continued to live in the South in 1980 (Watson, 1983). In many cases, their children have moved to larger cities and to the North and Midwest seeking better opportunities. Although the Black elderly have lived through major societal changes and positive gains, they continue to be a disadvantaged group that does not share equally in any facet of American society.

139

Hispanic Americans

Historically, Hispanic groups have been "ignored or considered as insignificant by social scientists and policy makers" (Maldonado, 1979, p. 176). The Census Bureau projects a 600% growth rate among elderly Hispanics in less than 50 years (Miranda, 1988). The needs of this population are increasingly important to recognize and address.

More than one out of 20 Americans is of Spanish or Latin origin. They share the common group label of "Hispanic" or "Latino" and Central and South America as a common ancestral home. Americans of Mexican, Puerto Rican, Cuban, and European descent (Spain) also share the Hispanic designation.

Mexican Americans, widely referred to as Chicanos, Latin Americans, and/or Spanish Americans are the largest Hispanic-American subgroup. They have a long history in the United States beginning in the early days of European exploration before the nation was formed. Historical accounts document the founding of Sante Fe, New Mexico more than a decade before the Pilgrims landed at Plymouth (Shaffer, 1984). Their ancestry can be traced back to the conquering of the Native-American population of Central America and the merging of these Spanish conquerors with the Native-American population to form the Mexican people.

Puerto Ricans are the second largest Hispanic subgroup and originate from the island of Puerto Rico, located about a thousand miles from Miami. The original Native-American inhabitants of the island became extinct while the Spanish settlers who imported African slaves merged with the slaves to form the group currently called Puerto Ricans (Shaffer, 1984).

Cubans came to the United States in large numbers in four major waves of immigration. The most recognized wave was the Cuban Refugee Program which was in operation from 1965 to 1973 (Cuban Refugee Program, 1974). During this period the United States and Cuba cooperated to run daily shuttle flights to the States to reunite families separated during earlier open immigration periods. Approximately 300,000 Cubans settled in the United States during this wave.

Considering the diverse origins of the three largest subgroups of Hispanic Americans it is obvious that when combined with the smaller subgroups of Spanish origin, the total Hispanic-American population is widely divergent.

The majority of Hispanic elderly have settled in four states. Those from Mexico and Central American are found predominantly in California and Texas. Florida has a large Cuban population, and New York has attracted many immigrants from Puerto Rico and the Caribbean Islands (American Association of Retired Persons, 1987).

Native Americans

Native Americans are recognized as the first inhabitants of North America and the first ethnic group to be subordinated to the Europeans. The majority of Native Americans who survived contact with European whites were removed from their ancestral homes and resettled on reservations restricted to certain areas in the country.

At that time and currently, Native Americans have a diversity of life styles, languages, religions, kinship systems and political organizations. For example, as Shaffer (1984) notes, at the time of the first European contact in North America, Native-American inhabitants spoke at least 300 tribal languages. Approximately half are still used among Native-American tribes in the United States.

Clusters of Native-American populations groups which include the elderly are located in such urban centers as Pittsburgh, Minneapolis, Tulsa, Denver, Oakland, and Tacoma. Other large population concentrations are located in Alaskan villages, in rural and semi-rural areas and on reservations in southern and southeastern areas of the United States.

In comparison with other racial and ethnic minorities in the United States, an understanding of the uniqueness of the Native-American population becomes crucial. Native Americans retain both a legal and constitutional status that differs from other minority groups. This difference impacts the provision of services to Native-American elderly (NICOA, 1981b).

The Constitution, a number of court decisions, and federal laws together award important powers of self-government to federally recognized tribes of Native Americans. Tribes living within the boundaries of federally recognized reservations possess many of the features of sovereignty that characterize American state and local governments. Tribes retain the right to adopt a form of government of their own choosing, to define tribal membership, regulate domestic relations of members, and to tax and control the conduct of tribal members through reservations. The National Indian Council on Aging (NICOA, 1981b) also suggests that the notion of self-determination is inherent in the possession of these powers. As distinct legal and cultural units, Native-American tribes are legally sanctioned to determine their own futures within the parameters of the United States law.

The elderly who live on reservations or in Alaskan Native villages are governed by tribal policies and may experience differences in the quality of life compared to the single Native-American elderly who lives in and is governed by the laws of individual states. As political jurisdictions, states have powers of taxation and are consequently able to legislate and support local programs for their elderly. Tribes do not have the resources to operate in this fashion. Congress and the Bureau of Indian Affairs make the final policy and financial decisions on questions of need for older Native Americans. As a result, there is actually less access to government assistance than for other minority groups (AARP, 1987).

Demographics

Size and Growth

The proportion of the population which is elderly varies considerably by race and ethnic origin. As is shown in Figure 1, there is a smaller proportion of older Blacks (8%) than Whites (12%). This difference is a result of Blacks having a higher fertility rate and a higher mortality rate than Whites. Among Blacks, more children are born and fewer persons live to reach 65 (AARP, 1987; Special Committee on Aging, United States Senate, 1986). At about age 70, an interesting phenomenon occurs. Blacks who survive to this age have a life expectancy almost identical to Whites. At more advanced ages, Blacks actually have a greater life expectancy so that the life expectancy for Black men (6.0 years) and women (7.4 years) at age 85 exceeds that for White men (5.2 years) and White women (6.5 years). No simple explanation has been given for this "age cross over" (U.S. Bureau of the Census, 1987). (See Figure 1.)

During the 1700s and 1800s slavery was a major force that changed the size of the Black population. In the first census of 1790, about 757,000 people were reported as Black. In 1860, just before the Emancipation Proclamation, the census counted almost 4.4 million Blacks, a six fold increase. This phenomenal increase was due directly to the importation and the encouraged high fertility rates of the slaves (Watson, 1983).

The increase in the Black population has continued although at a smaller rate than during slavery. In 1980, there were 26,488,000 Black Americans which is a 16% increase from 1970. During that same decade, the number of Blacks who are 65 and older increased by 34% from 1,5556,000 to 2,085,826. (Watson, 1983). The rate of growth among the Black elderly surpasses both that of the total Black population and of younger Blacks. Blacks have a higher proportion of elderly than any other minority of color. In 1982, about 12% of whites, 8% of Blacks, 6% of Asians and 5% each of Native Americans and Hispanic Americans were 65 and over (Markides & Mindel, 1987; U.S. Bureau of the Census, 1983).

Many of the current elderly Blacks grew up in the rural, agricultural south where they had few rights and privileges. Laws as well as customs prevented them from actively participating and receiving rewards from the larger society. The majority (59%) continue to live in the South in 1980 (Watson, 1983). In many cases, their children have moved to larger cities and to the North and Midwest seeking better opportunities. Although the Black elderly have lived through major societal changes and positive gains, they continue to be a disadvantaged group that does not share equally in any facet of American society.

Asian Americans are a relatively small group and are not dispersed throughout the United States. This group has accounted for less than 2% of the American population and have constituted 5% of American minorities of color. The large concentration (90%) of Asian Americans in the metropolitan areas of a few states supports the stereotype of an "invisible minority". The majority live in California and Hawaii (Beaver, 1983). Approximately 6% of the Asian/Pacific Islander population in America was 65 or over in 1980; 7% of this group were 85 and older. Asian Americans were less likely than Whites (12% in 1987) and Blacks (87% in 1985) to be 65 or older and more likely than Whites (1% in 1985) to be 85 and over (AARP, 1987; Special Committee on Aging United States Senate, 1986). (See Figure 1.)

The actual breakdown of Asian elderly residence is 55% living in the three western states of California, Hawaii and Washington, another 12% in two northeastern states of New York and New Jersey while only 10% live in rural areas (AARP, 1987; Kim, 1983; Yu, 1980). In Virginia and Louisiana, Asians constitute the smallest proportion of minority elderly since only 3.1% and 3.7%, respectively, were 65 and over in 1980 in these states (AARP, 1987). Overall, Japanese constitute the largest portion, one-third, of elderly Asian Americans.

Hispanics are the fastest growing minority population group in the United States. The greatest density in growth of Hispanics is concentrated in urban areas (Becerra & Shaw, 1984; U.S. Bureau of the Census, 1987). In March, 1987, there were 18.8 million Hispanics in the United States who were noninstitutional civilians. This figure represents an increase of approximately 700,000 since 1986 data were collected.

Approximately 5% or about 673,00 of the Hispanic elderly are 65 years of age or over. Of this number, approximately 6.6% or about 45,000 are 85 and older (AARP, 1987). Consequently, as a group, Hispanic-Americans are a relatively young population. (See Figure 1.)

The proportion of elderly among the Native-American population has grown faster than in other minority groups. Between 1970 and 1980, the number of elderly increased by 65%. This figure is twice the increase for Black or White elderly.

Native-American elderly comprise about 5% of the Native-American population in the U.S. Approximately 109,000 Native Americans are over the age of 65. Of these, about 6,100 are 85 years and over. Beginning at age 45, they suffer a higher incidence of chronic health problems and functional impairments than the general elderly population in the United States. Those individuals who are 45 and over show startling similarities across several dimensions, to the non-Native-American population over age 65 (NICOA, 1981a). (See Figure 1.)

Figure 1.
Socio-Demographic Characteristics of Minority Elderly Group

Race	Sex	Sex Ratio Men per 100 Women Age					Life Expectancy in Years	Income Median 65 Yrs.+	Group Poverty Status Below Official Poverty Line 65 Yrs. + - Percentage
		60-64	65-69	70-74	75-79	80+			
White	Male	87	81	72	61	43	71.7	$ 13,280	13%
	Female	100	100	100	100	100	78.7	$ 6,724	
Asian-American	Male	84	93	109	89	60	No Data	$ 5,551	14%
	Female	100	100	100	100	100		$ 3,476	
Black-American	Male	80	73	69	63	50	65.7	$ 7,092	32%
	Female	100	100	100	100	100	73.6	$ 4,350	
Hispanic-American	Male	86	76	77	76	61	No Data	$ 8,003	26%
	Female	100	100	100	100	100		$ 4,800	
Native-American	Male	87	77	82	74	59	65 years	$ 4,257	61%
	Female	100	100	100	100	100		$ 3,033	

Race	Age % 65+	85+	Education % of Group Little/No Formal	High School
White	12%***	1%	2%	41%
Asian-American	6%	7% of 6% aged 65 years and older	13%	26%
Black-American	8%**	7.5% of 8% aged 65 years and older	6%	17%
Hispanic-American	5%*	6.6% of 5% aged 65 years and older	16%	19%
Native-American	5%*	7.7% of 5% over 65 years	12%	22%

*1980 Data
**1985 Data
***1987 Data

Source: AARP, 1987

143

Education

Of all minority elderly, <u>Hispanics</u> have the highest illiteracy rate of any of the ethnic groups in the United States (See Figure 1). The proportion of Hispanics with little or no formal education is 16%, eight times as great as for White elderly (2%). In 1987, only 19% of Hispanic elderly 65 and older had completed high school (AARP, 1987; Becerra & Shaw, 1984).

Among the Hispanic subgroups, older Cubans were found to have a higher level of education than older Puerto Ricans or Hispanics of Mexican descent (Becerra & Shaw, 1984). This finding is explained by the large number of Cubans of higher socio-economic status who fled Cuba for this country during the unrest of the 1960s. Puerto Rican immigrants were found to have less formal education than any racial or ethnic group studied while Hispanics of Mexican origin living in the Southwest have the highest illiteracy rate in the Nation for elderly individuals. Three-fourths are functionally illiterate (Leonard, 1967).

<u>Native-American</u> elderly have the second highest percentage of little or no formal schooling. Approximately 22% are high school graduates and about 12% have no formal education at all (AARP, 1987). Only 6% of the <u>Black</u> elderly have had no formal education despite the severe limitations to educational resources they experienced in U.S. school systems. Black elderly with formal education fall significantly behind White elderly in achievement as only 17% of Blacks completed high school compared with 41% of White elderly (AARP, 1987).

Of all minority elderly, <u>Asian Americans</u> have the greatest percentage of high school graduates (26%). Yet, this figure is still significantly lower than the proportion of White elderly graduates (41%). Even though recent Asian immigrants include a significant proportion of well-educated professionals, the percentage of those lacking formal education (13%) is still substantially greater than for White elderly (2%).

Heterogeneity

Of the four minority groups discussed in this chapter, <u>Black Americans</u> are the only one that are not defined or described in any of the literature or government documents. The literature assumes that everyone knows who are Black Americans. This situation reflects the myth that Black Americans are a homogeneous population. In reality, Blacks vary on many dimensions including the amount of time they have lived in the United States, their country of origin and their immigration patterns. For example, some elderly Blacks have lived in the United States all their lives and may be eighth or ninth generation American. Others have recently immigrated to the United States from non-African countries like Haiti or from African countries such as Ghana or Nigeria and may not speak English. There is little or no appreciation of the rich cultural differences among the various ethnic groups within the literature. It is important for understanding and intervention to consider these differences. For example, an older Black who has recently moved to the United States from Haiti and speaks no English would likely have different concerns than an elderly Black person who has lived in this country all his or her life.

As in the total <u>Asian-American</u> population, the elderly are also diverse and can be divided into at least five groups (Lum, 1983):

1. retired single males, mainly Chinese and Filipino who were denied marriage because of immigration restrictions
2. elderly females, mainly Japanese who entered the country as picture brides
3. immigrants or Americans born during the early 1900s

144

4. parents who accompanied their children from China, Taiwan, Korea and the Philippines to America during the last two decades
5. persons who came to America in the last few years with their families as a result of the Vietnamese and Cambodian wars.

There are unique historical and contemporary influences on each of these five groups as well as on each ethnic group among the Asian Americans.

The Hispanic population in this country is racially heterogeneous and is comprised of several population subgroups of Spanish-origin. Each subgroup is identified by place-of-origin but may include Whites, Blacks, Native Americans, Asians, and Pacific Islanders of Spanish ancestry. Although demographic data on the subgroups are independently estimated, all subgroups are also statistically combined to comprise the larger minority group of Hispanic-Americans. Included in the Spanish surname group are individuals of Mexican, Puerto Rican, Cuban, Central American, South American, and Spanish origin (Torres-Gil & Negm, 1980).

Discussion of Native-American elderly as a group is difficult because "Indian groups are extremely diverse, with important tribal differences" (Gelfand, 1982, p. 29). Although most Native-American elders identify first on the basis of tribe, many of those who live on reservations further identify themselves with a particular band within their tribe (Dukepoo, 1980). For example, an elder may be a member of the Cahuilla band of the Mission tribe. Native-American elderly also differ in their "degree Indian." The concept of blood quantum or "degree of Indian blood" is a "means of establishing ties with the Indian community." However, this situation poses a unique and specific problem for Native Americans by inserting "legalisms into ethnic identification" which impact on one's eligibility for services (Dukepoo, 1980, p. 28).

Most research on Native-American elderly has been conducted on samples from reservations even though less than one-fourth of this group live on reservations (Stuart & Rathbone-McCuan, 1988). An important exception is a 1981 study that the National Indian Council on Aging conducted. Among its national representative sample of Native Americans, several lived in urban centers and a large concentration were also located in small, rural villages. The large number of tribes represented and the varied geographical residences underscore that Native-American elderly are as heterogeneous as their ethnic group counterparts (NICOA, 1981a). Efforts to estimate the characteristics and needs of Native-American elderly "are complicated by population dispersion and varying definitions of who is an Indian" (Stuart & Rathbone-McCuan, 1988, p. 240).

Economics

Income and Poverty

Inadequate income is the most prevalent concern for minority elderly. According to the National Caucus and Center on Black Aged during a 1987 hearing before the Select Committee on Aging, the lack of adequate economic resources is a primary cause of every other problem facing minority elderly (National Caucus and Center on Black Aged, 1987). While poverty tends to be a transitory state for many younger Americans, it becomes a continuing fact of life for many minority elderly. Employment and marriage, two strategies that move many beyond the poverty level, are less available to older persons and especially to minorities of color. Discrimination because of age, gender, and race restricts employment opportunities and the shortage of potential spouses limits marriage as an avenue to economic improvement.

Ethnic minority elderly have substantially lower earned incomes than their White counterparts. In 1985, for example, the median income of Black males aged 65-69 was $7,092 or 53% of White males who had a median income of $13,280. Elderly Hispanic males earned $8,003 or 60%

of that of White males. Black and Hispanic women had median incomes of $4,350 and $4,800, respectively, or 65% and 71% lower than that of elderly White women who earned $6,724. Data for Native Americans are from 1980, but show that the median income for Native-American men aged 65 or over was $4,257. For Native-American women in this same age group, the median income was $3,033. Asian-American elderly had a higher income than other minorities; $5,551 for Asian men and $3,476 for Asian women (AARP, 1987). (See Figure 1.)

Blacks are the poorest of the poor regardless of the indicator used. They have a higher poverty rate and a lower income than Whites (National Caucus and Center on Black Aged, 1987). For example, in 1985 the poverty rate among Black elderly (32%) was triple the rate of White elderly (11%). Hispanic elderly had double the poverty rate (24%) of White counterparts (Special Committee on Aging United States Senate, 1987). An aged person was considered poor in 1985 if his or her income fell below $5,156 ($6,503 for an elderly couple) (National Caucus and Center on Black Aged, 1987). These figures translate to a maximum total income of $99 per week or $125 for a couple. (See Figure 1.)

The harshness of the situation becomes more apparent when one considers the "economically vulnerable," those individuals with income between the poverty level and twice the poverty line. In 1985, 71% of older Blacks were either poor or economically vulnerable contrasted with 40% of the White elderly. The situation is especially bleak for women who fare less well than men among White and minority elderly. Of all major groups of older women, Black women are most likely to live in poverty. The highest rate of poverty is among Black women living alone. Almost all (88%) were poor or economically vulnerable in 1985 (National Caucus and Center on Black Aged, 1987).

The proportion of elderly Asian (14%) living below the poverty level is almost identical to Whites (13%). This proportion is at least half that of other elderly minorities. The rates are as high as 40% however, for those Asian Americans residing in rural areas (AARP, 1987). (See Figure 1.)

Hispanic elderly are particularly vulnerable to loss of employment income. They often do not collect income maintenance supplements. Language barriers, pride, lack of information about the bureaucratic process, and about available services, and distrust of the Federal government, because of past discrimination, all add to their reluctance to seek assistance. Fear of problems related to citizenship status is another major issue (Torres-Gil & Negm, 1980). For the elderly Hispanic illegal aliens who have worked in the United States, the fear of discovery prohibits their exploration of governmental income maintenance supplements.

Sixty-one percent of Native-American elderly 65 years old or over live below the official poverty line compared to 11% of Whites in this same age group. (See Figure 1.) Because the Native-American is "old" at age 45, the chronic ailments and disabilities suffered result in loss of economic earning power and a decrease in an already poor quality of life. The extended family is affected along with the individual (NICOA, 1981a). Interesting is that since the 1970 census a 10% increase of Native-American elderly have fallen below the national poverty level. Despite the fact that in the years 1970-1980 when Native-American elders were designated "a target population" to receive entitlement program services, more than 10,000 joined the ranks of the impoverished (NICOA, 1986).

Sources of Income

Employment

In general, as persons reach their late 50s, participation in the labor force falls and those who remain employed usually have higher unemployment rates and reduced occupational mobility. These trends are intensified for the minority elderly, especially <u>Blacks</u>. The extent of labor force participation for Black men over age 65 (13%) was lower in 1986 than the rate for older White (16%) men. This rate has fallen more rapidly than Whites in recent years. Historically, participation of Black women in the labor force has been considerably higher than for White women. Over the last 30 years, however, the rates have converged so that in 1986, only one percentage point separated the two groups (8% for the elderly Whites and 9% for elderly Blacks) (Special Committee on Aging United States Senate, 1986; U.S. Dept. of Labor, 1988).

The historically high unemployment rates for younger Black men help to explain the fact that older Black men have lower levels of lifetime labor force participation. Long periods of unemployment due to discrimination and other reasons cause many Black workers to leave the labor force altogether and stop looking for work. These persons are classified as discouraged workers and are not counted among the unemployed.

For older (55 years plus) workers who did not work at all during 1986, Black men (58%) are a little more likely than White (51%) to fall into this category. The differences among women are negligible with about three-fourths of Black women (73%) and White women (75%) not working during 1986. One distinct racial difference, however, is that Blacks are far more likely than White counterparts to cite illness or disabilities as their reason for not working. These physical ailments are often related to the heavy physical types of work Blacks have engaged in during their work lives (U.S. Department of Labor, 1988).

These findings and other research indicate that Blacks are more likely than Whites to retire involuntarily. Poor health and less demand for Black workers, as shown in the unemployment rates, force many Blacks to retire early. Because of inadequate retirement income, poor health status and other factors, Blacks are consistently more dissatisfied with retirement than Whites (Markides, 1985).

Despite their age, many older persons attempt to augment their incomes by working. Again, minorities fare worse than Whites. Black elderly workers, for example, are more likely than their White counterparts to be unemployed, underemployed or working in lower paying positions. For instance, in 1985 Blacks age 55 to 64 were at least twice as likely as Whites to be unemployed or earning as little as 56% of the wages paid to Whites (National Caucus and Center on Black Aged, 1987).

A significant portion of <u>Asian Americans</u> (30%) work after the traditional retirement age of 65. Thus their own earnings are a major source of income. About 30% of the Asian elderly over age 65 participated in the labor force (Kim, 1983). These people who were working or actively looking for work compares to 11% of all older workers (AARP, 1987). Even at 75 years of age and older, approximately 16% of Asian Americans work (Kim, 1983). Thus, earnings are a major source of income for a significant number of elderly Asian Americans. These persons are primarily self employed and working in service areas and farming. Asian Americans (8%) are also more likely than Whites (5%) to be unemployed (AARP, 1987).

The percentage of <u>Hispanic</u> elderly who are in the labor force is the same as for the White population. However, elderly Hispanics suffer from greater unemployment (9%) than Whites (5%) (AARP, 1987).

Approximately 12% of <u>Native Americans</u> continue working after age 65 (AARP, 1987). A national profile shows that of those Native-American elderly who were employed, 65% were semi-skilled, unskilled, or farm workers (NICOA, 1981b). The unemployment rate among reservation elders tends to be higher than for those living in urban areas (Dukepoo, 1980).

Social Security and Pensions

While Social Security benefits are a key source of income for most elderly, they are more crucial for ethnic minorities than Whites. The reason is that minorities are less apt than Whites to have other sources of income such as assets and private pensions. In 1984, for example, older White males (34%) were more likely than <u>Black</u> males (20%), White females (12%) and Black women (5%) to receive private pensions (National Caucus and Center on Black Aged, 1987).

For ethnic minorities, Social Security benefits are the major and sometimes only source of income. Nevertheless, minority elderly are still less likely than Whites to receive these benefits. Additionally, those recipients receive smaller amounts. In 1984, about 92% of all White persons 65 or over received Social Security, including 5% who collected both Social Security and Supplemental Security Income. In contrast, 86% of Blacks received Social Security including 19% who received both Social Security and SSI (National Caucus and Center on Black Aged, 1987). This disparity is primarily explained by the type of employment ethnic elderly held. They worked in minimum or low-wage occupations that were either not covered or only partially covered by Social Security or other Pension Program benefits.

During their entire work lives, <u>Asian Americans</u> are more likely to be self-employed. When this group does retire, they are usually ineligible for Social Security and private pension benefits.

<u>Hispanic</u> elderly are also less likely to receive retirement income from private pensions and private savings than are White elderly. Uneven work histories, low employment in manufacturing, professional or blue collar work associated with few pension plans and the inability to have accumulated savings are realities that preclude income from these sources (Becerra & Shaw, 1984). Older Hispanics who retire due to a disability face another economic barrier. The strict definitions of disability often preclude these people from eligibility for SSI benefits.

Another factor which reduces the level of benefits is the method by which Social Security is calculated. The amount payable is determined by adding incomeless years into an average yearly income. Consequently, elderly Hispanics like Blacks who may have not held regular employment or who were unemployed during the normally high earning period of late middle age are severely penalized (Becerra & Shaw, 1984).

Income for <u>Native-American</u> elderly largely comes from Social Security or Supplemental Security Income benefits. However, in keeping with the complex status of Native Americans in this country, several factors complicate or prevent these income supports under existing federal programs. With little formal education, many Native-American elderly fail to complete the application process or, because of the complexity of rules and regulations, do not apply for entitlements under Social Security or Veterans Administration programs. Further, some of the regulations create special hardships. For example, tribal dividends governed by treaty regulations must be counted as income when SSI eligibility is determined. In addition, the Social Security program requires documentation of quarters worked, of marriage, and of age (NICOA, 1981b). Needless to say, "story telling" and verbal renditions of births, deaths, and marriages do not substitute for official written documentation thereby aborting an application process.

Living Arrangements and Social Support

Housing

Housing is the most expensive budgetary item for the elderly. Almost half of the elderly spend at least 45% of their income for shelter (National Caucus and Center on Black Aged, 1987). The availability of suitable, affordable housing for minority elderly is rare. Long waiting lists exist, especially in urban areas where many minority elderly live. For example, one-quarter of the applicants for federally assisted housing for the elderly (Section 202 housing) wait a minimum of five years for an available unit. Such extended waiting periods discourage minority elderly from applying (National Caucus and Center on Black Aged, 1987).

Federal cutbacks and prohibitive rents further reduce the availability of suitable housing. The reduction in funding for housing has resulted in a substantial decline in the erection of federally assisted and other public housing for the elderly . For instance, between 1980 and 1985, Section 202 housing starts plummeted from almost 21,000 to less than 9,000 units. During the same period, rental expenses for these units jumped from 25% to 30% of a tenant's income. The scarcity of housing for minority older persons is underscored by the fact that only 13% of all poor elderly persons resided in federally-assisted housing in 1984 (National Caucus and Center on Black Aged, 1987).

Whether owners or renters, Black elderly have major housing problems. Those fortunate enough to own homes (58% of Blacks compared to 72% of Whites) may face unaffordable and escalating property taxes and maintenance costs. Among both homeowners and renters, Blacks are considerably more likely to have substandard and unsuitable housing (1/3 of elderly Blacks compared to 1/8 of older Whites). These housing units may lack plumbing, central heat, air conditioning, and kitchen facilities (National Caucus and Center on Black Aged, 1987).

Black elderly are more likely than White to be widowed, divorced and separated. They, however, usually reside in a household with family rather than live alone or with unrelated persons. It is not unusual to find children and younger persons residing in Black families headed by an elderly individual or couple. A Black elderly person living with a grown child, usually a daughter, is also a rather common occurrence (AARP, 1987; Beaver, 1983). The nurturing role, particularly among older Black women, seems to be a dominant one.

Although most Asian Americans prefer to live with family, many elderly live alone. As a group, fewer aged Asian Americans (19%) than Whites (30%) live alone. When one looks at subgroups, however, another picture emerges. Asian-Americans are more likely than Whites to live alone. Over one fourth (26%) of Chinese American elderly men and greater than two-thirds (67%) of the women, live alone. Half of all Japanese households outside of the West have only one person and 70% of these are women living alone. Almost one-third of the Filipino elderly live alone (Kim, 1983). Many of these people would like to share homes and help each other; however, specific social policies prevent such mutual interdependence. For instance, Supplemental Security Income is reduced if persons live with others whether they are ethnic friends or kin (Kim, 1983).

The actual physical living arrangements of Hispanic elderly such as sharing residences with kin either as primary household heads or as dependents, represent an important family characteristic. However, mutual aid and informal support within the extended network system are also significant for this cultural group. Hispanic Americans have a highly integrated kin network and tend to live in closer proximity to their kin (Mindel, 1980).

Seventy-two percent of Hispanic elderly were found to live with at least one family member. This figure is slightly higher than the 69% of comparable Whites who live with family (AARP, 1987). However, among the old-old, 80+, differences among the groups in living with a spouse disappeared (Lubben & Becerra, 1987). This finding is likely explained by the large number of widows among all ethnic groups in this older age category. In 1980, over 80% of the Hispanic elderly lived in metropolitan areas with high concentrations in Arizona, California, Colorado, New Mexico, Texas and the Eastern Seaboard. Earlier research indicates that the Hispanic elderly tend to be a relatively stable residential population (Sotomayor, 1978; Torres-Gil et al., 1977; Valle & Mendoza, 1978).

Compared with older Whites, elderly Hispanics live in poorer quality housing. Regional differences also have been observed. An early study cited housing as "best in the West and worst in the South" (Bell, Kaschau, & Zellman, 1976). Elderly Hispanics of Mexican descent living in the central United States were three times more likely to live in poorer quality housing than those Hispanics in California and Arizona. Elderly Hispanics from Southern states were about five times more likely to live in substandard housing when compared with elderly Hispanics in western states.

Becerra and Shaw (1984) point out that because low-income elderly Hispanics tend to live with kin more often than other minority elderly groups and Whites, the lack of housing units large enough to accommodate extended family living arrangements poses additional housing problems for several of the subgroups. For example, elderly Hispanics of Cuban descent have long lived in overcrowded conditions because of the extended family tradition and small housing size typically in low-income urban centers. Puerto Rican elderly also must move and find their own housing units because of limited space in crowded housing units in the inner cities of the northeast (Becerra & Shaw, 1984). Large numbers of these subgroups in inner city areas are seriously affected by the many economic and environmental problems that tend to characterize non-affluent urban areas. When compared to non-minority elderly, they usually are among the first groups affected by inflation resulting in forced relocations. Depending upon general demographic population shifts, elderly Hispanics may be among the first to be dispossessed and relocated (Torres-Gil & Negm, 1980).

Based on either a preference to live in close proximity to other Hispanics or the need to find low-income housing, many rural elderly Hispanics have moved to areas of high Hispanic concentrations. These ethnic enclaves or barrios embody characteristics of both rural and modern urban lifestyles. This type of community setting may soften the blow of culture discontinuities resulting from acculturation, urbanization and the move away from traditional neighborhood social interactions (Becerra & Shaw, 1984).

Approximately half or more of <u>Native-American</u> elderly live in the states of Oklahoma, California, Arizona, New Mexico and Texas. An additional one-quarter or more live on reservations and in Alaskan Native villages. The remaining elderly, somewhat less than one-quarter percent, live in states along the Canada border (AARP, 1987).

About 96% of Native-American elderly live in households in their communities. Housing stock is generally old and dilapidated and approximately 26% occupied by the elderly was built prior to 1939. The National Indian Council on Aging (1986) found that one-quarter of their sample of 712 elderly Native-Americans slept in bedrooms occupied by three or more persons. Few of these homes had heat (20%), water (24%) or indoor toilets (15%).

The proportion of Native-American elderly in nursing homes is low and decreases as age increases. This trend is most noticeable among those 85 years and over (oldest-old) where 13% live in nursing homes compared to 23% of White elderly (AARP, 1987). Shorter life expectancies contribute to this phenomenon.

Marital Status

The majority of minority elderly men are married while the majority of women are widowed. Overall, minority elderly are less likely than Whites to be married and more likely to be widowed and divorced. Asian men are an exception to this trend (AARP, 1987).

Minority elderly marital status is related to life expectancy. No matter what ethnicity or race, women outlive men. The life expectancy for minorities is usually less than for Whites. For example, the life expectancy at birth for White men is 71.7 years; White women, 78.7 years; Black men 65.7 years; and Black women 73.6 years. Since women outlive men, they are more likely to become widowed (AARP, 1987). (See Figure 1.)

As among Whites and other non-Asian minorities, the majority of elderly Asian-American men are married and the majority of women are widowed. Asian Americans, however, have a larger proportion (7.5%) of never married men than Whites or any other minority group. This situation is a consequence of immigration laws that prohibited Chinese women and children from accompanying men to the United States (Beaver, 1983).

Family Life

Familial support and expectations (Kobata, Lockery, & Moriwaki, 1980), vary within each ethnic group, social class, and subculture. For many ethnic communities, however, the role of family in all its forms is still a viable and significant support system (Alvarez & Bean, 1976; Price, 1976; Solomon, 1976).

In many Black families, the younger generation respects and revers the older persons. These favorable attitudes help account for the fact that fewer Black elderly (3%) than White (5%) are institutionalized (AARP, 1987; Beaver, 1983). The racial difference increases with age. For persons 85 and over, who are more likely to be widowed and in need of long term physical and medical assistance, 12% of Blacks as compared to 26% of Whites are institutionalized (AARP, 1987; National Caucus and Center on Black Aged, 1987). Other factors relating to Black underutilization of nursing homes and other long term care facilities are (National Caucus and Center on Black Aged, 1987):

- prohibitive high costs
- racial discrimination
- reluctance of Blacks to seek institutional care because of the media accounts of the poor conditions in the facilities
- the Black extended family provides a number of persons to share in the responsibility of caring for the ill elderly.

Family life among elderly Asian Americans can differ in many ways. Characteristics such as the length of stay in America, country of origin, socioeconomic status, geographical region, marital status, fluency in English, and history of conflict with the majority in America must be considered.

The current solo living situation of some Asian elderly is quite different from the historical family pattern. Traditionally, the Asian-American family has been a close social unit which provided support, security and a sense of meaning for its members. Roles were strictly and formally assigned. Elderly family members were respected and cared for in multi-generation households. The roles of the elderly included aiding their children and grandchildren in achieving positions of wealth and status. The elderly willingly sacrificed themselves to care for their descendants and to teach the younger generations. In return, the elderly were respected and consulted about all major family decisions. China, for example, has been described as a gerontocracy because of the revered position of the elderly in the family (Lum, 1983).

In addition to the family, the clan developed historically in the U.S. as an informal source of support. The associations representing various provinces of the old country or based on last names, developed in urban America. These organizations symbolized the power of a strong extended family. In some instances, they served as social service agencies, providing food, shelter, employment and protection to new immigrants, and an opportunity to socialize for persons who had been in America for longer periods (Lum, 1983). For various reasons, the clan has become less important and less able to cope with current social problems of the inner city, such as overpopulation due to immigration, inadequate housing, unemployment, crime and increasing health problems (Lum, 1983). The demise of clan associations and the increased mobility of second and third generation immigrants and American-born Asians have left many older Asian Americans without their traditional social supports. Many also have lost their important family role of guide and consultant for the younger generations. Some elderly have responded by using the familiar strategies of relying on other Asians, and in this case, on other elderly Asian Americans who remain nearby in the urban areas.

Various research has yielded contradictory results about the role of the elderly in the Hispanic family (Becerra & Shaw, 1984). The Mexican-American Hispanic subgroup is by far the largest and as a result the focus in the literature has mostly been on the Mexican-American elderly residing in the Southwest. As a result, existing data of elderly Hispanics can only suggest general patterns of family life because the lifestyles of the subgroups are different. However, a significant ethnic value is the idealized role given to the extended family members by relatives with the godparent playing an especially important family role (Becerra & Shaw, 1984; Lubben & Becerra, 1987).

Evidence suggests that Hispanic elderly in this country believe in the extended family orientation more than other minority elderly groups. This way of life is used as a determinant of family ties, of frequency of contact, and degree of closeness of family ties (Bengston & Burton, 1980). The ethnic value of family orientation for Hispanic elderly in both the country of origin and in the United States grew out of socio-economic needs. "Family" meant an extended, multi-generational group of persons with specific social roles ascribed to members of each group to help meet the requirements of survival for the entire family group. Thus, the extended family network has included grandparents, aunts, uncles, cousins, lifelong family friends, and godparents.

A very important characteristic of the traditional Hispanic-American family of Mexican descent is the subordination of the younger to the older. It is argued that older people receive more respect from youth and children than is characteristic in Anglo homes. Such respect is noted in the behaviors, manners and patterns of speech of younger to older Hispanics. This pattern is noted even among children where older siblings have higher authority and greater power in the family than do younger ones (Mindel, 1980).

Recent data, however, have pointed to the erosion of intergenerational and lateral interdependence or "familism" in the Hispanic family network (Mindel, 1980). In areas where neighborhood friends and churches provide some support services, the function of the family in providing for socio-economic needs is shifting as other institutions increasingly assume such functions (Becerra & Shaw, 1984; Torres-Gil, 1976). The plight of younger Hispanics looking for better employment opportunities is a factor that contributes to family erosion. Seeking better employment may force them to leave their elders behind. For example, in rural areas, a large percentage of elderly are still often members of extended family units at a significantly higher rate than their White counterparts. The socio-economic barriers that their younger family members experience may actually increase their dependency on natural support networks. Finally, the acculturation of the younger generation in a society which places a high premium on youth and on liberal mores may offset the once-valued roles of older Hispanics and devalue lateral interdependence.

Family-life among Native-American family networks also assumes a structure which is radically different from other extended family units in western society. For example, the accepted structural boundary of the European model of family life is the household. An extended family is defined as three generations within a single household. In contrast, Native-American family networks are structurally open and assume a village type characteristic. Family extensions include several households representing significant relatives in vertical and horizontal kinships. A large network may easily encompass 200 persons and span three generations. Such networks are characteristically divided in units with each unit having at least one responsible and obligated adult available as family head (Red Horse, Lewis, Feit, & Decker, 1978)

The extended family often serves as a major instrument of accountability. Standards and expectations which maintain group solidarity through enforcement of values are established. This structure contributes to a very conservative cultural pattern as the vehicle of transmission of cultural attributes prevents "contamination" from the wider society.

The elderly, or the grandparents, retain official and symbolic leadership in family communities. Each of these active processes is sanctioned by children and their parents. As Red Horse et al. (1978) suggest, official leadership is characterized by a close proximity of grandparents to family. Such leadership may be observed in the behavior of children who seek daily contact with grandparents and by grandparents who monitor parental behavior. Based on this structure, Native-American elders have an official voice in child-rearing methods. Parents rarely overrule corrective measures from their own parents.

Symbolic leadership, reflecting immense respect for the elderly, is seen in the incorporation of unrelated elderly into the family. This practice more frequently occurs during the absence of a natural grandparent but is not necessarily limited to or dependent on it. Symbolic leadership may be observed in the behavior of children and parents who select and virtually adopt elders as grandparents. Symbolic grandparents do not invoke strong child-rearing sanctions and because their acceptance is sought, their norm-setting standards are seldom ignored (Red Horse et al., 1978).

Regardless of the geographic movements of tribes and intertribal marriages occurring over time, Native-American family network dynamics have remained intact. The extended family network remains constant despite family lifestyle patterns which indicate the emergence of a distinct, closed Native-American community that does not easily admit outsiders. Thus the maintenance of cultural characteristics and values tend to be transmitted with relative ease.

The world of Native-American elderly to a large extent has been limited to reservations. This situation has been especially true for Native-Americans in the rural areas of the South and Southwest. Reverence and attachment to the land as well as treaties with the United States government which have provided designated areas of land have contributed to the value of the extended open family structure (Birren & Sloane, 1980). Family ties have been very strong and far reaching, contributing to decreased socializing outside the family among Native-American elderly. Despite close family ties, there appears to be less trust and more unhappiness about family relationships than among White elderly as Native Americans are challenged to allocate deficient resources among their large numbers (NICOA, 1981a).

Health

Physical and Mental Well-Being

Older **Blacks** have poorer health than elderly Whites no matter what criterion is used. Overall, Blacks have more illnesses and are more debilitated by an illness. For example, Blacks are more likely to develop high blood pressure and also have more kidney failure and deaths caused by stroke as a consequence of the hypertension (National Caucus and Center on Black Aged, 1987). Blacks seek medical care less frequently, receive less preventive care and rely more on self diagnosis and treatment. When they do obtain medical help, they are more likely than Whites to rate their health as "poor" or "fair" (National Caucus and Center on Aged, 1987).

Inadequate income is a pivotal factor in the poor health status of Blacks. Actually Blacks begin and end life in a poorer health state than Whites. This fact is supported by the differential life expectancy and death rates. The economic deprivation throughout their lives has a cumulative influence that peaks with old age. With less income, Blacks have poorer nutrition and few opportunities for preventive health measures. They tend to have worked in low status jobs which provide inadequate health insurance benefits. In addition, among those with limited resources and competing needs, health care is postponed and sought only when an illness reaches crisis proportion.

Relatively little data are available on the mental health status of older Blacks and their use of mental health programs. Much of the literature that does address the area of ethnicity and mental health uses a social stress explanation for mental illness (Dohrenwend, 1970, 1973, Dohrenwend & Dohrenwend, 1969; Fried 1975; Kessler, 1979, Kessler & Cleary, 1980). Findings show that poor persons are more likely to have mental problems. They are exposed to a greater number of stresses and have fewer psychological and sociological resources for coping with them (Kessler & Cleary, 1980). Furthermore, attempts of minorities to adapt to and cope with an alien and often hostile environment are another source of stress.

The Black elderly, then, would be expected to have higher rates of mental problems and to utilize mental health services more than the White elderly (Markides & Mindel, 1987). This expectation is supported to some extent. Blacks in general and older Blacks in particular do have higher rates of admission to county and state hospitals. In 1975, older Black men had a much higher admission rate than older White men (210.8 vs 130.9 per 100,000). Older Black women's rate was almost three times that of White women (143.7 vs 54.0 per 100,000).

While these figures may suggest Blacks have more mental health problems than Whites, other explanations are equally tenable (Markides & Mindel, 1987). An alternate explanation is that the data used do not reflect the total reality. Neighbors (1984) has shown that the admission rates to public institutions are only one part of the story. One also has to consider private mental health facilities where Whites are more likely to seek treatment. When both private and public facilities are considered, older Blacks do not have higher rates of utilization (Neighbors, 1984). They instead underutilize mental health services.

Another option is that the racial differences in admission rates, diagnosis and treatment are a reflection of socio-economic status differences between Blacks and Whites and not of race. Hollingshead and Redlich's (1958) early work pointed out the connection between social class and psychiatric diagnosis, treatment validity, and type of facility. These findings have been supported by other scholars who have also explicitly considered the variable of race (Adebimpe, 1981; Edwards, 1982; Owens, 1980; Pope & Lipinski, 1978). The findings indicate that there is a discrepancy between the diagnoses of Blacks and Whites who have comparable symptoms. Blacks receive more severe diagnoses such as schizophrenia and paranoid disorders than Whites. Clinicians seem to attribute more paranoid and psychotic qualities to Black clients for reasons unrelated to their actual psychopathology. The literature shows that Blacks are more likely to be hospitalized while comparable Whites are seen in outpatient treatment and Blacks are more likely to get medication while Whites are more likely to participate in "talk" therapy (Markides & Mindel, 1987). Diagnosis and treatment based on race rather than behavior lead to inappropriate intervention and/or mistreatment.

A fourth explanation is that racial differences in utilization patterns result from discriminatory practices. This perspective posits that older Blacks are actively steered to public mental health facilities and away from private psychiatric hospitals and nursing homes used by many Whites. Some researchers suggest that state mental hospitals function as nursing homes for Blacks since these facilities are the only ones routinely available (Butler & Lewis, 1977). It seems then that Blacks with severe, chronic physical problems as well as those with mental problems are equally likely to be hospitalized in a state mental institution.

Relatively little national data exist concerning the physical and mental health status of Asian Americans and few studies address these issues. Moreover, Asian Americans are reticent to discuss problems with persons who are not family. For some, discussion of physical and mental illness with anyone is a social taboo. Chinese Americans, for example, prefer not to talk about sickness or death for fear the discussion will result in the misfortune of illness or death. In addition, they distrust the federal government due to past injustices so are unlikely to use programs funded by the government (Kim, 1983; Kitano, 1969; Sue & Morishima, 1982).

Since Asian Americans are a minority group, one might suspect they have stressful lives and as a result may have more health and mental health problems than Whites. Studies have supported this hypothesis (Brown, 1973; Sue & McKinney, 1975; Sue & Sue, 1974). In one study, almost two-thirds (63%) of elderly Chinese Americans rated their health as fair or poor. Over one-third had never had a medical or dental examination. Twice as many Chinese (39%) as Whites (15%) reported health as their most severe problem (Carp & Kataoka, 1976). Other studies have found that the suicide rate among aged Chinese Americans was three times the national rate (Kart, 1981). Suicides were especially prevalent among elderly Chinese bachelors (Crandall, 1980). The suicide rate among aged Chinese women has also been reported as quite high (Lyman, 1974).

Many Hispanics do not perceive mental health services as a solution to emotional or family difficulties they may experience. The reasons for the underutilization of services are numerous. Language barriers, cultural and social class difference between therapist and clients, an insufficient number of mental health facilities, overuse or misuse of physicians for psychological problems, reluctance to recognize the urgent need for help, and a lack of awareness of the existence of mental health services and their purpose are reasons cited in the literature that tend to explain Hispanics' underutilization of both health and mental health services (Ho, 1987).

It has been noted that Hispanic Americans rely strongly on family and consider family members as primary sources of support. Accordingly, traditional family roles are important and responsibility taken seriously. This belief creates some difficulty for the male head of household to admit that he is experiencing problems in efforts to provide for the family. Before the seeking of outside help is considered, godparents or compadres usually are consulted prior to seeking external assistance. Seemingly, different problem areas direct the seeking of certain types of help. For example, if the family problem is marital, the compadre of marriages may be sought for mediation (Ho, 1987). In the Hispanic family of Puerto Rican origin, the padrino is used as a mediator. A padrino is an "individual in a higher position within the family structure and who has a personal relationship with the family for whom he provides material needs and emotional guidance" (Ho, 1987, p. 127).

Additionally, Catholicism plays a vital role in the lives of Hispanic-Americans and priests, folk healers, and religious leaders are often strong resources for families in times of difficulty and stress. The Hispanic-American family may distortedly view the mental health therapist as omnipotent because of a perceived association of roles between a healer, the priest and the therapist. A reliance on these sources of help and a less than clear understanding of the nature and type of mental health services offered by localities may contribute to a significant underutilization of mental health services.

On the other hand, the physical and mental health care services available to Hispanic elderly are inferior both in quality and quantity. Some observers have suggested that physicians are often perceived by some Hispanic elderly of Mexican descent as a cure all or as a centralized health resource for all illnesses not treatable in the home. When asked reasons for consulting a physician during the preceding year, men 60 and older cited diabetes, gastrointestinal diseases, musculo-skeletal arthritis, and hypertension as reasons to consult a physician. Women over 60 cited hypertension, diabetes, flu and colds. Approximately 50% of the respondents said they received home health care provided by a relative or friend. The relatively high use of this resource may be attributed to the cost of other care, alienation from or lack of access to various forms of institutional care, the positive support of family and friends, and the reliance on folk medicine or faith healers (Torres-Gil & Negm, 1980).

Native-American elderly have significant physical and mental health problems and, as has been noted, become functionally "old" before the general elderly population (NICOA, 1981a). Data from the Indian Health Service show that the average life expectancy for Native Americans is only 65 years, eight years less than that for Whites (AARP, 1987). Several factors may account for this difference. (See Figure 1.) The majority of Native-American elderly seldomly see a physician and when they do, they tend to be more ill than White elderly. A large number of those needing medical services often live in rural isolated areas and do not have access to transportation. For some elderly, where services are accessible, a different cultural understanding of disease processes and a tradition of ritual folk healing often prevent efforts to seek help from medical doctors.

The major health problems experienced by Native-American elderly are tuberculosis, diabetes, liver and kidney disease, high blood pressure, pneumonia, malnutrition and sight impairment (AARP, 1987; NICOA, 1986). In other conditions of health impairment, Native-American elderly are at least as impaired as a representative sample of comparable White elderly taken from Cleveland (NICOA, 1981a). Elderly Native Americans also perceive their physical health as poorer than their White counterparts.

Utilization of Services

Because of their stressful life experiences, Blacks are expected to have a greater need for mental health services than Whites, they actually underutilize mental health programs (Edinberg, 1985; Sue, 1981). In addition, a majority of those who seek services terminate prematurely and feel they are neither helped nor understood (Sue, 1981).

There are at least three interactive factors that largely determine the rate and the way in which Black elderly utilize mental health services: characteristics of elderly Blacks; characteristics of mental health programs and characteristics of mental health professionals. The issues related to each factor are listed on the following page.

Elderly Blacks

- mistrust mainstream institutions.
- rely heavily upon extended family ties, church organizations and other informal mutual aid.
- view therapy as "strange" and think it is as a service for "crazy" people.
- turn to formal services after all other sources of help have been exhausted; which is usually a time of crisis.
- distrust therapists, especially White therapists.
- prefer Black therapists, who are often not on staff, over White.
- feel therapists are not responsive to their needs and priorities.
- often have multiple concrete problems such as housing, low income that influence their psychological functioning but are not addressed in some intervention plans.
- may not have transportation to get to agencies.
- accept their problems as an inevitable part of old age.
  (Beaver, 1983; Edinberg, 1985; National Caucus and Center on Black Aged, 1987)

Mental Health Programs

- located in inconvenient and inaccessible areas outside the central cities where most Black elderly reside.
- do little or no outreach, education or publicity to the Black community.
- do not have elderly Blacks on advisory councils or in other roles where they could have input about service development and evaluation.
- have few or no Blacks on staff.
- do not train staff to work effectively with the Black elderly.
- have poor coordination of services with other programs and services that the Black elderly use or need.
- overlook concrete problems (housing, income, physical health) which influence the psychological functioning of the Black elderly.
- have physical settings which do not help Blacks feel welcome; for example, the lack of Black magazines in the waiting room.
- do not make home visits.
  (Beaver, 1983; Edinberg, 1985; National Caucus and Center on Black Aged, 1987)

Mental Health Professionals

- have negative attitudes about serving Black elderly which interferes with service delivery.
- are pessimistic about outcomes and communicate, often non-verbally, these feelings to the client.
- are ill at ease with elderly Blacks because they have had little previous contact with them and no training about effective intervention with Blacks.
- interaction with and diagnosis of Black elderly are often based on negative stereotypes.
- often communicate with jargon that the Black elderly do not understand and are too proud to ask for further clarification.
- view client problems as inevitable and a normal part of the aging process.
- have values and ways of interacting that are not congruent with the expectation of clients. For example, White professionals often call clients by their first name to show concern or closeness. Older Blacks, especially, prefer the use of titles and the last names (for example, Mrs. Jones instead of Susie, Mr. Moore instead of Joe)
  (Beaver & Miller, 1985; Brody, 1985; Edinberg, 1985)

This list is not exhaustive but does demonstrate that there are several contributors to low mental health utilization rates and premature service termination of elderly Blacks. This pattern of underutilization of services is not solely a mental health problem. While home health care, homemaker service, transportation, outreach, information and referral, congregate meals, and home delivered meals are specifically for the elderly, they attract few Black elderly. This situation occurs despite the fact that older minorities have needs that are typically 2 to 3-1/2 times as great as White elderly (National Caucus and Center on Black Aged, 1987).

Cultural and language differences, reliance on folk medicine, distrust of Western Medicine, and reliance on the family help to explain Asian Americans' hesitancy to use formal health and mental health services (AARP, 1987). Availability of preferred alternatives is also important. In larger cities of the United States where Asian Americans are concentrated, folk medicines are often available. Also, many Asian elderly still order folk medications from their old countries and keep them for emergencies (Kim, 1983).

The provision of services to the Hispanic elderly is often complicated by several variables. First, as has been pointed out, the Hispanic elderly are heterogeneous. The several subgroups have discrete nationalities with different dialects, cultures, and needs. Responses to services that are offered tend to cluster in different geographic locations, however, the reluctance of service organizations to develop appropriate interventions that are sensitive to the Hispanic culture act as barriers to services. Secondly, the needs of the subgroups usually remain unmet because there is a lack of trained bilingual, bicultural professionals to act as advocates in policy formulation and implementation. Consequently, the policies that are enacted and services that flow from them do not address group specific cultural factors.

A comprehensive network of services exists for the general population of Native Americans in self-governed communities. The unique relationship tribes have with the federal government commands an array of resources from The Bureau of Indian Affairs, Indian Health Service, and the Department of Housing and Urban Development. Therefore, Native-American elderly are more likely to say that they live in subsidized housing and receive health and nutrition services more than a comparable group of their White counterparts (NICOA, 1981a). They tend to use public services to a greater extent than whites largely because there are no other alternatives to care. However, in comparison to the representative sample of Cleveland White elderly , Native-American elderly actually utilized the service system less (NICOA, 1981a).

One significant explanation is that when extended family members have resources, Native-American elderly seek their help first. Mainstream health care system is used only after the resources of the family network are exhausted (Red Horse et al., 1978). Despite the comprehensive array of services offered, and the preference for indigenous services, a majority of Native-American elderly will say that more services are needed than are provided. It is thus possible to conclude that the extent to which actual needs are met is inadequate. Services such as transportation, coordination, education and employment were perceived as underprovided while others such as meal preparation, legal protection, personal care and checking were either not wanted or felt to be not needed even when they were provided (NICOA, 1981a). This leads one to question whether services to Native-American elderly are being provided under the assumption that their needs are the same as the dominant society and that cultural barriers do not affect the utilization of these sometimes indiscriminately offered services (NICOA, 1981a).

Participation in Medicaid and Medicare Programs

The fact that poverty status is still linked to poor health among the elderly is surprising since the Medicare and Medicaid Programs provide health services to this group. These programs are insufficient to combat accelerating health care costs of minority elderly and are frequent recipients of budgetary cuts. In 1984, for example, the elderly were spending the same proportion (15%) of their income on health care as they did before these programs were established in 1965. Furthermore, the amount of benefits Medicaid and Medicare offer is constantly eroding. For example, the Medicare inpatient hospital deductible charge escalated from $204 in 1981 to $520 in 1987 (National Caucus and Center on Black Aged, 1987).

Surprisingly, the majority of poor elders are not covered by these programs. In 1984, only one-third (36%) of the noninstitutionalized elderly poor had Medicaid protection. The amount of paper work and information, the complicated procedures, the desire to be self-sufficient as well as suspiciousness of bureaucracy probably result in many eligible elderly not applying for these programs. Another element in the health problems of minority elderly is the gaps in the Medicare and Medicaid Programs. Services of particular importance for the elderly are not covered in many states. These include prescription drugs, physicals, eye glasses, hearing aids, dentures, custodial nursing home care and homemaker services (National Caucus and Center on Black Aged, 1987).

Working with Minority Elderly

In general, the social worker must recognize and accept that many older ethnic clients concerned about survival issues seek intervention only as a last resort and with limited understanding of the helping process. The worker must use strengths and aspects of their culture to help the elderly minority client understand that the helping process is a mutual endeavor between two involved participants.

Assessment

In assessing the mental health status of ethnic minority elderly in general, social work practitioners must examine the total person and the physical and social environment. Not only the current presenting problem but the life situation, social and personal world, values and life history of the client must be explored (Beckett & Coley, 1987). In consideration of and respect for cultural values and traditions, this task may be far easier said than done. Specifically, for example, Asian culture dictates that inner negative thoughts, feelings and personal problems not be expressed (Tseng & Char, 1974).

Since the success of our traditional treatment modalities depends heavily on eliciting such information, work with Asian minority elderly using traditional models could be severely hindered. Further, even though unacceptable thoughts and feelings are suppressed, physical illness is acceptable and Asians who exhibit physical illness are given positive attention and concern. In addition, traditional Chinese medication links emotion to specific viscera such as the heart to happiness and the liver to anger and nervousness (Kobata, Lockery, Moriwaki, 1976). Such specific beliefs help to clarify and underscore the importance of close examination of the type of somatic complaints Asian elderly may present. The problem may be anxiety but expressed as discomfort in the lower back area, denoting possible problems with the liver. Such knowledge of Asian beliefs and customs would be significant if intervention with the elderly of Asian descent is to be responsive and helpful.

There is evidence that suggests that some Hispanic elderly believe old age comes early because they associate it with the end of the work role. Since they have usually been employed in physically demanding jobs, it has often been necessary to leave the work force relatively early.

These circumstances contribute to pessimism about the quality of life, often causing high levels of depression among the elderly. Also language barriers and poverty add to depression and must be considered both in assessment and in the planning stages of intervention with this group.

Assessment of Native-American elderly must consider that an individual Native-American's mental health is linked to a sense of selfhood which is accomplished by adherence to historical culture and transmitted primarily through family socialization (Levine, 1976). As Native-Americans leave the reservation to seek gainful employment, acculturation increases. Thus, the adoption of Anglo culture value, orientation and behavioral norms, the psychological impact of conflict in values and behaviors, and the individual's classification of the difficulty must be weighed carefully as intervention strategies are planned.

In summary, accurate assessment of the minority elderly client or client system involves the client's classification of the problem as either an illness, a physical disorder, or lack of skill or resources. Because the culture of the client influences perceptions and labeling of problems as well as shapes expectations for intervention, discrepancies between these expectations and the worker's culturally determined expectations may lead to the client's early termination of services. The worker's basic task is to elicit the client's explanatory model, to fully understand the client's beliefs about the issues at hand, the personal and social meaning attached to them, and the expectations about what the client will do and what the worker will do. Worker and client can then jointly determine the therapeutic goals (Brown & Gil, 1985).

Intervention

Social work intervention, in general, can be categorized into three types of preventive strategies: primary, secondary, and tertiary (Beaver & Miller, 1985).

Primary prevention is intervention in which the focus is the averting of problems before they occur. Primary prevention activities are those that promote well being. Examples are good nutrition, stress management, and education.

Secondary prevention is intervention given at the earliest sign of a problem. The aim is to avoid further deterioration as well as to assist people in developing coping mechanisms that will help prevent new occurrences of similar dysfunctions in the future. Examples of secondary prevention are problem solving, teaching new strategies and new behaviors.

Tertiary prevention is intervention that includes intensive actions to limit further disability and to rehabilitate. An example of this type of intervention is findings a safe living situation for the elderly who can no longer live at home.

While these three types of intervention indeed contribute to the effectiveness of the helping process, intervention with the older ethnic client carries additional considerations that cannot be ignored if the clients' needs are to be met in a responsible and responsive manner.

General considerations in working with the elderly client as noted by Beaver (1983) include recognition and understanding of (1) the likelihood of any physical changes due to impairment, (2) interrelated economic, social, and personal concerns, (3) the issue of multiple losses and coping with and accepting such losses, (4) the likelihood of negative self-stereotype related to age, and (5) generational values about help-seeking and help accepting behaviors (Mindel, 1980).

Further special considerations in working with the older ethnic client include sensitivity and understanding of racial cultural differences. For example, in working with the elderly Black client who has in all probability experienced overt and sanctioned discrimination, it becomes important to give formal respect to that client. Consequently, the use of titles and last names, and the communication of appreciation of the value of self-sufficiency by the presentation of the services in question as a right and not a need serve to convey respect for the client and his dignity.

Accordingly, work with the elderly Hispanic client would initially focus on concerns about politeness in language. The worker would use formal forms of "you" and consult with the client as to how to refer to his/her ethnic group since there are several Spanish-origin groups. Also important in work with the elderly Hispanic client is permitting a social relationship to develop as a prerequisite to further work with the client. Mindel (1981) suggests that the client be permitted to set the pace with the focus largely on service requested and not the underlying problem.

Because Hispanic sex roles tend to be rather strong with male dominant behaviors, elderly Hispanic clients may experience difficulty in sharing with a worker of the opposite sex. Thus, the arranging of same sex practitioners to work with the elderly client exhibits sensitivity and understanding to discrete ethnic/cultural values and practices as the elderly client has probably not adopted Anglo value orientations and behavioral norms. The worker's utilization of the aspects and strengths of the culture (roles and values) as part of the interventive strategy then becomes a specialized approach with attention to the client's own level of comfort.

In intervention with the elderly Asian client, it is also important for same sex workers to be assigned and for the worker to slow the pace of the helping process. It will take time for the elderly Asian client to develop a relationship with the worker and for formal services to be accepted or developed. The worker must pay attention to the cultural differences that signal respect. For example, the use of titles and the careful attention to issues of politeness as opposed to confrontation are likely to convey to the client he/she is respected. Older Asian clients tend to be very concerned with "saving face" and resultantly, the worker must be careful to limit or avoid eye contact--a sign of respect in sensitive issues. Also, work with the elderly Asian client, in many situations, calls for the avoidance of touch as well as the understanding that a polite nod does not at mean agreement.

Finally, intervention with the elderly Native-American must take into account various tribal differences. Each will vary in terms of the significance of touch and eye contact. Across the tribes, however, it is important to establish relationships with both formal and informal community leaders, to be honest, and to avoid aggressive behavior and excessive talking. Native-American elderly value listening and revere age. When invited into the home of the elder Native -American, respect must be conveyed by listening well, by accepting refreshments, and by not looking around the home which is a sign of disrespect (Mindel, 1981).

The consideration of family network structure in working with the Native-American elderly client is a major component in understanding the client. Without such understanding, normal ethnic behaviors within the network relational field may appear questionable and bizarre to an outsider. Such behaviors may lead workers to raise questions of competency and responsibility about familiar behaviors within the network structure and lead to negative labeling of the family and its behavior (Red Horse et al., 1978). For example, permitting a young adolescent girl to visit and sleep unsupervised in the homes of a succession of adolescent males may be labeled neglect in another culture. The elders who permit it may be questioned. However, the Native-American family relational field can be extensive. Such males offer protection and preservation of honor to the adolescent girl as her most loyal brothers. The absence of understanding in a situation of this type can lead to very serious gaffes by the social worker and create alienation in the helping attempt that may never be re-negotiated.

Chapter References

Adebimpe, V. (1981). Overview: White men and psychiatric diagnosis of Black patients. American Journal of Psychiatry, 138, 279-285.

Alvarez D., & Bean, F. D. (1976). The Mexican American family. In C. H. Mindel & R. W. Habenstein (Eds.), Ethnic families in America: Patterns and variations. New York: Elseveer Scientific Publishing Company.

American Association of Retired Persons. (1987). A portrait of older minorities. Washington, DC: Author.

Beaver, M. L. (1983). Human service practice with the elderly. Englewood Cliffs, NJ: Prentice-Hall.

Beaver, M., & Miller, D. (1985). Clinical social work practice with the elderly. Homewood, IL: Dorsey Press.

Becerra, R. M., & Shaw, D. (1984). The Hispanic elderly: A research reference guide. Lanham, MD: University Press of America.

Beckett, J. O., & Coley, S. M. (1987). Ecological intervention with the elderly: A case example. Journal of Gerontological Social Work, 11, 137-157.

Bell, D., Kaschau, P., & Zellman, G. (1976). Delivering services to elderly members of minority groups: A critical review of the literature. Santa Monica, CA: The Rand Corporation.

Bengston, V. L., & Burton. (1980). Familism, ethnicity and supports systems: Patterns of contrast and congruence. A paper presented at the Western Gerontological Association, San Diego, CA.

Birren, J. E., & Sloane, R. B. (Eds.). (1980). Handbook of mental health and aging. Englewood Cliffs, NJ: Prentice-Hall.

Brody, E. (1985). Mental and physical health practices of older people. New York: Springer.

Brown, L. B., & Gil, R. M. (1985). Social work practice with Hispanic groups. In L. Brown, J. Oliver, & J. Alva (Eds.), Sociocultural and service issues in working with Hispanic-American clients. State University of New York at Albany: School of Social Welfare.

Brown, T. R. (1973). Mental illness and the role of mental health facilities in Chinatown. In S. Sue & N. Wagner (Eds.), Asian Americans: Psychological perspectives. Palo Alto, CA: Science & Behavior Books.

Butler, R. N., & Lewis, M. I. (1977). Aging and mental health: Positive psychological approaches (2nd ed.). St. Louis: C. V. Mosby.

Carp, F. M., & Kataoka, E. (1976). Health care problems of the elderly of San Francisco's Chinatown. Gerontologist, 16, 30-38.

Crandall, R. C. (1980). Gerontology--A behavioral science approach. Reading, MA: Addison-Wesley.

Cuban Refugee Program. (1974). FACT sheet. Washington, DC: U.S. Government Printing Office.

Dohrenwend, B. P., & Dohrenwend, B. S. (1969). Social status and psychological disorder: A casual inquiry. New York: Wiley-Interscience.

Dohrenwend, B. S. (1970). Social class and stressful events. In E. H. Hare & J. K. Wings (Eds.), Psychiatry epidemiology (pp. 313-319). New York: Oxford University Press.

Dohrenwend, B. S. (1973). Social status and stressful life events. Journal of Personality and Social Psychology, 9, 203-214.

Dukepoo, F. C. (1980). The elder American Indian: A cross cultural study of minority elders in San Diego. San Diego State University: University Center on Aging.

Edinberg, M. A. (1985). Mental health practice with the elderly. Englewood Cliffs, NJ: Prentice-Hall.

Edwards. (1982). The consequences of error in selecting treatment for blacks. Social Casework: The Journal of Contemporary Social Work, 63, 429-433.

Fried, M. (1975). Social differences in mental health. In J. Rosa & I. Zola (Eds.), Poverty and health (2nd ed.). Cambridge, MA: Harvard University Press.

Gelfand, D. (1982). Aging: The ethnic factor. Boston: Little Brown and Co.

Ho, M. H. (1987). Family therapy with ethnic minorities. Newbury Park: Sage Publications.

Hollingshead, A., & Redlich, F. (1958). Social class and mental illness: A community study. New York: Wiley.

Johnson, E. S., & Williamson, J. B. (1987). Retirement in the United States. In K. S. Markides & C. L. Cooper (Eds.), Retirement in industrialized societies. New York: John Wiley & Sons.

Kart, C. S. (1981). The realities of aging. Boston: Allyn & Bacon.

Kessler, R. C. (1979). Stress, social status and psychological distress. Journal of Health and Social Behavior, 20, 100-108.

Kessler, R. C., & Cleary, P. D. (1980). Social class and psychological stress. American Sociological Review, 45, 463-478.

Kim, P. (1983). Demography of the Asian-Pacific elderly: Selected problems and implications. In R. L. McNeely & J. Cohen (Eds.), Aging in minority groups. Beverly Hills: Sage.

Kitano, H. (1969). Japanese-American mental illness. In S. Plog & R. Edgerton (Eds.), Changing perspectives in mental illness. New York: Holt, Rinehart & Winston.

Kobato, F. S., Lockery, S. A., & Moriwaki, S. Y. (1980). Minority issues in mental health and aging. In J. E. Birren & R. B. Sloane (Eds.), Handbook of mental health and aging. Englewood Cliffs, NJ: Prentice-Hall.

Leonard, O. E. (1967). The older rural Spanish people of the Southwest. In E. G. Youmans (Ed.), Older rural Americans (pp. 239-261). Lexington: University of Kentucky Press.

Levine, I. M. (1976). Ethnicity and mental health: A social conservation approach. Washington, DC: White House Conference on Ethnicity and Mental Health.

Loring, M., & Powell, B. (1988). Gender, race and DSM-III: A study of the objectivity of psychiatric diagnostic behavior. Journal of Health and Social Behavior, 29, 1-22.

Lubben, J. E., & Becerra, R. M. (1987). Social networks. In D. E. Gelfand & C. M. Barresi (Eds.), Ethnic dimensions of aging. New York: Springer.

Lum, D. (1983). Asian-Americans and their aged. In R. L. McNeely & J. L. Cohen (Eds.), Aging in minority groups (pp. 85-94). Beverly Hills, CA: Sage.

Lum, D. (1984). Toward a framework for social work practice with minorities. Social Work, 27, 244-249.

Lum, D. (1986). Social work practice and people of color. Monterey, CA: Brooks/Cole.

Lyman, S. (1974). Chinese Americans. New York: Random House.

Maldonado, D., Jr. (1979). Aging in the Chicano context. In D. E. Gelfand & A. J. Kutzik (Eds.), Ethnicity and aging: Theory, research, and policy (pp. 175-183). New York: Springer.

Markides, K. S. (1985). Minority aging. In B. B. Hess & E. W. Markson (Eds.), Growing old in America (3rd ed.). New Brunswick, NJ: Transaction.

Markides, K., & Mindel, C. (1987). Aging and ethnicity. Beverly Hills: Sage.

Mindel, C. H., & Haberstein, R. W. (1981). Ethnic families in America: Patterns and variations (2nd ed.). New York: Elseveer Scientific Publishers.

Miranda, M. R. (1988). Hispanic aging: Issues for policy development. Aging Network News, 5(8), 5-6.

National Caucus and Center on Black Aged. (1987). The status of the Black elderly in the United States. Washington, DC: U.S. Government Printing Office.

National Indian Council on Aging. (1981a). American Indian elderly - A national profile. Albuquerque, NM. Administration on Aging, Office of Human Development Services, Washington, DC.

National Indian Council on Aging. (1981b). Indian elderly and entitlement programs: An accessing demonstration project. Albuquerque, NM. Administration on Aging, Office of Human Development Services, Washington, DC.

National Indian Council on Aging. (1986). Research project to derive and disseminate information the the health, housing and safety status of Indian elders. Albuquerque, NM. Administration on Aging, Office of Human Development Services, Washington, DC.

Neighbors, H. W. (1984). The distribution of psychiatric morbidity in Black Americans: A review and suggestions for research. Community Mental Health Journal, 20, 169-181.

Owens, C. E. (1980). Mental health and Black offenders. Boston: Heath.

Pope, H. G., & Lipinski, J. F. (1978). Diagnosis in schizophrenia and manic depressive illness. Archives of General Psychiatry, 35, 811-828.

Price, J. A. (1976). North American Indian families. In C. H. Mindel & R. W. Haberstein (Eds.), Ethnic families in America: Patterns and variations. New York: Elsevier Scientific Publishing Co.

Red Horse, J. G., Lewis, R., Feit , M., & Decker, J. (1978). Family behavior of urban American Indians. Social Casework, 59, 67-72.

Shaffer, R. T. (1984). Racial and ethnic groups (2nd ed.). Boston: Little, Brown & Company.

Solomayor, M. (1975). Social change and the Spanish speaking elderly. In A. Hernadez & J. Mendoza (Eds.), The national conference on the Spanish-speaking elderly. Kansas City: National Chicano Social Planning Council.

Solomon, B. B., & Baber, B. (1976). Black empowerment social work in oppressed communities. New York: Columbia University.

Stuart, P., & Rathbone-McCuan, E. (1988). Indian elderly in the United States. In E. Rathbone-McCuan & B. Havens (Eds.), North American elders: United States and Canadian perspective (pp. 235-254). New York: Greenwood Press.

Sue, D. W. (1981). Counseling the culturally different: Theory and practice. New York: Wiley.

Sue, S., & McKinney, H. (1975). Asian-Americans in the community mental health care system. American Journal of Orthopsychiatry, 45, 111-118.

Sue, S., & Morishima, J. (1982). The mental health of Asian Americans. Special Committee on Aging, United States Senate. Development in Aging. Volume III. San Francisco: Jossey-Bass.

Sue, S., & Sue, D. W. (1974). MMPI comparisons between Asian-American and non-Asian students utilizing a student health psychiatric clinic. Journal of Counseling Psychology, 21, 423-427.

Torres-Gil, F., & Negm, M. (1980). Policy issues concerning the Hispanic elderly. Aging, 305/306, 2-5.

Torres-Gil, F. M., Newquist, D., & Simonia, M. (1977). Housing: The diverse aged. Los Angeles: Andrus Gerontology Center, University of Southern California

Tseng, W., & Char, W. (1974). The Chinese of Hawaii. In W. S. Tseng, J. F. McDeamott, & T.W. Maretzki (Eds.), People and cultures in Hawaii. Honolulu: University Press of Hawaii.

U.S. Bureau of the Census. (1983). America in transition: An aging society. Washington, DC: U.S. Government Printing Office.

U.S. Bureau of the Census. (1985). Current population reports. Washington, DC: U.S. Government Printing Office.

U.S. Bureau of the Census. (1987). Statistical abstract of the United States (107th Edition). Washington, DC: U.S. Government Printing Office .

U.S. Commission on Civil Rights. (1979). Civil rights of Asian and Pacific Americans: Myths and realities. Washington, DC: U.S. Government Printing Office.

U.S. Congress House Select Committee on Aging. (1987). The plight of the Black elderly: A major crisis in America. Hearing before the Select Committee on Aging, House of Representatives, 99th Congress, Second Session. Washington, DC: U.S. Government Printing Office.

U.S. Department of Labor. (1988). Employment in perspective: Women in the labor force (Report 756). Washington, DC: U.S. Government Printing Office.

U.S. Senate Special Committee on Aging in Conjunction with the American Association of Retired Persons, the Federal Council on the Aging and Administration on Aging. (1986). Aging America: Trends and projections (1985-86 ed.). Washington, DC.

Valle, R., & Mendoza, L. (1978) The elder Latino. San Diego, CA: The Campanile Press.

Watson, W. (1983). Selected demographic and social aspects of older Blacks: An analysis with policy implications. In R. McNeely & J. Cohen (Eds.), Aging in minority groups (pp. 42-49). Beverly Hills: Sage.

Weeks, J. (1984). Aging concepts and social issues. Belmont, CA: Wadsworth.

Yu, E. S. H. (1980). Philippino migration and community organization in the United States. California Sociologist, 76-102.

Discussion Questions

1. Why are ethnicity and race important variables in understanding and intervening with the elderly?

2. Compare the socio-economic characteristics of the four ethnic minorities of color (Asian Americans, Blacks, Hispanic Americans and Native Americans).

3. Design a social service program to serve one ethnic minority of color group. What need does each component of the program address? How does your program differ from a program already existing in your community?

4. Discuss five ways the aging experience for ethnic minorities of color differ from that of Whites.

5. To what extent do you think the situation of minority elderly is a consequence of: (a) individual factors; or (b) structural factors? Why?

6. Does the key to improving the conditions of the minority elderly lie in: (a) integration into the mainstream of American Society; (b) in strengthening the sense of cultural identity among the minority group; or (c) in a combination of both a and b? Why?

7. For what reasons do you think minorities of color are discriminated against and/or oppressed in American society?

8. How would you redesign the Social Security Benefits so they would be more equitable for the minority elderly who have a significantly shorter life expectancy than the White majority?

Learning Activities

Activity #1. Old people are . . .

A. Divide the class into five groups:

1. Older People
2. Black Older People
3. Asian-American Older People
4. Hispanic Older People
5. Native-American Older People

Do not tell the group which group they are in before distributing the materials. They can be referred to as "Group A," "Group B," etc. Each group will see from the form which group they will respond to. It is important, however, that they know only their group and not other groups that are being considered.

B. Distribute the appropriate "Old People Are" forms to each member of the group.

C. Ask each group member to complete the form and turn it face down.

D. Distribute a second copy of the same form. Tell the group to imagine themselves to be a 75-year-old member of the group described on their form. Group A (Older), Group B (Older Blacks), etc. Ask them to complete the form as they would respond at age 75.

E. Have each group report to the class their initial responses and how they changed on the second form. They may discuss the reason for the change. The results usually are that the "Old people are . . ." forms filled out first are critical and negative but that the forms filled out the second time are more positive and less harsh.

F. Have each group share with the class their real group identity, for example, Group A = Older people, Group B = Black older people, etc.

G. Have the class compare and contrast the responses of the five groups. Which group was seen most negatively? Most positively? Why?

H. Discussion: This exercise should provide and stimulate much thoughtful discussion. Some students will find it difficult to identify with a certain group. The discussion can explore the reasons for this. The reasons usually include lack of knowledge about or familiarity with the group. The students may suggest ways to get to know the older group better. Move the class toward feeling, understanding, and empathizing with what the older persons usually experience, but without moralizing, valuing or being judgmental.

Summarize broad issues as follows:

A. Aging brings changes.
B. Students will age also.
C. Aging patterns and issues may differ among different ethnic groups.
D. Aging may be another characteristic for which ethnic minorities are discriminated against.
E. There are many components to the aging process—biological, cultural, social, economic, etc.

GROUP A
Old people are ...

1. Old people should _____
   _____
   _____

2. Old people always _____
   _____
   _____

3. Old people look _____
   _____
   _____

4. Spending time with old people is _____
   _____
   _____

5. Old people need _____
   _____
   _____

6. Old people have rights to _____
   _____
   _____

7. As far as sex goes, old people _____
   _____
   _____

8. Old people can expect _____
   _____
   _____

9. Old people have power to _____
   _____
   _____

10. Old people 's small fixed incomes are _____
    _____
    _____

GROUP B
Old Black people are . . .

1. Old Black people should _____
    _____
    _____

2. Old Black people always _____
    _____
    _____

3. Old Black people look _____
    _____
    _____

4. Spending time with old Black people is _____
    _____
    _____

5. Old Black people need _____
    _____
    _____

6. Old Black people have rights to _____
    _____
    _____

7. As far as sex goes, old Black people _____
    _____
    _____

8. Old Black people can expect _____
    _____
    _____

9. Old Black people have power to _____
    _____
    _____

10. Old Black people 's small fixed incomes are _____
    _____
    _____

GROUP C
Old Asian-American people are . . .

1. Old Asian-American people should _____
   _____
   _____

2. Old Asian-American people always _____
   _____
   _____

3. Old Asian-American people look _____
   _____
   _____

4. Spending time with old Asian-American people is _____
   _____
   _____

5. Old Asian-American people need _____
   _____
   _____

6. Old Asian-American people have rights to _____
   _____
   _____

7. As far as sex goes, old Asian-American people _____
   _____
   _____

8. Old Asian-American people can expect _____
   _____
   _____

9. Old Asian-American people have power to _____
   _____
   _____

10. Old Asian-American people 's small fixed incomes are _____
   _____
   _____

GROUP D
Old Hispanic people are . . .

1. Old Hispanic people should _____
   _____
   _____

2. Old Hispanic people always _____
   _____
   _____

3. Old Hispanic people look _____
   _____
   _____

4. Spending time with old Hispanic people is _____
   _____
   _____

5. Old Hispanic people need _____
   _____
   _____

6. Old Hispanic people have rights to _____
   _____
   _____

7. As far as sex goes, old Hispanic people _____
   _____
   _____

8. Old Hispanic people can expect _____
   _____
   _____

9. Old Hispanic people have power to _____
   _____
   _____

10. Old Hispanic people 's small fixed incomes are _____
    _____
    _____

GROUP E
Old Native-American people are . . .

1. Old Native-American people should _____
_____
_____

2. Old Native-American people always _____
_____
_____

3. Old Native-American people look _____
_____
_____

4. Spending time with old Native-American people is _____
_____
_____

5. Old Native-American people need _____
_____
_____

6. Old Native-American people have rights to _____
_____
_____

7. As far as sex goes, old Native-American people _____
_____
_____

8. Old Native-American people can expect _____
_____
_____

9. Old Native-American people have power to _____
_____
_____

10. Old Native-American people's small fixed incomes are _____
_____
_____

Activity #2. Life Line Exercise

This exercise puts one's life span into clear perspective and focus.

birth date	sister born	began school	graduate high school	today's date	college graduation	marriage	first child	retire date	death
10/5/68	6/20/70	9/2/72	6/3/86	1/15/89	6/3/89	6/93	1996	2028	12/31/2050

SAMPLE LIFELINE

1. Instructions

   Instructor: Put a sample life line on the flipchart or blackboard.

   Student: On an 8-1/2" x 11" paper, draw a horizontal line lengthwise, in the middle of the paper. At the left end put a slash and your birthdate. At the right end put a slash and guess your deathdate. Between these two slashes, put a slash indicating today's date, choose significant future events and date them. That is, between today's date and your deathdate, place slashes and dates, indicating significant events that you want to happen between now and the time you die.

2. Discussion

   Members have no difficulty with their birthdates but are resistant and frightened about selecting a deathdate. This is a good place to talk about death and fears of dying, relating it to how much more older persons must think about dying. Stress that we all die, we need to begin to accept death as a fact, and talking about death is helpful. Merely doing this exercise helps move the group closer to the concept of death and its inevitability. It can be cathartic to talk for a few minutes about the fears and fantasies of what happens at death. Many members will acknowledge that they have never allowed themselves to think of their own death, or that this is like opening a door which they have always kept closed. As the discussion continues, you may hear responses such as, "I've never thought I'd die until recently.", "I had a hard time accepting death until my father developed cancer. Seeing him suffer has made me begin to think about dying, his and mine," or "it's not easy to talk about death over lunch, or at the dinner table."

   Members usually choose as the significant dates between birth and today's date such things as their graduation from high school, birth of a sibling or relocations. Other choices have included significant deaths, beginning college, serious illness, family changes such as divorce, and so on.

   The responses between today's date and the death date may included marriage, becoming a parent, losing weight, taking a world cruise, going back to school, moving into a home, retiring, beginning a career, caring for older parents, and so on. This future prediction helps mobilize students to consider options and choices which they have and points up how much control they do have in exercising those options.

   This simple exercise can be extremely effective . Students will usually refer to their reactions in subsequent classes and will usually indicate that as a result of the exercise, they are seriously considering changes and modifications in their lives.

3. Have students complete another life line. This time each should assume he/she is an ethnic minority (Asian American, Black, Hispanic or Native American). Make sure each ethnic minority is represented by at least two students. If there are minority students in the class, they should select another ethnic minority. For example, an Asian-American student could assume a Native-American identity.

4. Discuss the problems students may have in completing this life line, for example, assigning a deathdate, determining the education level and significant life events.

5. Have students compare and contrast the life lines of the four minority groups with their own life line.

6. Have students consider social work implications of the life lines. Issues such as differential life span, economic problems, and widowhood may be included.

Activity #3. Myths and Stereotypes

These are negative views that are held about the elderly and the process of aging. We often assume that once an individual reaches adulthood, there is little growing left to do and that physical decline and deterioration or "going down hill" cannot be escaped. These assumptions provide a basis for "ageism", defined as the prejudices and stereotypes that are applied to older people solely on the basis of age. As with any other prejudices, the effects of ageism are often subtle but always damaging.

Myths and stereotypes based solely on age affect the self-image or the perceptions that aged individuals have about themselves. Stereotypes that seemingly are held across all population groups of the elderly are not supported by the literature on aging but appear to be well entrenched in society.

Have students list stereotypes of minority elderly of color and the elderly in general. Students may be hesitant at first. If so, the instructor may give some examples such as:

> Asian-American elderly do not need help from social agencies.
> All Black elderly are in poor physical health.
> Native-American elderly are completely taken care of by the federal government.
> Elderly in general have little interest in sex; they want only companionship.
> Older Blacks are happy with their plight.
> Older persons cannot change.
> Aging inevitably leads to mental deterioration and senility.
> Elderly persons do not care about their appearance.

It is helpful to put the list of myths and stereotypes on the board or on a flip chart. Group members can discuss how each stereotype influences their personal perception of the elderly and how it might be counterproductive to effective social work practice.

Case Studies

(Please review Appendices A and B for guidelines on teaching
gerontological social work by using case studies)

Case #1: Mrs. Chan

Mrs. Chan, a 65 year old Chinese widow from Hong Kong, was referred to a community mental health center by a family physician, who had been unable to correct Mrs. Chan's insomnia and weight loss through medication. In addition to her physical problems, Mrs. Chan's symptoms included depression and lack of appetite and energy. She spent most of her time gazing motionlessly out the front window of her apartment.

The intake social worker described Mrs. Chan's reaction to her as mixed with shame and hopefulness. She remarked that Mrs. Chan feared "losing face" because of her situation and regretted greatly that she has been a "burden" to the social worker. Mrs. Chan spoke very little English and displayed limited cooperation, according to the social worker.

Eight months ago, Mrs. Chan's husband died in Hong Kong. Five months ago her only son invited her to live with him and his family in the United States. Mrs. Chan initially was apprehensive about leaving her home, close friends, and relatives in Hong Kong, but due to Chinese social pressure and customs, she yielded to the idea of living with her son. She had not wanted her relatives and friends to suspect that her son did not want to take care of her.

Living with her son and family did not work well for her. Mrs. Chan and her daughter-in-law, an American-born Chinese, never seemed to get along with each other. They had open conflict about the role of a wife and the proper manner in which children should be disciplined.

Mrs. Chan's son, caught in the middle, developed a severe case of sleep disturbance. To protect her son's health, Mrs. Chan agreed to live in an apartment by herself. Mrs. Chan explained that the idea of living apart from her son was difficult for her. She would never have conceded to his idea of her living alone if she still lived in Hong Kong.

Source: Ho, 1987

Case #2: Mr. Williams

Mr. Williams is a 58 year old Black man who was referred to a family service agency by his minister. Mr. Williams, a retired military man, works irregularly as a construction worker. When not working, he has a tendency to drink heavily. When he drinks he often stays away from home for a couple of days. During the past two weeks, Mr. Williams had two serious car accidents and he was found asleep in the car on a cold night. The minister felt Mr. Williams might be suicidal and in need of therapy. Mr. Williams refused to go to the local mental health clinic but the minister was able to persuade him to go to a family service agency.

He is married and has four children. Mrs. Williams, age 56, is a Licensed Practical Nurse. The two older children, a son, age 36, and a daughter, age 33, are married and live out-of-state. The two younger children, a daughter, age 20 and a son, age 17, are still at home. The daughter is a sophomore at a local college and the son attends high school and is an excellent athlete. Both are excellent students.

Mr. Williams disclosed that his family had adequate income - wife's employment, his retirement benefits, and his irregular construction work. He, however, felt "out of place" in his own home. He thought his wife was an excellent mother and a busy body working all the time and attending church activities several times a week.

He went on to say that no one at home seems to notice him except when he was not there for a couple of days. This he said had been the situation ever since he retired from the service four years ago. Mr. Williams has reacted by initiating "fairly close" relationships with females whom he calls his "drinking buddies".

Source: Ho, 1987

Case #3: Mrs. Alvarez

Mrs. Alvarez, a 69 year old motel housekeeper has experienced a number of significant losses over the past six years. Six years ago, her husband of 39 years died of a heart attack. The death was sudden and occurred shortly after Mrs. Alvarez returned home from work. Mr. Alvarez had been a laborer and had spent his last 3 years sporadically unemployed and unable to contribute to the family income. He routinely looked for work but was generally passed over for younger men in his neighborhood who seemed strong and in good health.

Mrs. Alvarez took her husband's death quite hard but managed to adjust to the loss with the help of her five grown daughters and a few close friends and relatives. She remained employed and found going to work kept her mind off her loneliness and the emptiness she experienced without Mr. Alvarez.

Approximately a year after Mr. Alvarez's death, Mrs. Alvarez's purse was snatched one evening as she walked to the bus stop from the motel on her way home. Although Mrs. Alvarez was not physically injured she was emotionally traumatized. Her weekly pay of $117.00 had been taken along with her house keys and other important insurance papers she always carried in her purse. She had no money for food and was terrified to return to work. She became very nervous and jumpy and was unable to sleep at night even though her oldest daughter had come over to the apartment and had seen to it that management had changed her locks and had issued Mrs. Alvarez a new set of keys.

Six months after the attack, Mrs. Alvarez gave up her apartment and moved in with her middle daughter. It was difficult for Mrs. Alvarez to give up her home in which she and Mr. Alvarez had raised their children. She had come to know the people and the neighborhood quite well but she knew her fears were threatening her physical and mental health.

Mrs. Alvarez secured part-time work at a motel in the neighborhood in which her daughter lived. However, her continued flashbacks of the prior attack and the vision problems she was experiencing made holding the job too difficult for her. After giving up her job, Mrs. Alvarez spent much of her time in the house. Even so, she managed to maintain regular phone contact with two of Mr. Alvarez's sisters from the old neighborhood and with friends who also visited her occasionally at her daughter's home. Mrs. Alvarez seemed to be adjusting relatively well to these major social stresses. Her appetite was good, she maintained contact with her family and friends, and she found time to take short trips with her daughter.

Then, six months later, Mrs. Alvarez's daughter, her favorite and only unmarried child, died unexpectedly of a heart attack. Mrs. Alvarez was devastated but, with the help of her other children, managed to make arrangements for the funeral and attend to all of the legal documents. Mrs. Alvarez then moved in with her oldest after some conflict among her children about who had the room to "take in" Mrs. Alvarez.

Mrs. Alvarez has lost quite a bit of weight since her daughter's death. She sits around the house all day, does not answer the phone, does not take interest in her personal appearance, and is totally withdrawn. She rarely, if ever, smiles at all.

Source: Adapted from Beaver & Miller, 1985

Case #4: Anita Thundercloud

Anita was the elder within the family. She was a direct descendent of the most renowned chief of her band and enjoyed high status. She lived alone in a trailer. Shortly after her 70th birthday, she became ill and unable to care either for herself or to perform routine household chores. A social worker arranged for Anita's admission to a rest home.

The family accepted this interventive plan without comment. Subsequently, however, this situation changed. Anita received regular visits at the rest home but these did not satisfy family needs. Anita became lonely for home and the family became lonely for her. A ritual feast was held which Anita attended. Family concerns regarding her absence were expressed and a decision was made that she should remain at home.

The family developed its own helping plan. Each member was given a scheduled time period to provide homemaker services for Anita. Through this shift system, the family network assumed service responsibility. In this case, the family in the immediate vicinity consisted of ten households. Service providers ranged from 13-year-old grandchildren to 58-year-old children.

Source: Red Horse et al., 1978

Audio-Visual Resources

Asian-Americans

Sam
20 min., 16 mm.

Explores themes of culture and class through the portrayal of a Japanese American whose public personna as the Japanese gardener in a White, Los Angeles suburb contrasts with glimpses of the private man, his past, and family. Sam recounts an agonizing tale of World War II detention while his wife tells a survivor's tale of the atomic bombing of Hiroshima.

CONTACT: Extension Media Center, University of California, 2176 Shaqtuck Avenue, Berkeley, CA 94704 (415-642-5578).

Wataridori: Birds of Passage
37 min., 16 mm., VHS or 3/4 AV tape

A portrait of three Iffei or first generation Japanese Americans and their experiences here in the United States. One is a fisherman, the second is a gardener, while the third is a widow.

CONTACT: Visual Communications, Los Angeles, CA (213-680-4462).

Black-Americans

On My Own: The Traditions of Daisy Turner   28 min., video, 1987

In the green hills of Vermont there lives an amazing Black woman of 102 whose memories go back almost to the Civil War. She is the daughter of Alex Turner, born a slave in Virginia who ran away from the plantation, crossed the Rappahannock and joined the Union Army. In 1872, he moved with his wife and their three children to Grafton, Vermont where he had been offered a job in a saw mill.

Daisy was one of 13 children in a family where days were spent on farm chores and evenings were spent storytelling and singing. In this way, the rich family traditions were passed down from one generation to the other. Her stories of growing up in rural Vermont show us that a Black family could flourish in a New England town. This portrait of Daisy is especially beguiling because of her skill at creating poetry to preserve memorable happenings. As we listen to her commanding voice, we realize that Daisy, like the bards of old, keeps alive the culture of her people.

CONTACT: Filmakers Library, 133 East 58th St., New York, NY 10022.

The Hundred Penny Box   18 min., color, 1979

This dramatic film is about a Black family: Michael, his 100 year old great-great-Aunt Dew, his mother, and the big ugly old box. The box holds a small sack with a hundred pennies in memory of each year of Aunt Dew's life. Michael likes to count the pennies and listen to the stories that each year evokes. When his mother, burdened by the care of a failing old lady who disrupts the order of her hours, wants to get rid of the big ugly old box, Michael is fiercely defiant. His small boy understanding of Aunt Dew is vastly greater than his mother's. At story's end, Aunt still has her old box and memories. Based on the book, The Hundred Penny Box, by Sharon Bell Mathis.

CONTACT: Churchill Films.

Hispanic Americans

LaFamilia: A Celebration of Love   22 min., color, 1979

Juan and Delores Venegas celebrate their 60th wedding anniversary with her very large family of 10 children, 55 grandchildren, 15 great-children, and over 200 in-laws and friends. This film is a celebration of love and love's power to hold together an entire society through the simple family unit. The Venegas Family sets an example for all. They offer a possible key to the rejuvenation of our social structure through a revived interest in the extended household.

CONTACT: Moctesuma Esparaza Productions.

Luisa Torres   43 min., color, 1980

This is a documentary film about an elderly Hispanic woman who lives a traditional life on a small farm in the village of Guadaluipta in northern New Mexico. Her life, close to the earth, is one that has remained virtually unchanged for generations. For her, growing old has further integrated everything she knows, and her role as teacher is a natural one. Her traditional culture has provided her with dignity and respect from her children, her community, her many friends. It is the respect of a culture that still treasures its old people because it is the old people who have values which remain true. When they die the world will be deprived of their example and of their accumulated wisdom.

CONTACT: Blue Sky Productions, P.O. Box 548, Sante Fe, NM 87501.

Native-Americans

Augusta

17 min., color, 1978

Daughter of a Shuswap chief, Augusta, now 88, was separated from her parents at age four, and sent away to a Catholic Mission school where only English was allowed to be spoken. When she married a White man in 1903, she lost her status as an Indian. Old photographs and her soft- voiced reminiscences bring alive moments that happened long ago. She lives alone now in a log cabin without running water or electricity in the Caribou country of British Columbia. It is her home, and she wouldn't be anywhere else.

CONTACT: National Film Board of Canada, Vancouver Productions.

Mother of Many Children

58 min., color

Agatha Marie Goodline, 108 years old, a member of the Obbeman tribe, contrasts her memories with the conflicts that most Indian and Inuit women face today. The film traces the cycle of their lives from birth to old age in a series of sensitive vignettes. Sarah looks forward to a picnic of raw Arctic char dipped in seal oil. Elizabeth is learning to make leaf dolls with one of her nine grandmothers. Sally who has brought up by her grandparents in the bush, remembers that "it was a good life. I never felt like I was poor."

CONTACT: National Film Board of Canada.

Annotated Bibliography

Adams, J. P. (1980). Service arrangements preferred by minority elderly: A cross-cultural survey. Journal of Gerontological Social Work, 3(2).

A study that explores and identifies common patterns in help-seeking behavior among minority elderly.

Becerra, R. M., & Shaw, D. (1984). The Hispanic elderly: A research reference guide. Lanham, MD: University Press of America.

This book details a list of Spanish language research instruments which have been used to assess the Hispanic elderly. The volume also discusses the knowledge gained from research among the elderly Hispanics and from Hispanics in general. There is an excellent overview of barriers that must be overcome when doing research with Hispanic elders. The book helps to bridge the gap between the Hispanic elders' needs and the provision of culturally sensitive human services.

Beckett, J. O., & Coley, S. M. (1987). Ecological intervention with the elderly: A case example. Journal of Gerontological Social Work, 11, 137-157.

This article discusses an intervention model, the ecological system's perspective, and a related tool, the eco map, which are particularly relevant for service delivery to the elderly, especially the Black elderly. The model is applied to a case of a Black family.

Brody, E. (1985). <u>Mental and physical health practices of older people</u>. New York: Springer.

This book is a compilation of several research studies with a major portion devoted to a study by Brody. Her chief finding is that the elderly tend to under-report their symptoms because the elderly do not believe that the health care providers care about aging patients. The chief value of this book lies in its presentation of practice research. The volume includes original survey instruments and checklists.

Carillo, C. (1982). Changing norms of Hispanic families: Implications for treatment. In E. E. Jones & S. J. Korchin (Eds.), <u>Minority mental health</u>. New York: Praeger.

This chapter examines the affective and cognitive process and rationales involved in Hispanic interactions. Widely held prejudicial views and their effect on the Hispanic community are explored.

Dressel, P. L. (1988). Gender, race, and class: Beyond the feminization of poverty in later life. <u>The Gerontologist</u>, <u>28</u>(2), 177-180.

The feminization of poverty has the potential for both limiting and distorting the issue of old age poverty. Diversity contained within age, race, and gender groups must be acknowledged in order to facilitate a more complete understanding of poverty among the elderly and its policy implications.

Edinberg, M. (1985). <u>Mental health practice with the elderly</u>. Englewood Cliffs, NJ: Prentice Hall.

The book is divided into four (4) sections: Processes of Aging (4 chapters); Psychopathology and Assessment (3 chapters); Interventions with the Aged (7 chapters); and Delivery of Mental Health Services (1 chapter). Each section has material relevant to the minority elderly. For example, one chapter in the first section has a discussion of characteristics and stereotypes of minorities of color and ways to overcome barriers to their receiving mental health services. A chapter in the third section has a useful paradigm for comparing and evaluating intervention with minority and majority elderly.

Gelfand, D. E., & Barresi, C. M. (Eds.). (1987). <u>Ethnic dimensions of aging</u>. New York: Springer.

This book is divided into three sections: theory, research and practice and policy. It includes chapters on each minority of color and other ethnic groups such as Amish, Greeks and Jews. The book has a very good discussion of the intersection of ethnicity and age and has a thirty page reference section.

Green, J. W. (1982). <u>Cultural awareness in the human services</u>. Englewood Cliffs, NJ: Prentice Hall.

A monograph that offers significant concepts regarding Asian, Black, Hispanic and Native Americans and the provision of social service. Types of help-seeking behaviors found among these groups and ethnic-sensitive social work practices are delineated.

Guttman, D. (1987). Ethnicity in aging: Perspective on the needs of ethnic aged. <u>Social Thought</u>, <u>13</u>(1), 42-51.

This study discusses the needs of older ethnic Americans, with reference to the existing literature on the subject. On the national level, concrete needs and their alleviation must be addressed through the building of coalitions and partnerships between often competing groups of minority representatives. On the local level, the leaders of the ethnic community must become aware of the real daily needs of the elderly and search for ways in which these needs can be met.

Ho, M. K. (1987). Family therapy with ethnic minorities. Newbury Park: Sage.

Although this book focuses on family therapy with ethnic minorities, it is also a repository of important information about these groups. For example, it addresses the following for each of the four minorities of color: values, socio-cultural and demographic descriptions, family interaction and help seeking patterns. In addition, it compares and contrasts the four groups on these measures. It presents cases and discusses intervention with each minority group.

Jackson, J. S., Newton, P., Ostfield, A., Savage, D., & Schneider, E. (Eds.). (1988). The Black-American elderly: Research on physical and psychosocial health. New York: Springer.

This state-of-the-art volume gathers, for the first time, what is currently known about aging Black populations in the United States. Topics range from epidemiology and demography to cultural, behavioral, economic, social, and biomedical aspects of aging. The authors compare Black elderly to the elderly of other racial and ethnic groups as well as discuss research.

Lee, J. K. (1986). Asian-American elderly: A neglected minority group. Journal of Gerontological Social Work, 9, 103-116.

This article discusses the historical experiences, structural difficulties, and cultural barriers that prevent the Asian-American elderly from obtaining needed social services. It describes eight pieces of discriminating legislation passed by federal and state governments from 1853 to 1942 which has negatively impacted the political, social and economic status of Asian-American elderly. It also explains this group's underutilization of social services.

Markides, K. S., & Mindel, C. H. (1987). Aging and ethnicity. Newbury Park, CA: Sage.

Organized into 10 chapters, this book explores elderly Americans who are neither White nor middle class. The purpose of the book is synthesizing ethnic research in social gerontology. It also includes an extensive reference section and an author's index. It is a valuable overview of the issues of today's ethnic minority elderly.

National Indian Council on Aging. (1981). American Indian elderly: A national profile. Albuquerque, NM. Administration on Aging, Office of Human Development Services, Washington, DC.

A comprehensive research effort that examines in detail and documents the conditions of life of Native-American people in the United States, including Alaska.

Okura, Y., Ziller, R. C., & Osawa, H. (1985-86). The psychological niche of older Japanese and Americans through auto-photography: Aging and the search for peace. International Journal of Aging and Human Development, 22(4), 247-259.

Thirty Japanese and 30 Americans participated in a study that drew on autophotography to understand aging in a cross-cultural context. The subjects, who averaged 73 years, were asked to take (or have someone else take) six photographs that describe "who you are." A content analysis of the photographs indicated that older Japanese appear to be inwardly oriented and aesthetically oriented and that older Americans are more oriented toward other people. The study concluded that peace was sought through self-harmony in the Orient and through social harmony in the Occident.

U.S. Commission on Civil Rights. (1987). <u>Asian-American discrimination issues, population and employment characteristics, and Indochina refugees by detailed origin, 1970s-85</u>. Washington, DC: U.S. Government Printing Office.

This report examines Asian-American population characteristics and factors contributing to anti-Asian activity in the U.S. and presents demographic and socio-economic data.

Yu, E. S. (1986). Health of the Chinese elderly in America. <u>Research on Aging, 8</u>, 84-109.

This paper reports and compares death rates, causes of death, and socioeconomic characteristics of Chinese Americans and American whites. While the Chinese had a lower death rate than Whites, place of birth had a greater effect than gender on the Chinese Americans. Suicide rates were higher for older Chinese-American women than for Whites but there was no difference for men.

<u>General Bibliography</u>

Alvarez, D., & Bean, F. D. (1976). The Mexican-American family. In C. H. Mindel & R. W. Habenstein (Eds.), <u>Ethnic families in America: Patterns and variations</u>. New York: Elseveer Scientific Publishing Company.

Beaver, M., & Miller, D. (1985). <u>Clinical social work practice with the elderly</u>. Homewood, IL: Dorsey Press.

Brown, L. B., & Gil, R. M. (1985). Social work practice with Hispanic groups. In L. Brown, J. Oliver, & J. Alva (Eds.), <u>Sociocultural and service issues in working with Hispanic-American clients</u>. State University of New York at Albany: School of Social Welfare.

Devore, W., & Schlesinger, E. (1981). <u>Ethnic-sensitive social work practice</u>. St. Louis, MO: C. V. Mosby.

Dukepoo, F. C. (1980). <u>The elder American Indian: A cross cultural study of minority elders in San Diego</u>. San Diego State University: University Center on Aging.

Ho, M. H. (1987). <u>Family therapy with ethnic minorities</u>. Newbury Park: Sage.

Kim, P. (1983). Demography of the Asian-Pacific elderly: Selected problems and implications. In R. L. McNeely & J. Cohen (Eds.), <u>Aging in minority groups</u>. Beverly Hills: Sage.

Kobato, F. S., Lockery, S. A., & Moriwaki, S. Y. (1980). Minority issues in mental health and aging. In J. E. Birren & R. B. Sloane (Eds.), <u>Handbook of mental health and aging</u>. Englewood Cliffs, NJ: Prentice Hall.

Lubben, J. E., & Becerra, R. M. (1987). Social networks. In D. E. Gelfand & C. M. Barresi (Eds.), <u>Ethnic dimensions of aging</u>. New York: Springer.

Lum, D. (1986). <u>Social work practice and people of color: A process-stage approach</u>. Monterey, CA: Brooks/Cole.

Markides, K., & Mindel, C. (1987). <u>Aging and ethnicity</u>. Beverly Hills: Sage.

National Caucus and Center on Black Aged. (1987). <u>The status of the Black elderly in the United States</u>. Washington, DC: U.S. Government Printing Office.

National Indian Council on Aging. (1981). <u>American-Indian elderly: A national profile</u>. Albuquerque, NM. Administration on Aging, Office of Human Development Services, Washington, DC.

Solomon, B. B. (1983). Social work with Afro-Americans. In A. Morales & B. W. Sheafor (Eds.), <u>Social work: A profession of many faces</u>. Boston: Allyn & Bacon.

Sue, D. W. (1981). <u>Counseling the culturally different: Theory and practice</u>. New York: Wiley.

CHAPTER 6

OLDER WOMEN: SOCIAL WORK PERSPECTIVE

by Joyce O. Beckett
and Robert L. Schneider

Introduction

Although legislation has been enacted to foster equal treatment of women in all areas of society, the need for attention to women's issues continues. Even though women in general, and older women in particular, comprise a numerical majority in America, they are oppressed and in other ways treated as a minority group. Women are discriminated against in many areas including the economic, education, health, mental health, and criminal justice systems.

Possibly the single most significant fact about aging is that the population of older persons is overwhelmingly female; 60% of those 65 years of age and over are women . These women are the fastest growing segment of the U.S. population (Report of the Mini Conference on Older Women, 1981). Among persons seventy-five and older, women comprise two-thirds of the population (U.S. Bureau of Census, 1985). The ratio of women to men increases over the life span. Large numbers of women outlive their husbands, often by as much as two decades; and a significant number outlive their eldest son. The problems associated with aging such as greater risk of chronic illness, reduced economic resources, increased poverty, increased caregiving and care needing, surviving one's relatives and closest friends, increased risk of death and institutionalization are predominantly the problems of women (Doress et al., 1984; U.S. Bureau of the Census, 1984).

Despite the rapidly rising number of older women, research, and social policy usually overlook this important group of the elderly. Attention to women and the elderly has usually failed to take the particular needs of older women into account. For example, a 1986 gerontology textbook does not include the word "women" or "gender" in the index (Hendricks & Hendricks, 1986). Thus, the reader is not directed to the few places in the text where these issues are discussed. While it devoted a chapter to ethnic minorities, the book does not have a chapter on women. Furthermore, the discussion of minorities for the most part overlooks minority women.

Learning Outcomes

After completing this chapter, students will be able to:

- compare and contrast the life situations of elderly men and women

- identify and give example of biases that older women face

- give examples showing the heterogeneity among elderly women on such socioeconomic variables as class, ethnicity, marital status, race and region

- analyze personal beliefs, attitudes and biases about elderly women

- use sociocultural variables in the assessment and social work intervention with elderly women

Outline of Key Topics and Content Areas

Definition of Elderly Women

Discrimination and Bias

Demographic Profile of Older Women

Family
- Living Arrangements
- Marital Status
- Family Relations
- Caregiving
- Homosexuality

Economics and Older Women
- Socialization
- Economic Dependency
- Economic Insecurity
  - Limited Employment Opportunities
  - Pay Inequity
  - Marital Dissolution
  - Problems with Social Security
  - Limited Access to Pesnions

Housing

Labor Force Participation
- Employment
- Part-time Employment
- Out of the Labor Force

Health
- Physical Health
- Mental Health
- Long-term Care
- Obstacles to Good Health Care

Summary of Key Topics and Content Areas

Definition of Elderly Women

Who constitutes older women? This is a difficult question to answer. Traditionally, age 65 has been the benchmark for delineating the elderly; it was used because it was the age at which most men retire from the labor force and the age when full Social Security benefits begin. The lives of many of the current cohort of older women follow a pattern unlike that of men. These women may have worked before marriage and before the birth of the first child, but many withdrew from the labor force and returned home to care for their children. As the children matured and left home, and perhaps the husband died or divorce occurred, women often returned to work outside the home.

There are exceptions to this intermittent pattern of work. Many black women, for example, have a lifelong pattern of work similar to men and some upper class white women have never been employed outside the home. Nevertheless, the employment pattern for most older women differs from the traditional male norm. The result is that retirement is not a good benchmark for the age at which women move into the status of the elderly.

In addition, age is more than a chronological occurrence. It has cultural, social, as well as biological components. In general, there seems to be a double standard about age which considers women old at an earlier age than men (Sontag, 1972). Furthermore, women in the poorest stratum may be physically old by their thirties due to successive pregnancies, inadequate nutrition and overwork (Crooks, 1986). This chapter will use the age of the sources and literature discussed; which is usually 62 or 65.

Midlife, the years between ages 45 to 64, is a very important life stage for women and should also be the target for research and study. Midlife women face significant alterations in all areas of their lives--family, occupation, social, education, medical and financial. While it is a time for expansion and growth, it is also a period of role change as children usually grow up and leave home and parents and parents-in-law begin to have medical complications associated with the aging process. During this life stage, an appropriate foundation for personal and economic security must be built or expanded in order to prevent economic dependency and poverty in the subsequent life stage.

Discrimination and Bias

Most older women are confronted with the double jeopardy of discrimination because of age and gender. Unlike white men who may be initially subjected to prejudice because of age only in later life, white women cope with gender discrimination throughout their lives and age compounds their oppression. Other women face additional oppression because of characteristics such as race, class and residence. An older, lower class, black woman who lives in the central city is likely to face multiple jeopardies.

In addition to discrimination, there is also age-sex bias. Troll and Turner (U.S. House of Representatives, 1979) have classified three types of such bias:

1. Expectation and distortion - belief that certain behaviors fit certain ages according to sex. As a result, people tend to make the perceptions congruent with the expectations. For example, if one expects women to be ill during menopause, one sees them that way even though this view may be inaccurate.

2. Restrictiveness - people's behaviors are limited by what is perceived to be appropriate actions for their age and sex. For instance, a 60-year-old woman beginning to work on a graduate degree or a 50-year-old woman having her first child would likely be considered as "deviant."

3. Negative attitudes - people classified as old, no matter what age standard is used, may be seen as intellectually inferior, narrow-minded, ineffective and/or infirm.

Demographic Profile of Older Women

The cohort of older women in America has been largely invisible and the realities of their lives obscured by myths and neglect (Older Women, 1980). Their life experiences are very different from those of men and even the Women's Movement did not define aging as a feminist issue until the late 1970's (Hooyman, 1986a). Nevertheless, older women are the fastest growing segment of the American population. As Peter Morrison, a Rand Corporation demographer puts it, "Aging is disproportionately a woman's problem in our society" (Otten, 1984, p.1).

The following profile provides a description of the status, the conditions and the actual circumstances of many older women. These facts produce an overview of the reality confronted by older women in American society.

- Elderly women now outnumber elderly men 3 - 2. This disparity is even higher at age 85 and older where there are only 40 men to every 100 women. In 1986, there were 17.4 million older women and 11.8 million older men. At age 65, women have an average of 18 years of life remaining (Aging America: Trends and Projections, 1985-86).

- In 1986, older men were nearly twice as likely (77%) to be married than older women (40%) (AARP, 1986). Among those who married after age 65 there were nine bridegrooms to every bride (Report of Mini White House Conference, 1981). Older men are several times more likely to remarry than women. The higher remarriage rate of widowers is the result of social norms supporting men's marriage to younger women and discouraging the opposite for women and the surplus of women in the marriage market (Older Women - The Economics of Aging, 1980).

- Widowhood is the marital status of the majority of older women and is also long-lasting. The average widow who does not remarry and dies a natural death will spend 18 1/2 years in this last portion of life. This period, as a woman alone following marriage, is longer than the period from entrance into first grade until marriage (Older Women - The Economics of Aging, 1980).

- Half of all older women in 1986 were widows (50%). There were over five times as many widows (8.1 million) as widowers (1.5 million) (AARP, 1987).

- While most women over 75 are widowed, most men over 75 are married. The divorce rate for men over 65 is more than double the rate for women of the same age group. For men, that means a surfeit of women available for dating or marriage, but also, because there are few other unattached men around, there can also be stretches of intense loneliness. For older women, the situation is just the opposite. They often find a supportive community of other older women in similar situations, but they are less likely to find a spouse (Ricks, 1986).

- The majority (67%) of older noninstitutionalized persons lived in a family setting in 1986. Approximately 9.3 million (83%) of older men and 9.1 million (57%) of older women lived in families. The proportion living in a family setting decreased with age. About 14% (7% of men, 18% of women) were not living with a spouse, but living with children, siblings or other relatives (AARP, 1987).

- About 30% (8.3 million) of all noninstitutionalized older persons in 1986 lived alone. They represented 6.6 million (41%) older women and 1.7 million (5%) older men. Older persons living alone increased in number by 68% between 1970 and 1986. Almost half of women 75 years and older live alone compared to 21% of men (AARP, 1980). Eighty percent of the elderly who live alone are women (U.S. Bureau of the Census, 1984).

- Women outnumber men not only among the older population generally but particularly among the population living in institutions where women outnumber men 2 to 1; for example, over two thirds of nursing home residents are female (Otten, 1985).

- About three million older workers were in the labor force in 1986 including 1.8 million men (16%) and 1.2 million women (7%). They constituted 2.6% of the labor force (AARP, 1987).

- Approximately half (54%) of the workers over 65 in 1986, 49% of men and 61% of women, were employed part-time (AARP, 1987).

- The educational level of the older population has been steadily increasing between 1970 and 1986. Their median level of education increased from 8.7 years to 11.8 years (11.7 years for males and 11.9 years for females) and the percentage who had completed high school rose from 28% to 49%. About 10% in 1986 had four or more years of college (AARP, 1987).

- In 1984, thirty-three percent of older women had difficulty with one or more home management activities such as preparing meals, shopping, managing money, or doing house work (AARP, 1987).

- Of the 18.6 million households headed by older persons in 1986, seventy-five percent were owners and twenty-five percent were renters. Older male householders were more likely to be owners (83%) than were females (65%) (AARP, 1987).

- Among women 75 and older, three out of four paid more than 35% of their cash income for housing (Report on Mini White House Conference, 1981).

This demographic profile of older America illustrates many of the particular problems and circumstances facing elderly women. It is evident that older women are primarily the ones who experience loneliness, isolation, widowhood, part-time employment, few opportunities to remarry, and life in long-term care institutions. Service providers such as social workers must be aware of these data and intervene in ways that take into account the needs of this increasingly large group of elderly individuals.

Family

There have been many changes during the twentieth century which influence the family life of older women. These include: an increase in life expectancy; the tendency until the 1960s toward earlier marriage; couples having fewer children; an increase in the education level, especially for women; increases in the number of women who work outside the home; increases in the divorce rate and the removal of a mandatory retirement age (Hendricks & Hendricks, 1986; Rix, 1987). These events interact in complex ways to affect family life. For example, the increase in life expectancy

188

has augmented the amount of time a couple is alone after the last child leaves home. It is also related to a greater likelihood of middle age and older women caring for their and/or their spouses' parents often at a time when these caregivers have returned to the labor force.

Living Arrangements

The overwhelming majority (95%) of elderly persons live in the community, mostly with family members. Below are some facts about the living arrangements in 1986 (AARP, 1987).

- Older men are much more likely than women to live in a family setting, 83% of men and 57% of women.

- Older men are more likely to live with a spouse than older women, 75% of men and 38% of women.

- More older women than men live with other family member--children, siblings and other relatives, (18% of women and 7% of men).

- A small proportion of men (3%) and women (2%) live with nonrelatives.

- Older women (41%) are almost three times as likely as older men (15%) to live alone.

- The number of older persons living alone increased 68% between 1970 and 1986.

- Although a small percentage (5%) of older persons lived in nursing homes in 1985, the percentage increases drastically with age, ranging from 1% for persons 65 to 75, 6% for persons 75-84 and 22% for persons 85 and older.

Marital Status

Both age and gender are important determinants of marital status. Older persons are less likely than younger to have never married and older women are less likely than men to be currently married (Hendricks & Hendricks, 1986). Below are some facts concerning the marital status of older persons with an emphasis on gender differences (AARP, 1987):

- In 1986, older women were almost one half as likely as older men to be married, 40% of women and 77% of men.

- Older women were almost four times as likely as older men to be widowed, 50% of women and 14% of men.

- In absolute numbers, there were five times as many widows (8.1 million) as widowers (1.5 million) in 1986; 85% of surviving spouses were women.

- About the same proportion of older women as older men were never married (5%) and divorced (4%). The number of women who were widowed or divorced was substantially larger than the number of men, however.

- The number (1.1 million) of divorced older persons is increasing dramatically; it soared nearly four times as fast as the older population as a whole during the period of 1976 to 1986, 3.7 times for men, 4.0 times for women.

Divorce and Widowhood. Older women are increasingly living without a spouse. Because of divorce and widowhood, more than 40% of the current generation of older women live alone for nearly one-third of their adult lives. Women's average age of widowhood is 56 years and at age 65, females have an average life expectancy of 19 years (AARP, 1987; Hooyman, 1986a).

The primary negative consequence of widowhood and divorce is poverty which is experienced by one-third of older widows living alone. Older divorced women usually do not share their ex-husband's pension or social security benefits. In addition, less than one-half of these women receive any property settlement (Bureau of the Census, 1980). Moreover, divorced older women have poorer health, higher mortality rates and lower levels of life satisfaction than divorced men or married and widowed women (Hess & Waring, 1983).

Remarriage. Once widowed or divorced, older women are much less likely than men to remarry. Remarriage rates for older men are 17 per 1000 compared to only 2 per 1000 for women. The possibility for remarriage dramatically decreases as women age. Among persons 75 years and older, 70% of the men are married compared to only 22% of the women (Hess & Waring, 1983). There are several barriers to older women's remarriage; these include the substantial deficit of older men because of their lower life expectancy, a small proportion of unmarried older men, the cultural norm against women marrying younger men and the societal expectation that men will marry younger women (Cherlin, 1987; Hendricks & Hendricks, 1986; Hess & Waring, 1983). The sex ratio dramatically underscores the scarcity of older men. It increases with age and ranges from 121 women to every 100 men for the 65-69 group to a high of 253 women per 100 men for persons 85 and older (Cherlin, 1987).

Family Relations

The gender differences in marital status influence family relations among the elderly. Because of the prevalence of widowhood, divorce and rare instances of remarriage, older women's family interactions revolve around vertical kinship ties to children, grandchildren and the older woman's parents. In contrast, older men more often have strong horizontal ties to their current spouse (Hagestad, 1986). Older women are not usually active in the day-to-day decisions of their children and grandchildren. But in times of crisis such as a child's divorce, older women often provide important assistance. Since mothers are more likely to retain custody of children following divorce, maternal grandparents become more involved with their daughters and grandchildren (Cherlin, 1987).

A relatively large portion of older women have no children; 25% of the women in their seventies have no surviving children. In addition to relationships with their surviving parents, interaction with female peers and friends have added importance for these women (AARP, 1987). Childless widows, however, are often more lonely and dissatisfied than widows with grown children. The absence of children and spouse also increases their probability of institutionalization (Treas, 1977).

Whether married or not, older women who have children have frequent contact with them. Sixty-two percent of these women have at least weekly visits and 76% talk on the phone at least weekly with their children. Moreover, 66% live within 30 minutes of a child (AARP, 1987). Whether spouse, parents or children, family members are an important dimension in the lives of older women.

Caregiving

The family ties of women are possibly stronger than those of older men. Women are socialized to adopt a nurturing role in which they provide support to their families throughout their life. In their later years, the caring roles of women usually include spouse, mother, grandmother and caregivers to their own aging parents and parents-in-law and increasingly to their dependent children (Gross, 1985; Jennings, 1987). Due to the rising life expectancies, more older women than in prior generations become great grandmothers or even members of five-generation families (AARP, 1985).

Women, some of whom may be 60 or 70 years of age, constitute almost 80% of the caregivers of elderly relatives (Brody, 1985). These women usually are daughters, wives and other relatives. Some of these caregivers provide services to persons who reside in their household while others care for relatives who live elsewhere. These women are the invisible laborers without whom neither the health system nor the patient could survive (Hooyman, 1986a).

Women's caregiving activities in the family are in addition to their own life stage tasks. Older women's multiple roles and multi-generation caregiving responsibilities place them at risk of depression, exhaustion, financial difficulties and physical and mental illness. They are sometimes referred to as the "hidden patient" (Fengler & Goodrich, 1979, p. 11). Their own illness or death tends to result in institutionalization of the person(s) for whom they cared (Teresi, Toner, Bennett, & Wilson, 1980).

Just as caregivers are predominantly women, so are the formal caregivers of services to the elderly. The staff of social service agencies, nursing homes, hospitals and other institutions that serve the elderly are primarily female. Throughout the life cycle, then, women are dependent on other women whether they are unpaid caregivers, underpaid employees in social agencies or recipients of the services. The result is that the conditions of older persons, who are primarily women, must be central to the consciousness of all women.

Homosexuality

Although there has been an exponential increase in research and literature on sexuality and sexual orientation, studies of older gay men and lesbians are rare. This is so despite the fact that in 1982 it was estimated that there were about 3.5 million homosexual men and women over sixty (Dawson, 1982). The available research is primarily descriptive, examines myths and stereotypes and concentrates on gay men rather than lesbians (Berger, 1982; Friend, 1987).

The neglect of women is particularly problematic since some literature suggests the experiences of older lesbians is quite different from that of older gays. For example, lesbians tend to socialize in private circles and avoid public institutions of the gay community (Berger, 1982). As lesbians age, it is reported that they are less concerned than gay men about a youthful appearance and sexual activity (Minnigerode & Adelman, 1976).

Some refer to older lesbians as an invisible minority group (Almvig, 1982; Kimmel, 1978). Most older lesbians spent the majority of their lives in a time where they were forced to conceal their sexual orientation. A result in old age is that these lesbians may be more isolated than gays from their age peers and younger homosexuals (Friend, 1987). Like other minority elderly, lesbians often face multiple jeopardy and discrimination due to age, gender, and an unpopular sexual orientation. The oppression is compounded even further for lesbians who are ethnic minorities of color. For example, the black community is much less accepting of homosexuality than the white community (Dawson, 1982; Friend, 1984; Kimmel, 1978).

The ageism, heterosexism, genderism and racism that lesbians face create unique conflicts and problems as well as successful coping mechanisms (Friend, 1987). Lesbians who live together, for example, have to contend with the economic pressure of having a combined female income and/or pension which is usually less than the amount for male couples or heterosexual couples.

Older lesbians face the compounded consequences of expectable age-related issues. For instance, a lesbian may find it difficult to manage a terminal or chronic illness when many health facilities exclude all except blood relatives. Fear of institutionalization may be intensified for at least two reasons. First, lesbians are less likely to assume their families will provide for them in old age (Dawson, 1982). Thus, they anticipate the greater likelihood of institutionalization. Secondly, nursing homes and rehabilitation centers are often perceived to be unsupportive and hostile toward a homosexual life style (Friend, 1987). Another problem is the loss of a lover or partner. Families of a deceased lesbian may actively exclude the lover and homosexual friends of the deceased from funeral plans and participation in the services. This isolation frequently intensifies the grief process and increases the anger.

As among other minorities, the problems and conflicts faced by lesbians may result in effective coping mechanisms which can facilitate successful aging. Homosexuality is reported to be functional in adjusting to old age in several ways. First, the successful handling and resolution of the sexual orientation and identity struggle that usually occurs in adolescence may provide a sense of "crisis competence" (Kimmel, 1978). That is, the "coming out process" provides the individual with coping mechanisms which can be used in other crises in later life.

The consequences of the "coming out" may include family disruption, intense feelings and sometimes alienation from family. Lesbians may subsequently rely less on nuclear family members and more on accepting extended family, friends and other lesbians. These resources tend to serve as a "surrogate family" (Bell & Weinberg, 1978).

Another consequence of a lesbian lifestyle that may be helpful in the aging process is role flexibility. It is reported that homosexuals are more likely than heterosexuals to achieve the potential for greater freedom to learn skills associated with society's stereotypical views of males and females. Greater flexibility in gender roles among lesbians suggests they are more likely to weather the life stage crisis and to have skills to manage loss and independent living (Dawson, 1982; Friend, 1987).

Crisis competence, gender role flexibility, and a broad family and community network can be helpful to older lesbians. The literature that discusses these supports seems to assume that the women had a homosexual lifestyle at least since adolescence. It does not address the women who initially participate in homosexual relationships in their later years. These women often have been married, and have grown children. They may turn to other women for emotional and sexual gratification after the death of their spouse and partly because of the lack of men. These homosexual experiences may cause ambivalence, depression, uncertainty and shame. These consequences often exacerbate the normal crisis and tasks of the later life stages.

Economics and Older Woman

Socialization

The lifelong socialization encouraged by church, state, school and family for passive, dependent female roles in marriage make women particularly vulnerable in old age when they may be alone. Traditionally, their role in marriage has been characterized by economic, social and psychological dependency. Many accepted the societal norm of women as caretakers - wives, mothers, accountants, homemakers, unpaid family physicians, assistants, etc., and did not enter the world of work outside the home. Most women and men do not anticipate that women may spend years alone as widows or that women may have to function independently. The years they may have devoted to being wives, mothers, homemakers and the skills they have developed have been given low economic value in American society. Even among the never married and long term divorced women, society reinforces a dependent role (Older Women, 1980).

Economic Dependency

There are significant differences between older women and men that indicate a need for special attention to the particular situations in which so many older women live. Women tend to be poorer and have fewer financial resources with which to support themselves in their later years. The low incomes of older women are largely associated with a pattern of lifelong economic dependence on men and with status changes that occur with old age (Aging America, 1985). The median income of older persons in 1986 was $11,544 for males and $6,425 for females. After adjusting for a 1985-86 inflation rate of 2%, these figures represent a gain of 4% in real incomes for males but no change for females (AARP, 1986). Older women in every age group were substantially more likely to be poor than men at the same age. Overall, only about 8.7% of the men 65 and older were poor compared to 15% of the women. The oldest women were the poorest. Nearly 1 in 3 women 85 years of age and older was poor or within 125% of poverty in 1984. While women accounted for more than half (58.9%) of the elderly population in 1984, they accounted for nearly three-quarters (71.2%) of the elderly poor (Aging America, 1985).

The phrase "feminization of poverty" is also associated with older women. Consider the following facts (Older Women, 1980):

- 2.8 million women over 65 live in poverty compared with less than a million men;

- 12.2 million women of retirement age have no access to pensions;

- 60% of women over 65 living alone have Social Security as their only income;

- 4 million women between 45 and 65 have no health insurance (Klemerrud, 1982);

- women who are single (widowed, divorced or separated), those of ethnic minority background, and the very old are particularly at risk of falling into poverty;

- the sharp contrast between race and sex groups can be seen most easily when all older white men are compared with all older black women; 41% of black women lived in poverty while only 8% of white men of this age group were poor.

Economic Insecurity

Economic security is essential for the well being of every older person. It is important to understand the causes of economic deprivation experienced by so many older women. Listed below are factors that have determined the economic status of many older women in America.

Limited Employment Opportunities. Although mature women, aged 45-64, are participating more substantially in the work force, their occupational distribution is one of over-representation among part-time workers and concentration in low paying occupations and lower status jobs. Women over the age of 54 are disproportionately employed part-time or seeking part-time work. This is attributed to their inability to secure full-time work rather than a preference for part-time employment.

Pay Inequity. Historically and currently, in America, as in other countries, women's wages are less than men despite the Equal Pay Act of 1963 and the Civil Rights Act of 1964. The focus of this legislation was ending the discrimination in employment based on sex, race and national origin. Most women work out of economic necessity yet white women earn about 61 cents for every dollar earned by white men. Minority women fare worst with black women paid 58 cents, and Hispanic women 53 cents for every dollar paid to white men. The wage disparity increases with age and education level. While white men's earning potential increases with age, women's earning potential stagnates and even declines in later years. Since women live longer than men and often have longer work careers, the wage discrimination is a crucial issue for older women (Elimination of Sex and Race-Based Wage Discrimination, 1987.)

Older women are often victims of a particular synthesis of sexist, racist and ageist prejudice in the labor market. They find employers unwilling to credit previous work experience and activities while out of the work force. Unwarranted assumptions of reduced trainability and productivity are often used to exclude the older woman from jobs (Crooks, 1986; Older Women, 1980).

The economic status of older women is a problem for which there are few easy answers. Policy makers in the public and private sectors are continuing to review alternative plans to reduce the economic deprivation experienced by so many older women. Social workers will continue to face obstacles in assisting older female clients to achieve economic security. Advocacy on their behalf should clearly be a priority in all forums of decision making, such as, legislatures and advocacy groups.

Marital Dissolution. The problems of income-maintenance among survivors of deceased workers or among divorced spouses affect primarily women since they tend to live longer, do not remarry as frequently, and have traditionally been in roles of economic dependency. For widows, the economic consequences may be as follows:

- Income from the husband's employment upon which the wife may be dependent is lost.

- The financial resources of the couple may have been greatly diminished or totally exhausted by the high costs of the husband's final illness and death. The total average death benefit left by husbands to widows is only $12,000 which includes all income from life insurance and Social Security and perhaps veteran's pensions. Fifty-two percent of all widows will have used up all available insurance benefits within 18 months and 25% have exhausted this resource within two months. Twenty-five percent of widows never receive all of their husband's benefits usually because they lack information to get access of these benefits. Social Security and benefit pensions may be inadequate or unavailable.

For women who are divorced at mid-life or later, there are also economic consequences which may determine the quality of their remaining years:

- Usually the husband has the highest and often the only income. When divorce occurs, that income is removed and child care and alimony payments are usually only a small part of the husband's income. Divorce and loss of the husband's income is a major cause of the movement of wives and children from middle class or lower class into poverty (Burkhauser, Holden, & Feaster, 1988).

- Contrary to popular mythology, there are only a few wealthy divorcees. Most divorced women are thrown upon their own resources not only to support themselves but their children. Thus, they may be handicapped by limited employment opportunities, low wages and the high costs of child-rearing in meeting current expenses and in building up economic security for their later years.

- Provisions for payment of Social Security and pension benefits to divorced wives are limited.

- Other benefits such as health insurance may be lost upon the termination of a marriage. Older divorced women may have difficulty in securing alternative health coverage before they are eligible for Medicare at age 65. In no-fault divorce cases, the assumption is that the woman can find employment and support herself, but the older a woman is and the longer she has remained out of the paid labor force, the more difficult is her search to find satisfactory employment (Older Women, 1980).

Problems with Social Security. The Social Security system does not cover everyone in the system equally. Someone who has been solely a homemaker or both an unpaid homemaker and a paid worker does not receive as good of coverage as a person who has had a long-term and consistent employment pattern. Retirement benefits are based on average earnings over a lifetime. At the current time, benefits are averaged over a 23 year period and after 1991, over a 35 year period. This long averaging period results in lower average earnings for women compared to men because married women typically spend time out of the work force in homemaking and child care activities.

A widow's benefits from Social Security is related to the standard of living that existed at the time of her husband's death rather than the standard of living at the time she went on the benefit rolls. Her benefits are based on his earnings index up to the year of his death. These benefits may be worth substantially less by the time the widow is eligible to receive them, at age 62.

A divorced woman's benefits under Social Security are usually 50% of the former husband's benefit. This amount may be inadequate for a person living alone since the spouse's benefit was intended as a supplement for a married couple. A divorced homemaker cannot receive a divorced spouse's benefit until the divorced husband reaches age 62 and retires. If he elects to continue working, she is ineligible for benefits until he retires.

A major equity issue is the relative worth of Social Security benefits given to a dependent spouse who receives benefits through her husband's employment, and the benefits awarded to spouses who have themselves earned benefits, as a paid employee. The system clearly favors women who have remained at home and couples who have earned an income from the husband's work alone rather than when both spouses worked. The protection that an older woman receives based on the years she was a paid worker cannot be added to the protection based on the years she was an unpaid homemaker. As a result, a previously employed woman may get no or only slightly higher benefits than she would have received as a dependent who had never worked. The money she personally pays into the system as a result of her own employment is not returned to her in benefits (Older Women, 1980).

Limited Access to Pensions. In terms of pensions, less than half of the private sector is presently covered by an employee sponsored pension plan; however, women are affected disproportionately (Older Women, 1980). A study revealed that 49% of men, but only 21% of women employed in the private sector were covered by a pension plan on their longest job. Only about 1 in 10 women received money from a private pension in 1981, and the average benefit for men was over

70% greater than that for women. The different working patterns of men and women are reflected in the pension system because a large number of women work in retail or service industries which typically provide low pension coverage. Moreover, women often interrupt their careers for family obligations and they are usually paid less than men which shows up in their pension checks.

Many women depend on their husband's pension to help see them through retirement. But what happens to the pension if the husband dies first? In many cases, the surviving spouse will receive no benefits even if her husband worked 20 or 30 years for the same company. For example, in a single life annuity arrangement that many companies use as a pension, payments will cease when the husband dies. If the husband has chosen a joint and survivor annuity, the monthly payment generally will be reduced, but the company will continue to pay after the death of either husband or wife. Many women do not learn until after the funeral that their husband gambled on a higher benefit single life option, leaving the widow without any benefits at all (Richmond Times-Dispatch, 1984).

Housing

Home ownership is one of the American dreams. While it can be an asset for some, it becomes a serious liability for some elderly persons, especially women living alone. Some facts about housing for the elderly are listed below with gender differences highlighted where possible.

- A majority of elderly men and women who were heads of households in 1986 owned their homes (75% owners, 25% renters) (AARP, 1987).

- Older male householders were more likely to be owners (83%) than were females (65%) (AARP, 1987).

- About 83% of older homeowners in 1983 owned their homes free and clear (AARP, 1987).

- Homes of elderly women living alone tend to be older and of lower market value than of elderly men or elderly couples (Older Women: Economics of Aging, 1981).

- Housing costs of older women living alone are a greater portion of their resources than for older men or married couples (Older Women: Economics of Aging, 1981).

With fixed or diminishing incomes and the steadily rising costs of owning and renting, many older persons, especially women, face "shelter poverty." "Shelter poverty" results when the costs of housing and fuel result in insufficient funds for other basic needs such as food and clothing. In almost two million households, total shelter costs comprise 85% of the total budget. Shelter poverty is even more likely among black and Hispanic women, who are almost twice as likely to rent as are all other elderly (Chauncey, 1987).

Labor Force Participation

Possibly the greatest social change of the 20th century has been the influx of women into the work force. The movement of women out of the home was a progressive rather than a sudden change and reflected differential patterns by age. It began about the turn of the century but has increased at a faster pace since World War II (Beckett, 1982; Evans, 1987). Older women spearheaded the addition of the work role outside of the home. Their primacy reflects public attitudes about the activity of women as much as anything else. Attitudes about women working shifted first for older women because they generally did not have young children; thus it was thought, their home responsibilities would not be too adversely affected. In 1913, only 10% of all 40 year old women worked compared to approximately 50% in 1987 (Licht, 1988). During the postwar period the labor force rate of women 45 to 54 escalated from about 30% in 1946 to 50% in 1960 to almost 70% in 1987 (Shank, 1988).

Some older women have worked for pay throughout their lives. Women with this employment pattern are more likely to be single, black and/or from working class families. Urban black women are the only group of married women who often have a high lifetime work rate. These women were excused from the prevalent attitude that a wife's place was in the home. Black women responded by eagerly taking the opportunity to work, usually in low paid service jobs, to help their family survive economically and to provide for their children's education (Evans, 1987).

Older women who wish to enter or reenter the work force meet formidable barriers. New and continuing family responsibilities, lack of documented employment experience and disrupted work histories prevent many, especially the recently separated, divorced and widowed, from securing employment outside the home (Benokraitis, 1987; Older Women and the Labor Force, 1984).

The movement of women into the work force is remarkable when one considers the discrimination they have had and continue to face. In addition to sex discrimination in employment, many women also face discrimination due to race, class, sexual orientation or disability. When they reach middle age, the discrimination women face throughout their lives is compounded by age discrimination. Despite the fact that older women are reliable workers with low turnover and low absentee rates, and laws that prohibit age and gender discrimination, differential treatment persists for older women (Woody, 1983).

Employment

- Middle-aged women (55-64) are entering the world of work in record numbers (Women and Aging Around the World, 1985).

- Middle-aged women (55-64) show a stronger preference than men to continue working even if they can afford to retire. In addition, many women in this age group who are not in paid employment, regret their situation.

- About three million older Americans (65 and over) were in the labor force in 1986; they comprised 11% of the labor force (AARP, 1987).

- While the labor force participation of older men (65+) has decreased steadily (from 66% in 1900 to 16% in 1986), the rate for women has fluctuated (from about 8% in 1900 to 10% in the 50's to 7% in 1986 (AARP, 1987).

- Women accounted for 40% of the older (65+) workers in 1986.

Part-time Employment

- Older men and women are more likely than younger persons to work part-time (in 1981, 48% for men 65+ vs. 6% for men 45 to 64; 60% for women 65+ vs. 25% for women 45 to 64). Regardless of age, women are more likely than men to work part-time (U.S. Bureau of the Census, 1983).

- Among women, unemployment is higher for blacks and Hispanics than among whites; it is also higher for persons with less education (Hendricks & Hendricks, 1986).

- Compared to younger people, older male and female workers stay unemployed longer periods (20 vs. 15 weeks), are more likely not to find reemployment, and earn less in subsequent jobs (Beckett, 1988; Stein, Doress, & Fillmore, 1987; U.S. Bureau of Census, 1983).

- While unemployment is the most important factor in men becoming poor, family disruptions--separation, divorce, widowhood--are the most important factors in women's poverty level (United Nations Development Program, 1979).

Out of the Labor Force

- In 1983, about 60% of the official discouraged workers, meaning those who give up job searching due to repeated rejections, were women (Older Women and the Labor Force, 1984).

- "Displaced homemakers" are a growing concern among older women. This label describes women in their middle and older years who must support themselves for the first time because of separation, divorce or widowhood. They often have little or no skills (Benokraitis, 1987; Stein et al., 1987).

- Almost one third of older women leave the labor force entirely by taking early retirement, despite the permanent reduction in Social Security Benefits that results from retirement prior to age 65 (Older Women and the Labor Force, 1984).

- Family responsibilities are the primary reason women give who remain outside the paid work force or who prematurely leave their jobs. In 1987, seventy-six percent of nonworking women age 45 to 54, seventy-four percent of those 55 to 59, and sixty-nine percent of the 60 to 64 cited this reason. In contrast, the nonworking men in these age categories indicated ill health, retirement or no desire to work as their primary reasons (Shank, 1988).

Health

Physical Health

The majority of older women live active, healthy lives. Despite the gender differences in mortality rates, women die from the same primary causes as men: cardiovascular disease, cancers, cerebrovascular disease and respiratory disorders (Women and Aging Around the World, 1985). The primary causes of death are the only health item on which men and women show similar behavior yet some specific gender differences exist; for example, women are more likely to die of breast cancer, while men more often have respiratory cancer (National Center for Health Statistics, 1985; Women and Aging Around the World, 1985). The secondary causes of illness vary by gender. Older men are seven times as likely as women to die of suicide; while women are more likely than men to die of diabetes (Hendricks & Hendricks, 1986).

Furthermore, there are gender differences in the incidence and severity of illness. Older women experience higher rates of potentially disabling illness such as arthritis, osteoporosis, hypertension and diabetes. Women are more likely than men to have mobility problems, to be bedfast and unable to perform essential self-care tasks. Because of the longer life expectancy, women often have to cope longer with chronic illness than do men (Doress, et al., 1984; Women and Aging Around the World, 1985)

These situations suggest that women's longevity brings risk of serious impairments in functioning and ability to perform the tasks of daily life. It is important to note that elderly women who face severe health problems are usually much older than elderly men. Men have health problems at an earlier age than women and are unlikely to reach the advanced age at which many women begin to have serious health problems. In addition, women are more likely than men to receive and comply with medical care when ill; for example, hypertensive women were twice as likely as men to be on medication (Women and Aging Around the World, 1985).

Race, income, and education also are important determinants of a woman's health status as well as the quality of the health care she receives. Low income and education are correlated with poor health status. Since older women are disproportionately represented among the elderly poor, they are more likely than men to have poor health and receive inferior and inappropriate health care (Women and Aging Around the World, 1985). Insufficient income has several additional effects (Boston Women's Health Book Collective, 1984; Women and Aging Around the World, 1985):

- increases the daily stress level as one attempts to get basic needs met;

- reduces the likelihood of sufficient exercise which can reduce stress levels and prevent physical and mental health problems. Many live in neighborhoods where they do not feel safe on the streets and have no access to indoor exercise facilities;

- reduces the possibility of adequate nutrition and the ability to purchase food for special diets;

- results in four million women 45 to 65 having no health insurance benefits.

Since the poverty rate among minorities of color is greater than that for white women, the minority elderly have a disproportionate number of health related problems. In addition, the incidence of illness varies by race and ethnicity. Osteoporosis, for example, affects about 25% of American women; while quite common among white and Asian women, it is rare among blacks (Women and Aging Around the World, 1985). About 1 in 165 blacks have sickle cell anemia, a debilitating illness that lessens the life span, but the disease is seldom seen among whites. (Pincus, Swenson, & Poor, 1984). Another example is that homicide is the eighth cause of death among black women while it is not in the top ten causes of white women's deaths; black women are less likely than whites to die of cancer and more likely to die of diabetes (National Center for Health Statistics, 1985).

Mental Health

Especially among the elderly, there is a close relationship between mental health problems and physical health status. Psychological symptoms may be a result of a physical illness and/or side effects from over the counter or prescribed medications as well as environmental changes and losses. Older persons are more likely than younger to receive psychoactive drugs for their psychological symptoms and drug therapy is the most commonly used and, often, the only treatment for psychiatric problems (Kermis, 1986). Prescribing psychoactive medication for the elderly can be problematic for several reasons:

- all psychoactive drugs have dangerous side effects for elderly persons (Glantz, Peterson, & Whittington, 1983; Jones-Witters, & Witters, 1983);

- there is no standard dosage for older people; each dose must be determined individually; prescribing drugs for the elderly is an art not a science;

- complicated dosage regimens exist for multiple symptoms and illness;

- the elderly's use of multiple medications (polypharmacy);

- the dosage may need to be changed as the person ages;

- psychoactive drugs have a high addiction potential;

- insufficient pharmacological knowledge among physicians since there is little or no formal training in this area and in the use of psychotrophics for the elderly;

- physicians often do not explain side effects of drugs to patients; when side effects do occur, patients make their own decision about medication or see another physician who is not told about the previous medication;

- lack of communication and coordination between mental health and medical personnel (Kermis, 1986).

There are several gender differences among the elderly with mental health problems. Gender variations appear in diagnosis, treatment, prescription of psychotherapeutic drugs and reaction to stress. The biases of the medical and mental health professions are often more of a factor in these distinctions than are the actual conditions of elderly men and women (Hendricks & Hendricks, 1986). Some of the variations by gender are noted below:

- After age 65, women have a lower risk than men for mental health problems (Hendricks & Hendricks, 1986);

- women are more likely to receive mental health services (Hendricks & Hendricks, 1986);

- women receive mental health services for a longer period of time than men;

- men are at least three times as likely to attempt and to succeed in suicide (U.S. Bureau of the Census, 1985);

- women are more likely to be given psychoactive drugs; older women comprise 6% of the U.S. population but receive 17% of the prescriptions for thorazine, a major tranquilizer, and 20% of those for sedatives (Jones-Witters and Witters, 1983);

- females have a lower hospitalization rate in county and state mental health facilities than men (President's Commission on Mental Health, 1978); but when private facilities are also considered, women comprise the majority of all hospitalized mental health patients (Raymond, 1982);

- over 70% of those undergoing electroshock therapy are women (Raymond, 1982);

- older women are more likely than men to lose their spouse and are better able to successfully work through the normal grief and depression (Marshall, 1980).

Long-term Care

Although older persons have more chronic illness than younger people, most with long-term care needs live in the community. Families provide the care to an overwhelming majority (84% of men and 79% of the women) of the disabled elderly who reside in the community (Hooyman, 1986a). Only 5% (about 1.4 million) of all elderly reside in institutions (Hooyman, 1986a; U.S. Senate Special Committee on Aging, 1987). The proportion in institutions increases with age; for example, 2% of those 65 to 74, but 9% of those 75 and older are in institutions (Beaver, 1985).

In contrast to earlier periods when most disabled elderly were confined to mental institutions, currently almost all (96%) of the institutionalized elderly reside in places other than mental hospitals (Older Women Economics of Aging, 1981). These institutions vary from homes for the elderly which provide custodial care and general supervision, to skilled nursing facilities (Hendricks & Hendricks, 1986).

Most (70%) of the disabled institutionalized elderly are women; for those 85 years old and above, 80% are women (Hendricks & Hendricks, 1986; Hooyman, 1986a, b, c; Older Women Economics of Aging, 1981). The existence of family can be a prime factor of institutionalization. Almost all (90%) of elderly women in nursing homes have no spouse and almost half have no close relatives (Hooyman, 1986a; Hooyman, 1986b; Women & Aging Around the World, 1985). These characteristics suggest women are more likely to be institutionalized for social rather than medical reasons.

Despite the fact that the majority of institutional care residents are women, little has been written in America about the qualitative differences in men's and women's experiences in these institutions. Some literature shows that women are given more types of medication than men but that male residents are more likely than female to be given drugs as "chemical restraints" or "chemical straightjackets" (Brink, 1979; Glantz et al., 1983; Milliren, 1977). Research in Great Britain indicates men and women in long-term care facilities have a different profile: men enter at an earlier age, are in better health and are more mobile; women are less satisfied with residential life and feel more lonely and less useful. Women in institutions have lost a role that most men do not have - the domestic, housekeeper, or caretaker role (Women and Aging Around the World, 1985).

For both men and women, misuse of drugs in long-term care facilities is problematic. They are among the highest users of medication and are also the greatest victims of drug misuse (Brink, 1979, Glantz et al., 1983). The average nursing home resident receives 5 to 12 different drugs per day. Doses are missed, multiple doses given and drug interactions are all too often. Drugs are given to counteract the side effects of other medications. A resident may receive a medical order for two drugs, one that treats diarrhea and the other for constipation; or one that is a diuretic and another for incontinence (Lamy, 1978). These problems are related to 30,000 long-term care resident deaths a year (Brink, 1979).

Another problem is that long-term care is expensive. Many (80%) elderly and their families mistakenly think Medicare and/or private supplements cover the cost. Less than 2% of the costs are paid by these benefits (AARP, 1987). To receive Medicaid, a benefit that does pay for some long-term care in institutions, a person must either be poor or reduced to poverty in the process of trying to pay for care.

The long-term care of the elderly in institutions is increasingly a women's industry but administered by males. Low income women are both residents and low wage caretakers--persons without much power. The management and administration, tasks that command higher salaries, are usually done by younger men, however (Boston Women's Health Book Collective, 1984; Hooyman, 1986b; Women & Aging Around the World, 1985).

Obstacles to Good Health Care

As older women turn to the health care system, they face some special obstacles to good care. (List taken from Boston Women's Health Book Collective, 1984)

Inadequate Research. Until recently, medical research paid little attention to the health concerns of older women. Currently, medical literature focuses on menopause as the primary midlife health issue. For post-menopausal women, medical research seems to lump mental and physical problems under the rubric of senility, an incurable problem (Butler, 1975; Butler & Lewis, 1976).

Medical research pays little attention to other issues such as occupational health concerns. Since medical research does not address many important health concerns of older women, health care practitioners have inadequate information about diseases facing older women and about the treatment and prevention of these medical and psychiatric problems.

Practitioner Attitudes. Physicians and other health care staff share our culture's negative attitudes, myths and stereotypes toward older persons. Medical personnel, like the general public, are personally ambivalent and frightened by aging and death. This ageism is complicated by sexism. Medical staff more frequently dismiss older women's complaints and problems as neurotic and/or imaginary than those made by men. As one nurse put it: When a man complains of dizziness, he gets a workup; an older woman gets valium (Boston Women's Health Book Collective, 1984). Classism and racism are other factors. Poor and minority women are more likely to be subjected to the negative attitudes and behaviors. These practices are less blatant with women who have ample financial resources and who have private physicians.

Limits of Medical Model to Chronic Illness. Diseases of the elderly are more often chronic rather than acute; they develop slowly, without a marked crisis point, linger for extended periods, often involve a number of body functions, have no single cause, and no cure (Hendricks & Hendricks, 1986). These illnesses do not respond to the daring surgery or high technological interventions that medical staff are trained to prefer. Some treatment is boring and ordinary - diet, braces, physical therapy, aspirin, environmental changes - but often time consuming and expensive. These treatments seldom spark the interest of health care providers and often the elderly are not seen as worth the time, energy and cost.

If practitioners begin to see and acknowledge the limitations of the medical model, other and better solutions may be found for women's health concerns. For example, as long as menopause is seen as a deficiency disease or an endocrinological disorder, surgery (hysterectomies) or drugs (estrogen or tranquilizers) seem like reasonable remedies. If, however, menopause is seen as a transition or a turning point on the way to a new life stage, other remedies - exercise, diet, or stress reduction - may be more appropriate (Report of the Mini Conference on Older Women, 1981). In addition, Medicare, Medicaid and private insurances do not adequately cover chronic conditions unless they require institutionalization.

Inappropriate Sources of Care. Presently no single medical specialty specifically addresses the health problems of older persons or older women. Although there is growing interest in the area of geriatrics, there is also a debate as to whether geriatrics should be a medical specialty or integrated with other medical specialities. Internists, family practitioners and primary care physicians who are skilled in the medical problems of older women and who have a positive attitude are the most appropriate physicians for older women. There is a shortage of physicians, however, for these specialty areas as well as for psychiatry (U.S. Senate Special Committee on Aging, 1987).

There is also an insufficient number of geriatric centers and clinics. Those that do exist are usually located in large urban medical centers and thus not available to many elderly who live in the inner city or remote rural areas (U.S. Senate Special Committee on Aging, 1987). They may have limited hours, for example, the recently developed clinic at Medical College of Virginia in Richmond is available only one afternoon a week.

Misdiagnosis. Health care persons tend to assign the physical and emotional problems of the elderly to one cause: aging or senility. Treatable causes such as poor nutrition, physical malfunctions, grief, or side effects of medication are rarely considered. These practices result in failure to treat reversible conditions or inappropriate treatment such as tranquilizers, sedatives, antidepressants and hormones.

Overprescription of Drugs. Many older persons take several medications daily for multiple chronic conditions, often prescribed by different physicians. While the dosage may be technically correct, it may be inappropriate for several reasons. First, persons over 60 and women are more sensitive to many drugs and should take lower doses than younger persons and males. Second, the drug may have side effects such as depression and confusion. Thirdly, drugs may interact with each other and cause additional health problems. Some medications are especially problematic for older persons: reserpine, methyldopa, digitalis, procainamide, beta-blocking agents, all barbiturates, alcohol and tranquilizers. Sharing a list of all medications with all physicians and coordination of health care can help alleviate these problems (Comfort, 1976).

Insufficient Attention to Prevention. Treatment rather than prevention is usually the focus of health care. Thus, illnesses such as osteoporosis that are prevalent among women get little attention despite the fact that they are in great part preventible. For example, the following help to prevent osteoporosis: increased calcium intake, vitamin C & D supplements, increased exercise, not smoking, reducing the intake of alcohol, and refraining from the long-term use of steroid medications such as cortisone prescribed for diseases such as arthritis (AARP, 1985; Boston Women's Health Book Collective, 1984).

Chapter References

A profile of older Americans. (1987). Washington, DC: AARP.

A profile of older Americans. (1985). Washington, DC: AARP.

Aging America: Trends and projections 1985-86. (1985). Washington, DC: U.S. Department of Health and Human Services.

Almvig, C. (1982). The invisible minority: Aging and lesbianism. Utica, NY: Syracuse University.

Beaver, M. (1983). Human service practice with the elderly. Englewood Cliffs, NJ: Prentice Hall.

Beaver, M., & Miller, D. (1985). Clinical social work practice with the elderly. Homewood, IL: Dorsey Press.

Beckett, J. O. (1982). Working women: A historical review of racial differences. The Black Sociologist, 9, 5-27.

Beckett, J. O. (1988). Plant closings: How older workers are affected. Social Work, 33(1), 29-33.

Before you buy: A guide to longterm care insurance. (1987) Washington, DC: AARP.

Bell, A., & Weinberg, M. (1978). Homosexualities. New York: Simon & Schuster.

Benokraitis, N. (1987). Older women and reentry problems: The case of displaced homemakers. Journal of Gerontological Social Work, 10, 75-92.

Berger, R. (1982). The unseen minority: Older gays and lesbians. Social Work, 27, 236-241.

Boston Women's Health Book Collective. (1984). The new our bodies, ourselves. New York: Simon & Schuster.

Brink, T. L. (1979). Geriatric psychotherapy. New York: Human Sciences Press.

Brody, E. (1985). Women in the middle and family help to older people. The Gerontologist, 25, 19-30.

Bureau of the Census. (1980). A statistical portrait of women in the United States: 1978. Washington, DC: U.S. Government Printing Office.

Burkhauser, R. V., Holden, K. C., & Feaster, D. (1988). Incidence, timing, and events associated with poverty: A dynamic view of poverty in retirement. Journal of Gerontology: Social Sciences, 43(2).

Butler, R. (1975). Why survive: Being old in America. New York: Harper-Colophon.

Butler, R., & Lewis, M. (1976). Sex after sixty. North Miami, FL: Merit Publications.

Chauncey, C. (1987). Shelter poverty and displacement. In P. Doress & D. Siegel (Eds.), Ourselves growing older (pp. 146-147). New York: Simon & Schuster.

Cherlin, A. (1987). Women and the family. In S. Rix (Ed.), The American Woman 1987-88 (pp. 67-103). New York: W. W. Norton.

Comfort, A. (1976). A good age. New York: Crown Publishers.

Crooks, L. D. (1986). The situation of older women around the world: An emerging issue. Paper presented at International Conference on Social Welfare, Tokyo.

Dawson, K. (1982). Serving the older community. SIECUS report (pp. 5-6). New York: Sex Education and Information Council of the United States.

dePatie, C. (1980). Social security and the older woman. In V. C. Little (Ed.), Women, work and age: Policy challenges. Ann Arbor, MI: Institute of Gerontology.

Doress, P., Swenson, N., Cohen, R. Friedman, M., Harvis, L., & MacPherson, K. (1984). Women growing older. In The Boston Women's Health Book Collective, The new our bodies, ourselves (pp. 435-472). New York: Simon & Schuster.

du Rivage, V. (1984). Increasing poverty through federal policy change. In E. Snyder (Ed.), Women, work and age: Policy challenges. Ann Arbor: Institute of Gerontology.

Elimination of sex and race based wage discrimination: Policy statement. (1987). Silver Spring, MD: NASW.

Evans, S. (1987). Women in twentieth century America: An overview. In S. Rix (Ed.), The American woman 1987-88 (pp. 33-66). New York: W. W. Norton.

Fengler, A. & Goodrich, N. (1979). Wives of elderly disabled men: The hidden patients. The Gerontologist, 19, 175-183.

Friend, R. A. (1984, June). A theory of accelerated aging among lesbians and gay men. Paper presented to the combined annual meeting of American Association of Sex Educators, Counselors and Therapists, and the Society for Scientific Study of Sex, Boston, MA.

Friend, R. A. (1987). The individual and social psychology of aging: Clinical implications for lesbians and gay men. Journal of Homosexuality, 14, 305-331.

Gelfand, D., & Barresi, C. M. (1987). Ethnic dimensions of aging. New York: Springer.

Glantz, M. D., Peterson, D., & Whittington, F. J. (Eds.). (1983). Drugs and the elderly adult: Research issues. Washington, DC: U.S. Department of Health and Human Services.

Growing numbers, growing force: A report from the White House mini-conference on older women. (1980). Oakland, CA: The Older Women's League.

Hagestad, G. (1986). The aging society as a context for family life. Daedalus, 115, 119-139.

Hendricks, J., & Hendricks, C. D. (1986). Aging in mass society. Boston: Little, Brown & Company.

Hess, B., & Waring, J. (1983). Family relationships of older women: A women's issue. In E. Markson, Older women. Lexington, MA: Lexington Books.

Holden, K. C. (1988). Poverty and living arrangements among older women: Are changes in economic well being under estimated? Journal of Gerontology: Social Sciences, 43(1).

Hooyman, N. (1986a). Family caregiving of the elderly: A fact sheet. Unpublished paper. Seattle: University of Washington, School of Social Work.

Hooyman, N. (1986b). The older woman in America. Paper presented at International Conference on Social Welfare, Tokyo.

Hooyman, N. (1986c). Taking care: Supporting older people and their families. New York: Free Press.

Jennings, J. (1987). Elderly parents as caregivers for adult dependent children. Social Work, 32(5), 430-433.

Jones-Witters, P., & Witters, W. (1983). Drugs and society: A biological perspective. Monterey, CA: Wadsworth Health Sciences.

Kermis, M. (1986). Mental health in late life. Boston/Monterery: Jones & Barrett.

Kimmel, D. (1978). Adult development and aging: A gay perspective. Journal of Social Issues, 34, 113-130.

Klemesrud, J. (1982, November 22). Older women: Their league gains strength. New York Times, B-12.

Lamy. (1978). Therapeutics and the elderly. Addictive Disease: An International Journal, 3, 311-335.

Lamy, P. (1983). Pharmacology and therapeutics. In M. D. Glantz et al., Drugs and the elderly adult (pp. 121-129). Washington, DC: U.S. Department of Health and Human Services.

Licht, W. (1988, February). How the work place has changed in 75 years. Monthly Labor Review, 19-25.

Marshall. (1980). Last chapters: A sociology of aging and dying. Monterey, CA: Brooks/Cole.

Milliren, J. W. (1977). Some contingencies affecting the utilization of tranquilizers in long-term care of the elderly. Journal of Health and Social Behavior, 18, 206-211.

Minnigerode, F., & Adelman, M. (1976, October). Adaptations of aging homosexual men and women. Paper presented at the Annual Meeting of the Gerontological Society of America, New York, NY.

National Center for Health Statistics. (1985, September 26). Annual summary of births, marriages, divorces and deaths, United States, 1984. Monthly Vital Statistics Report, 33, Department of Health and Human Services, Publication No. (PHS) 85-1120. Hyattsville, MD: U.S. Public Health Service.

National Center for Health Statistics. (1985). Monthly Vital Statistics Report, 34, Department of Health and Human Services, Hyattsville, MD: U.S. Public Health Service.

Number of U.S. elderly growing rapidly. (1984, May 31). Boston Globe.

Older women and the labor force. (1984, June 6). Testimony of the Older Women's League (OWL) before the Joint Economic Committee.

Older women - The economics of aging. (1980). Washington, DC: George Washington University, Women Studies Program and Policy Center.

Older women - The economics of aging. (1981). Washington, DC: George Washington University, Women Studies Program and Policy Center.

The Older Women's League. (1980).

Otten, A. L. (1984, July 30). The oldest old: Evermore Americans live into 80s and 90s, causing big problems. Wall Street Journal.

Otten, A. L. (1985, June 5). Women continue to outlive men, but the female edge is narrowing. Wall Street Journal.

Pincus, J., Swenson, N., & Poor, B. (1984). Pregnancy. In The Boston Women's Health Book Collective, The new our bodies, ourselves (pp. 329-360). New York: Simon & Schuster.

President's Commission on Mental Health. (1978). Final report: Vol. 2, Task panel reports. Washington, DC: U.S. Printing Office.

Raymond, J. C. (1982). Medicine as patriarchal religion. Journal of Medicine and Philosophy, 7, 197-216.

Report of the mini-conference on older women. (1981). Prepared for the 1981 White House Conference on Aging, Washington, DC, MCR-18.

Report on the status of midlife and older women in America. (1986). Washington, DC: Older Women's League.

Ricks, T. E. (1986, April 22). Men who live to a ripe old age find unexpected bonus: Lots of single women. Wall Street Journal.

Rix, S. (Ed.). (1987). The American woman, 1987-88. New York: W. W. Norton.

Sex differences and aging. (1981). Washington, DC: National Institute on Aging.

Shank, S. (1988, March). Women's link to labor market grows stronger. Monthly Labor Review, 3-8.

Sontag, S. (1972). The double standard of aging. Saturday Review of the Society, 95, 29-38.

Stein, E., Doress, P., & Fillmore, M. (1987). Work and retirement. In P. Doress & D. Siegel (Eds.), Ourselves growing older (pp. 163-180). New York: Simon & Schuster.

Teresi, J. A., Toner, J., Bennett, R., & Wilson, D. (1980, November). Factors related to family attitudes toward institutionalizing older relatives. Paper presented at the 33rd Annual Scientific Meeting of The Gerontological Society of America, San Diego, CA.

Treas, J. (1977). Family support systems for the aged: Some social and demographic considerations. The Gerontologist, 17, 486-491.

U.S. Bureau of the Census. (1983). America in transition: An aging society. Current Population Reports, Series P-23, No. 128. Washington, DC: U.S. Government Printing Office.

U.S. Bureau of the Census. (1984). Current population reports and the statistical abstract of the United States. Washington, DC: U.S. Government Printing Office.

U.S. Bureau of the Census. (1985). Marital status and living arrangements: March 1984. Current Population Reports, Series P-20, No. 399. Washington, DC: Government Printing Office.

U.S. House of Representatives Select Committee on Aging. (1979). Midlife women: Policy proposals on their problems. Washington, DC: U.S. Government Printing Office.

U.S. Senate Special Committee on Aging. (1985). Developments in aging: 1984, Vol. I. Washington, DC: U.S. Government Printing Office.

U.S. Senate Special Committee on Aging. (1987). Developments in aging: 1986, Vol. I. Washington, DC: U.S. Government Printing Office.

United Nations Development Program. (1979). Women and the international economic order. Development issue paper for the 1980s, No. 12. New York: UNDP, Division of Information.

Women and aging around the world. (1985). Washington, DC: American Association of Retired Persons and International Federation on Aging.

Women still have a tough time qualifying for pension plans. (1984, May 13). Richmond Times-Dispatch.

Woody, B. (1983). Uncertainty and risk of low income black working women: Project summary. Wellesley, MA: Wellesley College, Center for Research on Women.

Discussion Questions

1. Imagine you are in charge of the U.S. Department of Health and Human Services. How could information on gender differences in the elderly be useful to you? Describe one way you would use this information for policy development.

2. Discuss three demographic differences between older men and women. How might each difference influence service delivery to older persons?

3. Discuss two problems older women face in securing physical and mental health services. What steps can be taken to overcome the problems?

4. Imagine you are the administrator of a multi-service agency. Plan a program that would be helpful to minority elderly women. What concerns would the program address? Why?

5. Do you think Social Security and other governmental benefits should be determined differently for women than men? Why?

6. Discuss two differences in the experiences of older lesbians and older gays. What significance do these differences have for the development of services targetted for homosexuals?

7. Divorce often has severe economic consequences for older women. Explain how this social event is related to the economic status of older women.

Learning Activities

Activity #1. Older Women's Facts on Aging Quiz

Instructions: Give each student a copy of the quiz. Give the class about 15 minutes to answer the 20 True/False questions. Afterwards, give the students the correct answers. Use the quiz to initiate a discussion about the status and perception of older women in our society.

Activity #2. Spending a Social Security Check

Instructions: Give each student a copy of the Itemized Expense Sheet and Case Study. Instruct the students to work individually on budgeting their money. As a group, have them discuss the problems of trying to live on a fixed income. Also discuss how personal preferences and choices can influence budget allotments.

Older Women's Facts on Aging Quiz

True/False

1. _____ At age 65, women have an average of 18 years of life remaining.
2. _____ 85% of surviving spouses are female.
3. _____ The average age of widowhood is 64.
4. _____ There are five bridegrooms to every bride over 65.
5. _____ Three-fifths of all women over 65 are unmarried, while three-fourths of men are living with their spouses.
6. _____ Two-thirds of all widows live alone.
7. _____ 1/4 of widows live below the official poverty line.
8. _____ Of women 66 and over, 91% are white, 9% are black, and 2% are of Spanish origin.
9. _____ Almost half of women 75 and older live alone, compared to 21% of men.
10. _____ Women earn 75% of what men earn on the average.
11. _____ Sixty-three percent of aged Social Security beneficiaries are female.
12. _____ Eighty percent of retirement age women have no access to private pensions.
13. _____ One-third of all employed women are in jobs without a pension plan.
14. _____ Less than 10% of widows receive pension survivor's benefits.
15. _____ Over age 75, there are three times as many women as men.
16. _____ Over two-thirds of nursing home residents are female.
17. _____ Women have five years longer life expectancy than men.
18. _____ The number of elderly black women has increased 26% since 1971.
19. _____ Among women 75 and older, three out of four paid more than 35% of cash income for housing.
20. _____ Women retire on less than half of what men do.

Key to Older Women's Facts on Aging Quiz

1. True.
2. True.
3. False. The average age of widowhood is 56.
4. False. There are 9 bridegrooms to every bride over 65.
5. True.
6. True.
7. False. One-third (1/3) of widows live below the poverty line.
8. True.
9. True.
10. False. Women earn 59% of what men earn on the average
11. True.
12. True.
13. False. One half (1/2) of all employed women are in jobs without a pension plan.
14. True.
15. False. After age 75, there are twice as many women as men.
16. True.
17. False. Women have an eight year longer life expectancy than men.
18. True.
19. True.
20. True.

Statistics from: Older Women: The Economics of Aging. (1980). Washington, DC: The Women's Study Program and Policy Center, George Washington University, 1980.

Case Study for Activity #2

You are a 71-year-old woman whose sole income is a $_____ per month social security check. You own you own home, a two-bedroom house, which has taxes of $510, and insurance of $480 per year. You get no financial support from your children. Sometimes you eat at a nutrition site for $1.00 per meal. At other times you cook and eat alone. Your life savings is $3,500. You are a diabetic and have arthritis, which is worse when it is cold and rainy.

You are in the process of making out your average monthly budget. Listed below are the areas in which you'll incur expenses. Your task is to assign an average monthly figure for each category, and to perhaps eliminate some items that you feel you can't afford.

Itemized Expense Sheet

$/month	Housing	$/month	Food
_____	taxes	_____	eat at home alone
_____	gas	_____	eat at nutrition site
_____	eligibility	_____	eat out
_____	water	_____	other _____
_____	garbage		
_____	house insurance		
_____	home repair		
_____	appliances		
_____	other _____		

$/month	Clothing	$/month	In-Town Transportation
_____	new clothes	_____	bus
_____	washing	_____	taxi
_____	Goodwill	_____	own car/upkeep
_____	dry cleaning	_____	friend
_____	other	_____	walk

$/month	Leisure Time	$/month	Medical Expenses
_____	movies	_____	supplemental insurance
_____	plays	_____	prescriptions
_____	concerts	_____	doctors
_____	senior center	_____	new glasses
_____	other _____	_____	dentist
		_____	other _____

$/month	Gifts	$/month	Travel
_____	10 grandchildren	_____	save for trip to Montana
_____	3 children	_____	to visit
_____	friends	_____	other _____
_____	other _____		

Activity #3. Clarifying Values: Old Versus Young

What would you do in the specific situations listed below? What <u>criteria</u> do you use in responding to the circumstances? Are you <u>consistent</u> in your reasoning and logic? Are you more or less <u>comfortable</u> in the different situations? Do you avoid responding at all?

What would you do if:

1. _____ came to you and said she was contemplating marriage?
   a. Your 21-year-old niece _____
   b. Your 71-year-old grandmother _____

2. _____ told you he wanted to become a nurse?
   a. Your 21-year-old nephew _____
   b. Your 60-year-old uncle _____

3. _____ said she wanted to learn how to bowl?
   a. Your 18-year-old cousin _____
   b. Your 80-year-old mother _____

4. _____ said she was joining an art class?
   a. Your 16-year-old sister _____
   b. Your 73-year-old mother _____

5. _____ was planning to campaign actively for a presidential candidate?
   a. Your 22-year-old niece _____
   b. Your 75-year-old patient _____

6. _____ was going to start college after being out of school for years?
   a. Your 30-year-old aunt _____
   b. Your 60-year-old aunt _____

7. _____ wanted to learn a trade?
   a. Your 20-year-old client _____
   b. Your 65-year-old client _____

8. _____ started coming home at two and three in the morning?
   a. Your 21-year-old sister _____
   b. Your 70-year-old grandmother _____

9. _____ became an old-movie buff and started to travel around to see old movies wherever they were shown?
   a. Your 16-year-old brother _____
   b. Your 65-year-old grandfather _____

10. All _____ ever did for recreation was play cards?
    a. Your 25-year-old cousin _____
    b. Your 70-year-old aunt _____

Activity #4. Autobiography

This assignment is particularly helpful in aiding students to evaluate stereotypical views of the elderly and to learn how important the family is in the development of attitudes and values. The students are asked to describe their families of origin and their position in the network. Below is a guide for students to use in writing this autobiography.

Guide for Autobiography

These questions are meant as a <u>guide</u> for your autobiography. You may feel that some of this information is personal in nature. Be assured that it will be treated as such. You will need to make a choice regarding what you are comfortable including and what you want to think about in private.

1. Describe your family of origin including information on: (a) compostion/members (parents, siblings, birth order, etc.); (b) ethnic identity; (c) race; (d) sociocultural background; and (d) neighborhood, etc.

2. Describe the intergenerational network in your family including information on: (a) frequency and type of contact; (b) your perception of the affective quality of relationships and; (c) what you feel you learned about becoming or being "old."

3. Describe what you feel you have learned from your family about the process of dying or the meaning of death.

4. Describe your role in your family. What "part(s)" do you usually assume? How did you come to assume the role of "helping person"? How is this role related to your age and gender?

5. Identify specific family expectations and values that you feel contributed to your career choice and/or interest in a "helping" profession. Who are the significant others that might have influenced career choice?

6. Identify the family's style of adaptation as seen in their problem-solving techniques, reaction to stress and communication style. Have you felt comfortable in adopting and/or rejecting various "life solutions"?

7. Describe how your (family) life history impacts on your current functioning as a student social worker. How might these past experiences affect your philosophy of what constitutes "good" social work practice?

Adapted from Roberta Greene, 1982, "Step on a Crack, Break an Old Man's Back: Learning Assignments for Social Work Students in the Field of Aging." Unpublished course syllabus.

Case Studies

(Please review Appendices A and B for guidelines on teaching
gerontological social work by using case studies)

Case #1. Mrs. Tish and Past Memories

It took us quite a while after Mrs. Tish's admission to understand that when she sat by the elevators, although blind, there was something in this situation that stimulated in her a desire to travel. It is not the usual kind of feeling that occurs in one of the residents when they become confused and dependent and want to accompany a departing volunteer or visitor. In these cases, the social worker can help by meeting the resident's need to be with somebody. After the visitor has departed, the social worker will tell the resident where she lives, what meals is next, and resettle her without any real difficulty.

However, Mrs. Tish's reaction was of panic and deep agitation. Although blind, Mrs. Tish hears very well. She heard the elevator doors open and close, and people coming and going. I was trying to picture what was making her so upset when she heard the sounds. When she said she wanted to get on "the train" and mentioned the name of a little town in Russia, I knew she had transported herself back in time to when she was a young girl, sitting in a railroad station, waiting for a train. She seemed to be reliving the anxiety of having to get aboard despite all obstacles. We were not able to calm her by offering her reality information at that moment. We walked with her a long time until her agitation seemed to wear off and she was tired and ready to nap. I made sure when she awoke that she was told where she was, and how long she had lived here. She would say, "Yes, I am an old woman now, and I do need help to put on my shoes." She would be back with us again.

We realized Mrs. Tish is a person who can slip easily into her past when things are too confusing. When she is able to understand what is going on, she is very clear about where she is and her present capabilities.

Now we do not take her to the elevators to sit and be with many other people to experience all the traffic and commotion, which triggers associations with which she cannot cope. We were wrong in thinking that everyone who is blind needed so much social stimulation. It might be right some some nonsighted people, but it was not right for Mrs. Tish. Now we seat her outside her room on the bench nearby, where the surroundings are simple for her to comprehend. She knows her bed, her table and her clothing are nearby, and she is next door to Mrs. David. She recognizes the voices of the nurses who come by and talks with them while they are working.

Adapted from Edelson, J. S., & Lyons, W. (1985). Institutional care of the mentally impaired elderly. New York: Van Nostrand.

Case #2: Confusion and Care

"Miss, Miss!" she beckoned to me. "Tell me, please, where am I?" "Mrs. London," I said, "you are sitting outside your room, third floor of the Stuart Home for the Aged." "What am I doing here?" "You live her now, Mrs. London." "I just woke up," she said; "I don't know anything anymore. How long have I been here?" "I think you and I have been here about the same length of time," I replied.

"How long is that?" she interrupted, looking at me more closely. "About three and a half years." "Do my children know that I am here?" "Yes, your sons, Arthur and Joseph, come to visit you here, usually in the evening or on weekends." "I think I am going crazy," she said with a heavy voice; "I can't remember anything." "Mrs. London," I said, "there is nothing the matter with your ability to think very clearly." She seemed to be reflecting on what I had said.

"So," she replied, "I live here . . . so, what do you do here?" "I work here. I work with the volunteers and the residents on the third floor." "Do the nurses know me?" "Yes, Mrs. London, they do know you, and they are here to help you. When you forget, they will help you." "Do my children know I am here?" she asked again. "They know," I said again, "and they visit you. Your sons who live in Beal City come to visit as often as they can. Your daughter Sarah lives out of town and she cannot come to Beal City very often." "Are you sure?" "Yes," I said. "Remember you used to live with Sarah and then you needed to have medical care and nurses to help you follow the doctor's instructions. The children and you decided that this was the best place to have people to look after you, and you came here to the Stuart Home for the Aged to live." She nodded.

I continued, "I can't remember the name of the university where Sarah's husband teaches, where you used to live It is in the Midwest." "Yes," she said, "I know where you mean, but my mind is like a cat; I can't remember the name either." "That is why the nurses are here, Mrs. London, to help you remember other things you need to know, and to help you do things you need to do."

"Thank you," she said. She pointed to a door: "That is my room?" I nodded. "Tell me," she asked, "what time is it?" "It is three-fifteen p.m. At four p.m., it will be time for supper and the nurse will come and invite you to eat." "Well, I guess I could wait," she said, trying to make a joke; "I wouldn't starve. Thank you."

As I left her, I heard her calling to a nursing aide in the corridor in a characteristic fashion with which the staff is most familiar. "Nurse, nurse! When you do they feed you here? I am hungry!"

Adapted from Edelson, J. S., & Lyons, W. (1985). Institutional care for the mentally impaired elderly. New York: Van Nostrand.

Case #3. Decision Making and Long-term Care for Miss Perkins

Miss Perkins was a very small, seemingly fragile woman who dressed in a stylish but dated fashion. She had been living in the same house for over 40 years. After the deaths of her two older, unmarried sisters who had shared the home with her, she continued to live alone. In spite of her many eccentricities, Miss Perkins was likable and personable. A well-to-do, socially prominent first cousin helped her financially, but took no sustained personal interest in Miss Perkins.

Spry and active all her life, Miss Perkins became increasingly anxious as she felt herself growing older and less steady on her feet. At the age of 75, she reached out for help by applying for admision to a nearby nursing home. The idea of planning for the move was distasteful to her. The prospect of dismantling her beloved home, with its accumulated and cherished possessions of over half a century, was overwhelming and threatening to her.

Miss Perkins was quite lonely, had little money, and was undergoing tests for bleeding from the bowel. When the tests proved negative she decided not to enter the nursing home. Nevertheless, she was afraid to withdraw her application for fear she might need to be admitted at some future time. The social worker at the nursing home offered her deferred status. This meant that the nursing home encouraged her to remain in the community for as long as possible, that the social worker would be available to her when needed, and that she could be admitted if and when her circumstances required.

At intervals during the next few years, Miss Perkins' bowel problem would flare up; a flurry of phone calls and home visits would ensue and help to alleviate it. With each such incident Miss Perkins went through the process of conflict, doubt, hesitation, and indecision. She would review a number of alternatives and express her fears about group living--especially with people she didn't know. Repeatedly, the situation was resolved in favor of Miss Perkins staying in her own home a little longer. During this period the nursing home provided Miss Perkins with a variety of supportive services including telephone reassurance, friendly visiting, a hot lunch program, and transporation services whenever she needed to go to the doctor.

Miss Perkins was sustained by the knowledge that she could enter the nursing home if and when it became necessary. With the help of supportive services she remained in her own home for the next nine years, at which time she suffered a massive stroke and was immediately hospitalized. She died in the hospital less than three weeks later.

Adapted from Beaver, M., & Miller, D. (1985). Clinical social work practice with the elderly. Homewood, IL: Dorsey Press, p. 59.

Audo-Visual

All of Our Lives   29 min., videocassette, color, 1984

This multiple awards winning film is a celebration of elderly women who have achieved much despite their situation as they banded together to fight for senior citizens' rights.

CONTACT: The Extension Media, University of California Center-Berkeley, 2176 Shattuck Avenue, Berkeley, CA 94704 (415-642-0460).

Brittle Bones: Should You Worry?   11 min., videocassette, 1/2" VHS, color, 1986
                                                                                      #3D0855, VH

This film on osteoporosis is from the ABC 20/20 Series. Because medical science is unable to rebuild weakened bones due to the loss of calcium, the focus on this film is on the only known treatment - prevention of calcium loss. This film discusses bone development, the nature and effects of osteoporosis, and current prevention strategies of calcium supplements and estrogen replacement therapy.

CONTACT: Direct Cinema Limited, 445 West Main Street, Wycoff, NJ, (800) 345-6748, in New Jersey (201-891-8240).

The Challenge of Aging: Jewish Ethnicity in Later Life   29 min., videocassette, color, 1985

The film utilizes group discussions at a senior citizen housing project and the life review of four women members to highlight the place of ethnic heritage in helping Jewish elders to cope and adjust to aging. The permanency of ethnic heritage is stressed and the anti-Semitism issue is addressed by the women who are all immigrants. Other issues include intermarriage, significance of orthodox rituals, advocacy, and social action. The film would be useful for sparking discussion among a group of senior citizens or students.

CONTACT: Mirror Productions, 335 Greenwich Street #7B, New York, NH 10013 (212-925-7760).

Going Home: A Grandmother's Story   26 min., videocassette, color, 1987

This film focuses on the return of a Native-American grandmother, after 27 years in Los Angeles, to the Pine Ridge Reservation in South Dakota. Her return exemplifies the lives of other retired relocates who return to their native communities to live out the rest of their lives with friends and family. The film does an excellent job of portraying ethnicity as a positive resource in old age. The film will be useful in classes that seek to understand more fully the diversity and influence of culture on aging.

CONTACT: Joan Weibel-Orlando, Dept. of Anthropology, University of Southern California, Bruce Hall-102, University Park, Los Angeles, CA 90089-0661 (213-743-7100).

I Know a Song   24 min., 16 mm, color, 1987
                                     #7D0900, 16

This upbeat documentary film shows how the loving relationship of a daughter for her mother is kept in tact over the years of the mother's physical and mental decline with Alzheimer's. Through song and touch, the daughter seeks to keep an emotional rapport with the essence of her mother which she senses existing underneath the affliction. The film is useful for all primary caregivers of Alzheimer's patients, both professionals and families.

CONTACT: University Film & Video, University of Minnesota, 1313 Fifth Street, SE, Suite 108, Minneapolis, MN 55414 (800-542-0013 in state), (800-847-8251 out-of-state).

I Want to Go Home   12 min., videocassette, color, 1986

This is an intensely personal and powerful statement about life in the mind of one whose coherence (the ability to "know" oneself and the world in a recognizable and consistent way) is disintegrating. For eight years, Ms. Walsh documented her mother who was a victim of Alzheimer's disease. It is one of the most visual presentations currently available and is highly recommended for health care and social service providers who work with Alzheimer's patients. The film is probably too strong and/or disturbing to be used for family support groups. It is a vivid reminder that the first victim of Alzheimer's disease is the sufferer himself/herself.

CONTACT: Alida Walsh Productions, 69 Mercer Street, New York, NY 10012 (212-966-5944).

On My Own: The Traditions of Daisy Turner   28 min., videocassette, color, 1986

This film is a portrait of a 102-year-old black woman living in rural Vermont. Both life history and family history are shared through the oral traditions of family stories, songs and poems. The film is basically a biography but is also an object lesson in creative listening to the elderly for family history and family traditions.

CONTACT: Filmakers Library, Inc., 133 East 58th Street, New York, NY 10022 (212-355-6545).

<u>Portrait: Maggie Kuhn</u>   29 min., 3/4" U-matic cassette, color, 1979

As the national convener of the Grey Panthers, Maggie Kuhn discusses projects, issues, and achievements of this organization of older Americans. The film can be used to both document the influence of elderly women in policy making and the progress of aging legislation since 1979.

CONTACT: Michigan Media, University of Michigan, 400 Fourth Street, Ann Arbor, MI 48109 (313-764-8228).

<u>A Rose by Any Other Name</u>   15 min., sound, color, 1981

The focus of the film is sexuality and intimacy among the elderly. The story concerns a 79-year-old woman and her loving relationship with an equally old man. Both are residents of a nursing home. The film explores the reactions and pressures to end the relationship by both family and nursing home staff. The impact of the institutional structure is also explored. This film is highly recommended and suitable for older adults, families, health care workers, persons in management positions who make decisions about aging, and adults and students in a variety of disciplines.

CONTACT: Adelphi University, Center on Aging, Garden City, NY 11530 (can be obtained in 16mm film or videocassette) and University Film & Video, University of Minnesota, 1313 Fifth Street, SW, Suite 108, Minneapolis, MN 55414 (800-542-0013 in state), (800-847-8251 out-of-state).

<u>Silent Pioneers: A Documentary</u>
<u>of Gay and Lesbian Elders</u>   30 min., 16 mm, videocassette, color, 1985

This film is an honest portrayal of the aging of eight gay and lesbian individuals. The issues of death, love, friends, and life are examined and the role of SAGE (Senior Action in a Gay Environment) in providing social, emotional, and physical support are explored. The film shows the universality of forming relationships, earning a living, and finding a place in society. The film is appropriate for both gay and non-gay audiences of professionals and/or students. The film is especially recommended for courses in aging, for social service practitioners, and for policy makers.

CONTACT: Filmakers Library, Inc., 133 East 58th Street, New York, NY 10022 (212-355-6545).

Annotated Bibliography

Beckett, J. O. (1988). Plant closings: How older workers are affected. <u>Social Work</u>, <u>33</u>(1), 29-33.

This article discusses an increasingly common type of unemployment that results from plant closings. The effect of plant closings on older workers, their families and the community is discussed through a review of the literature. A case example that explored the mental health effects of a closing on older workers is presented. Gender differences are described: for example, women's psychological functioning was adversely affected while men's physical health status decreased. Implications for social work intervention on several levels (the individual, the family, the workplace, and the community) are presented.

Berger, R. M., & Kelly, J. J. (1986). Working with homosexuals of the older populations. Social Casework, 67(4), 203-210.

This is a descriptive article discussing clinical social work with older lesbian women and gay men. The article discusses issues which are unique to this population such as effects of harmful stereotypes, concealment problems and relationship patterns. Included are possible advantages homosexuals may have in adjusting to aging.

Doress, P., & Siegel, D. (1987). Ourselves growing older: Women aging with knowledge and power. New York: Simon & Schuster.

This thirty chapter book is written by the authors of the popular book, Our Bodies, Ourselves. Using a feminist perspective, it examines the neglected health and well-being concerns of middle-aged and older women, It is one of the most in-depth and easily read books on the topic. It is divided into three sections: aging well; living with ourselves and others; and medical problems. While discussion of minorities of color are included, it would be easier for the reader if this material had been put together in one chapter. Nevertheless, this should be a required reading for all social workers. Written by and for women, any person would find the volume helpful.

Dressel, P. L. (1988). Gender, race, and class: Beyond the feminization of poverty in later life. The Gerontologist, 28(2), 177-180.

The feminization of poverty has the potential for both limiting and distorting the issue of old age poverty. Diversity contained within age groups and within gender groups must be acknowledged in order to facilitate a more complete understanding of poverty among the elderly and its policy implications.

Goldburg, G. S., Kantrow, R., Kremen, E., & Lauter, L. (1986). Spouseless, childless elderly women and their social support. Social Work, 31(2), 104-112.

This is a study of 52 spouseless, childless, elderly females living in a metropolitan area. The women included never married, widowed, divorced, and separated individuals. Most of the women were young elderly (aged 65-74) who were in reasonably good health. Most of the women had developed substitute supports for the close kin they lacked. Implications for women who become less healthy are discussed along with the need to develop support from the younger generation.

Golub, S., & Freedman, R. J. (Eds.). (1985, Summer/Fall). Health needs of women as they age: Women and health. The Journal of Women's Health Care (entire issue), 10(2/3).

The health needs of women as they age is the theme of this special double issue. Together, the ten articles provide an informative and thorough overview of the major health problems that confront women beyond middle age, of how these health needs are being met, and of the problems that are not being adequately addressed by the medical care system. Problems such as osteoporosis, reproductive cancer, societal myths, negative stereotypes, psychological concerns of aging women, and issues relating to social policy are discussed. Together, the articles in this special issue emphasize the need for the health care delivery system to be prepared to meet the special health care needs of the aging woman.

Hess, B. (1985). Aging policies and old women: The hidden agenda. In A. S. Rossi (Ed.), <u>Gender and the life course</u> (pp. 319-331). New York: Aldine.

Discusses the impact of social policies on aged women and effectively argues that public policy regarding the aged discriminates against women. It discusses the gender differential impact of past and present policy in such areas as income maintenance, health care and housing.

Hooyman, N. R., & Lustbader, W. (1986). <u>Taking care: Supporting older people and their families</u>. New York: Free Press.

This book is a real treasure of practice wisdom. It suggests what to do and why, as well as give details for specific caretaking situations. Included are situations rarely mentioned in other volumes like caregiving for gay or lesbian couples. It abounds in checklists to be used in assessment situations. The utility of the book for the profession is excellent, but the quality of the book is such that it extends itself well beyond the limits of the social work profession.

Hunter, L. R., & Memhard, P. H. (1981). <u>The rest of my life</u>. Stamford, CT: Growing Pains Press.

Supplemented by her daughter's description of her final days and by a medical history, this is primarily a candid, humorous, and moving journal written by a nursing home resident. The author, aged 80, was "bedridden, arthritic, and crotchety," and was admitted voluntarily. The book provides excellent case study material for practica sessions including: attitudes toward aging of the practica members; depression and older adults; health care alternatives, including the nursing home; and death and dying. It could also serve as a good bibliography or self-help tool for family members of older adults.

Jennings, J. (1987). Elderly parents as caregivers for adult dependent children. <u>Social Work</u>, <u>32</u>(5), 430-433.

This article discusses some of the issues of a neglected group of caregivers (usually women) in our society--the elderly who are providing care rather than receiving it. Elderly caregiver parents of adult disabled children have similar concerns, when compared to other caregivers, including social isolation, lack of respite care, financial/economic needs, inadequate counseling and planning for the future of their dependents (adult disabled child). Research and practice implications are discussed.

Kahne, H. (1985-86). Not yet equal: Employment experience of older women and older men. <u>International Journal of Aging and Human Development</u>, <u>22</u>(1), 1-13.

Women aged 45 and older make up almost 30 % of the female civilian labor force and 40 % of the labor force consisting of older, civilian workers. The employment-related experience of older women is not only different from that of men but frequently disadvantaged. A discussion examines the growing importance of the issue of market equality of older working women. It then considers six ways in which their employment-related experience differs from that of men: rates of participation in the labor force, occupational distribution, earnings, unemployment, poverty, and retirement income. Directions for policy are suggested that would improve the status of older women, and, in some cases, meet the employment needs of older men.

Loewinsohn, R. J. (1984). <u>Survival handbook for widows: And for relatives and friends who want to understand</u>. Glenview, IL: Scott, Foresman.

The author, a family therapist and coordinator of a Widowed Persons Service, speaks directly to widows in this concise and personal resource. Loewinsohn addresses the grief process and offers practical ideas and suggestions for coping. Distributed by the American Association of Retired Persons, this book is recommended as self-help bibliotherapy for widows and their family members.

Nolan, J. (1986). Developmental concerns and the health of midlife women. Nursing Clinics of North America, 21, 151-159.

Reviews the literature of factors affecting the psychological health of middle-aged women. Topics considered include the impact of menopause, the empty nest syndrome, and the influence of work on midlife women.

Porcino, J. (1983). Growing older, getting better: A handbook for women in the second half of life. Reading, MA: Addison-Wesley.

This self-help book includes a discussion of many possible transitions for women 40 years of age and older: grandparenthood, separation, divorce, widowhood, coping with aging parents, and securing employment. The second half ("Our changing bodies") discusses both normal developments, such as menopause, and common diseases (e.g., hypertension and various cancers). Well-researched and very well-written, Porcino's work could be a text for a practicum on predictable transitions of aging, and also excellent bibliotherapy.

Sherman, S. R., Ward, R. A., & LaGory, M. (1988). Women as caregivers of the elderly: Instrumental and expressive support. Social Work, 33(2), 164-167.

A study focused on two types of support provided by caregivers of the elderly: (1) instrumental, defined as tangible aid and service referral; and (2) expressive, defined as role models and confidants who provide a form of sharing. Interviews were conducted with a probability sample of 1,185 persons 60 years of age and older to determine the availability and gender of their caregivers. A majority reported having both instrumental and expressive support. Men were more likely than women to name their spouses as an instrumental helper; and the majority of caregivers and confidants named by the subjects were women. Implications for social workers of the predominance of women in support networks are outlined.

Shulman, S. C. (1985). Psychodynamic group therapy with older women. Social Casework: The Journal of Contemporary Social Work, 66(10), 579-586.

Psychodynamically oriented groups can be an effective catalyst of growth for older patients. The discussion describes the first six years of an ongoing group for women, aged 55-70, who were outpatients of a community mental health center. The formation of the group, the selection and orientation of its members, and the process that evolved are examined. Object relations theory is used to organize observations about the development of the group. Countertransference issues are discussed.

Verbrugge, L. M., & Madans, J. H. (1985). Social roles and health trends of American women. Milbank Memorial Fund Quarterly: Health and Society, 63, 691-735.

Examines the relationship between the social roles of employment, marriage and parenthood and the physical health of black and white women aged 17 through 62. It also assesses changes in women's health from the mid-1960s to the late 1970s. Results showed women with the triple roles of employee, spouse and parent had the best physical health. Those with the poorest health were unemployed and unmarried and usually childless. Blacks have poorer health than whites. Over the last three decades, the health of older (45-64) unmarried, jobless women has worsened. In contrast, the health of employed, married women was stable or improved.

General Bibliography

Almvig, C. (1982). _The invisible minority: Aging and lesbianism_. New York: Utica College of Syracuse University Press.

Bell, M. (1987). _Women as elders_. New York: Haworth Press.

Essex, M. J., & Nam, S. (1987). Marital status and loneliness among older women: The differential importance of close family and friends. _Journal of Marriage and the Family_, 49, 93-106.

Fulani, L. (Ed.). (1988). _The politics of race and gender in therapy_. New York: Haworth Press.

Garner, D., & Mercer, S. (Eds.). (1989). _Women as they age_. New York: Haworth Press.

Gass, K. (1987). Health of conjugally bereaved older widows: The role of appraisal, coping and resources. _Research in Nursing and Health_, 10, 39-47.

Gibson, M. J. (Ed.). (1987). _Income security and long term care for women in midlife and beyond_. Washington, DC: American Association of Retired Persons.

Goldberg, G., Kantrow, R., & Kremen, E. (1986). Elderly women and their social supports. _Social Work_, 31, 104-112.

Golub, S., & Freedman, R. (Eds.). (1985). _Health needs of women as they age_. New York: Haworth Press.

Grau, L. (Ed.). (1989). _Women in the later years_. New York: Haworth Press.

Haug, M., Ford, A., & Sheafor, M. (1985). _Physical and mental health of aged women_. New York: Springer.

Hoeffer, B. (1987). Predictors of life outlook of older single women. _Research in Nursing and Health_, 10, 111-117.

Lesnoff-Caravaglia, G. (Ed.). (1984). _The world of the older woman_. New York: Human Sciences Press.

Magaziner, J., Cadigan, D., Hebel, R., & Parry, R. (1988). Health and living arrangements among older women: Does living alone increase the risk of illness? _Journal of Gerontology_, 43, 127-133.

Miller, J. (1986). _Toward a new psychology of women_ (rev. ed.). New York: Harper & Row.

Minkler, M., & Stone, R. (1985). The feminization of poverty and older women. _The Gerontologist_, 25, 351-357.

Verbrugge, L., & Madans, J. (1985). Social roles and health trends in American women. _Milbank Memorial Fund Quarterly: Health and Society_, 63, 691-735.

Warlick, J. (1985). Why is poverty after 65 a woman's problem? _Journal of Gerontology_, 40, 751-757.

HOW CASE STUDIES CAN IMPROVE YOUR CLASSES

by Dr. Robert L. Schneider

Introduction

Give social work students a choice between a lecture or a look-over-the shoulder of a skillful, experienced faculty member into complex, real-life service situations, and the students will choose the latter almost without exception. Today's social work educators are more concerned than ever that our programs produce individuals who have not only learned a body of knowledge and a repertoire of interventive skills, but who also make decisions applying the most valid theories and practice principles. The profession also expects students to demonstrate a commitment to proper values and standards. Ideally, we hope for a personal integration by students of these values, knowledge, skills and standards before they graduate from our programs.

All schools of social work use supervised field instruction as a major means of enhancing professional education. In the field placements, students actually apply their knowledge and skills to real life problems and clients under the supervision of an experienced social work practitioner. Social work students thus learn from doing.

Definition of Case Study

One additional applied strategy which social work educators are using to strengthen professional education and individual integration is the case study. The case study is a brief description of a professional social work decision or problem normally written from the point of view of the decision maker. For educational purposes, it is the record of a complex situation that must be literally pulled apart and put together again by students and faculty members before the situation can be understood. A good study is a vehicle by which a chunk of reality is brought into the classroom to be analyzed and discussed by the class and the professor (Leenders & Erskine, 1978).

Purpose

to:

The purpose of a case study in social work education is to provide students with opportunities

- analyze issues, problems and complex professional situations
- prepare for decision making and action steps
- increase self awareness and independent thinking
- develop plans and alternative recommendations
- integrate social work theory with practice realities.

Benefits

Incorporating into a classroom the analysis of a series of case studies will improve professional education because:

- Students are provided with opportunities to solve real life situations and obtain immediate feedback on their answers and behavior.

APPENDICES

- Students can look over the shoulder of an instructor who inquires skillfully into complex situations.

- Learning through cases is dynamic. It requires the cooperation of the learner. It goes beyond listening to wise statements and advice which promote little, if any, learning.

- Student participation is achieved by opening a channel of communication between students and students and students and teacher. Students are expected to make contributions to the understanding of the group, and they get enthusiastically involved.

- Students can integrate social work theory and practice while increasing their self-awareness and independent thinking. Schools fulfill their mission of preparing students for decision making and action.

What the Professor Needs to Know and Do

- As the instructor, you must accept the role of an involved participant in the analysis of the study.

- Realize that there are no right or wrong answers and solutions, but that there may be a number of feasible strategies to follow or judgments to make.

- Focus the discussion around the primary social worker in the study. The students should identify with this individual and begin to assume responsibility for decisions or steps under consideration.

- Realize that all the studies have been based on real life situations, but are disguised for purposes of confidentiality.

- Clues and indicators of some of the issues in the studies are often found in the final paragraph. By using APPENDIX B and the suggested questions which it contains, you will identify many other issues that can be incorporated into a discussion and proposed recommendations.

- Lead the discussion by asking a series of questions of the students, drawing out the facts of the case, and evaluating alternative recommendations.

- Introduce theory and research into the sessions and demonstrate how an analysis of a complex situation can benefit from the use of conceptual materials and applied research.

What the Professor Must Tell the Students

Inform your students that:

- They should review and use APPENDIX B, Suggested Tasks for Analyzing Case Studies.

- They should do a quick, initial analysis and fast reading of the study by skimming through the materials. After getting a general sense, students should do a careful second reading and then begin to answer questions found in APPENDIX B.

- Not all information is equally reliable and/or relevant, but the case writer is **not** deliberately misrepresenting data or facts in order to trick them.

- It is helpful to discuss the case and the guidelines with a small group of classmates before the class and/or during class. Students can test out their ideas and arguments. Remind them that they are not necessarily striving for consensus, but trying to clarify and refine their use of theories and experiences.

- They should come to class prepared to discuss the significance of the study with the instructor and their colleagues. Students are expected to be active participants, not passive note takers. Significant learning takes place when students become involved in the analysis and recommendations. This requires an active engagement in the process.

- They must identify with the key social worker in the study and put themselves in his or her place. They must reflect on the decisions under consideration and prepare next steps based on a professional rationale.

- If they come to class well prepared, are willing to commit themselves to a well reasoned set of analyses, and are receptive to constructive criticism, they will find the analyses of the studies challenging and exciting.

Bibliography

Leenders, M. R., & Erskine, J. A. (1978). **Case research: The case writing process** (2nd ed.). London, Canada: University of Western Ontario.

SUGGESTED TASKS IN ANALYZING CASE STUDIES
of
GERONTOLOGICAL SOCIAL WORK

Directions	Questions to Ask Yourself
Identify the important elements of the case study	What are the important facts? What is happening to whom? Is all relevant information accessible?
Specify the major issues	Who is responsible for making decisions? What decisions need to be determined? What issues and consequences need to be considered?
Evaluate constraints and resources	Which forces support and oppose which actions? What are the major barriers? Which resources are available for plans/actions?
Determine objectives and goals to be achieved	Which results are possible? Which are desirable? Which objectives are most important to whom?
Evaluate the behavior of professionals and clients	Does the social worker exhibit leadership? Is the client involved in the decision making?
Assess the conflicts or professional dilemmas	In what do the conflicts or dilemmas consist? Can conflicting plans be reconciled? Can dilemmas be resolved?
Identify alternative plans or programs	Are there plans, ideas, or programs that have not been identified? Are the alternatives mutually exclusive?
Assess the consequences of possible decisions and actions	What outcomes are likely to result from the decisions made? What are the short and long term consequences for the individuals and the profession? What unintended consequences might evolve?
Review appropriate strategies	What are the most effective ways of achieving the goals sought? What recommended actions seem appropriate now? in six months?

AUDIO-VISUAL RESOURCE CENTERS
in
VIRGINIA AND LOUISIANA

The following institutions offer audio-visual aids, films, video-cassettes, etc. in the field of aging. Each has its own policies and procedures. A media resource listing is also included.

Virginia

Virginia Center on Aging
Information Resources Center
P.O. Box 229 - MCV Station
Richmond, VA 23298

Virginia Department of Mental Health, Mental
    Retardation and Substance Abuse Services
Office of Geriatric Services
P.O. Box 1797
Richmond, VA 23214

Virginia Department for the Aging
700 Center
700 East Franklin - 10th Floor
Richmond, VA 23219

John Tyler Community College
Resource Library
Chester, VA 23831

Veterans Administration Medical Center (142D)
Medical Library
Richmond, VA 23249

Veterans Administration Medical Center
Library Services
Hampton, VA 23667

Veterans Administration Medical Center
Library Services
Salem, VA 24153

Presbyterian School of Christian Education
Center on Aging
1205 Palmyra Avenue
Richmond, VA 23227

University(s) Consortium

This consortium includes: University of Virginia, Virginia Commonwealth University, J. Sargeant Reynolds, John Tyler Community College, Virginia State University, Union Theological Seminary, Virginia Union University, Richard Bland and Randolph Macon College.
Loan Policy: All A/V resources at these institutions can be obtained only by consortium members. The usual interlibrary loan process can be followed.

Center for Gerontology
Virginia Polytechnic Institute and State University

There are only a few items in the Center's collection. However, the Virginia Cooperative Extension Office has a Learning Resource Center and audio-visual resources are available through the local extension officer, who is located in most cities and counties in Virginia.

Louisiana

The Governor's Office of Elderly Affairs
P.O. Box 80374
Baton Rouge, LA 70898-0374

Tulane University
Center on Aging for Research,
    Education and Services
P.O. Box 5085
New Orleans, LA 70118-5698

Northeast Louisiana University
Institute on Aging
Monroe, LA 71209

Grambling State University
Gerontology Center
P.O. Box 904
Grambling, LA 71245

Media Resource Guides

American Association of Retired Persons. (1987). <u>Free-loan audiovisual programs</u>. Washington, DC.

Lists a number of media products on various topics concerning aging that AARP loans free of charge. Each entry is described and includes a purchase price. Most are slides with audiocassettes although some videotapes and 16mm films are included. Presentation/ discussion guidelines and handout materials for participants are available from:

> AARP
> Program Scheduling Office
> Program Resources Department/AW
> 1909 K Street, NW
> Washington, DC 20049

National Video Clearinghouse, Inc. (1988). <u>Video source book</u> (10 ed.). Syosset, NY.

This guide has a compilation of videotapes and films. They are organized both by title and subject area; many of the items are related to aging. The guide gives important information--date, description, format, length, publisher and distributor, appropriate audience, etc. -- about each entry. It is available from:

> National Video Clearinghouse, Inc.
> 100 Lafayette Drive
> Syosset, NY 11791

Yahnke, Robert E. (1988). <u>The great circle of life</u>. Owings Mills, MD: National Health Publishing.

This is the first comprehensive guide to the use of films and videotapes that specifically addresses the topic of aging. It contains a synopsis of each film, discussion questions, activities, and worksheets.

> It is available from:

> National Health Publishing
> A Division of Williams and Wilkins
> 99 Painters Mill Road
> Owings Mills, MD 21117
> (301) 363-6400
> (800) 446-2221

ADVISORY BOARD

Mrs. Ruby Adler
AARP State Coordinator for Health Advocacy
Benton

Mr. Bobby Cooper*
Executive Director
Louisiana Association of Councils on Aging
Natchitoches

Ms. Nancy Covey
Executive Director
Virginia Association of Homes for Adults
Richmond

Mr. Joe Donchess
Executive Director
Louisiana Nursing Home Association
Baton Rouge

Ms. Kathy Donoghue
Executive Director
SEVAMP
Norfolk

Mr. Douglas Elgin
Director, Social Work Services
The Memorial Hospital
Danville

Ms. Wilda Ferguson
Commissioner
Virginia Department for the Aging
Richmond

Ms. Donna Foster
Assistant Director
Fairfax Department of Social Services
Fairfax

Ms. Vicki Fowler
Social Worker
Westminster Canterbury House
Richmond

Mr. George Gates
New Orleans Council on Aging
New Orleans

*deceased

Dr. Elizabeth Hutchison
Director, BSW Program
School of Social Work
Virginia Commonwealth University
Richmond

Ms. Delores Jones
Special Populations Coordinator
Louisiana State Mental Health Department
Baton Rouge

Mr. Thomas C. Laughlin
Jefferson Council on Aging
Metairie

Ms. Francis Littman
Director
Social Work Department
St. Mary's Hospital
Richmond

Ms. Alice Lowry
Supervisor
Social Services Department
New Orleans Charity Hospital
New Orleans

Dr. Ron Marks
School of Social Work
Tulane University
New Orleans

Dr. William McAuley
Director
Center for Gerontology
Virginia Polytechnic and State University
Blacksburg

Dr. Chris N. Miaoulis
Director
Social Work Program
Southeastern Louisiana University
Hammond

Dr. Iris Parham
Chairperson
Department of Gerontology
Virginia Commonwealth University
Richmond

Ms. Edna Paylor
Executive Director
Virginia Association of Nonprofit Homes for the Aging
Richmond

Mr. Thomas P. Perkins
Christopher Homes, Inc.
New Orleans

Ms. Wilma H. Salmon
Governor's Office of Elderly Affairs
Baton Route

Mr. Justin Schleis
Executive Director
Louisiana Association of Home and Services for the Aging
Baton Rouge

Ms. Karen Selden
Assistant Director
Instructive Visiting Nurse Association
Richmond

Mr. Brad Smith
President
Louisiana Aging Network Association
Baton Rouge

Ms. Beverly Soble
Director of Education and Residential
Services
Virginia Health Care Association
Richmond

Dr. Gordon Walker
Executive Director
Jefferson Area Board for Aging
Charlottesville

Ms. Bonita Williams
Director of Nursing Services
Instructive Visiting Nurse Association
Richmond

FACULTY LIAISONS

The following individuals served as Faculty Liaisons between their undergraduate social work programs and the Virginia-Louisiana Undergraduate Curriculum Project in Gerontology.

Dr. Malcolm Braudaway
Northwestern State University (LA)

Dr. Jean Cobbs
Virginia State University

Dr. Molly Davis
George Mason University (VA)

Dr. Beverly Favre
Southern University at New Orleans

Ms. Sara Hood
Virginia Union University

Dr. Elizabeth Hutchison
Virginia Commonwealth University

Dr. Lon Johnston
Virginia Intermont College

Dr. Lula King
Hampton University (VA)

Dr. Maryjo Lockwood
Southeastern Louisiana University

Dr. Ervin J. Mast
Eastern Mennonite College (VA)

Ms. Cheryl Mathews
Christopher Newport College (VA)

Dr. Judy Noel
Northeast Louisiana University

Dr. Jane Shannon
Radford University (VA)

Dr. Audrey Sistler
Southern University and A & M College (LA)

Dr. Evelyn Slaght
Ferrum College (VA)

Dr. George Stonikinis
Longwood College (VA)

Ms. Grace Tatem
Grambling State University (LA)

Dr. Greg Versen
James Madison University (VA)

Dr. Alvin Walter
Norfolk State University (VA)

362.6
Sc58
1989
v.2

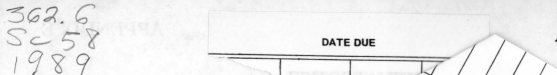

DATE DUE

HIGHSMITH 45-220

The following individuals served as edit...
Undergraduate Social Work Education and...
School of Social Work at Virginia Commor...

Editor: Robert L. S...
Professor

Associate Editor: Nancy P. Krop...
Doctoral Candidate...

AUTHORS

Joyce O. Beckett, PhD
Professor

Nancy P. Kropf, MSW
Doctoral Candidate/Instructor

Debbie Costigan, MA
Doctoral Student

Edward A. McSweeney, PhD*
Associate Professor

Patrick Dattalo, MSW
Doctoral Student/Instructor

Jane Reeves, MSW
Assistant Professor

Delores Dungee-Anderson, PhD
Assistant Professor

Amy Rosenblum, MSW
Assistant Professor

Rosemary L. Farmer, MSW
Doctoral Student/Assistant Professor

Robert L. Schneider, DSW
Professor

Marcia P. Harrigan, PhD
Assistant Professor

Michael J. Sheridan, PhD
Assistant Professor

Elizabeth Hutchison, PhD
Assistant Professor

Stephen D. Stahlman, MSW
Doctoral Candidate

*deceased